The handbook of play therapy

There is renewed interest in the use of therapeutic play to prevent or repair emotional damage among all those working with children, from workers in family centres to social workers dealing with the consequences of child abuse. There is an urgent need for developing skills in using play to communicate with children in order to establish facts and make assessments of their needs, for example following divorce or where abuse is suspected.

Workers in a wide range of fields are already using play in therapeutic work with children and families. Some have inherited skills from earlier generations of workers; some are developing their own highly innovative and creative approaches. But many are working in isolation, often unaware of similar kinds of work going on elsewhere, yet eager for new ideas. Accounts of current work are locked up in specialist journals or lacking because workers are too busy to write. Other professionals working with children who would like to learn about play therapy, the theory behind it and the basic skills and understandings needed to practice it, are offered little training or guidance. This book has been written for both these groups of people.

The handbook of play therapy provides a comprehensive introduction to play therapy. It gives a clear outline of the theory of play and of play therapy, gives guidelines for practice and examples of good practice in different settings and situations, makes practical suggestions for training and includes useful information on further resources. It will be an invaluable handbook to all those working with children, including social workers , those working with the under-fives, teachers, hospital play specialists, occupational therapists, and also some psychologists, speech therapists and nurses.

Linnet McMahon is Lecturer in Therapeutic Child Care in the Department of Community Studies at Reading University and also a freelance play therapist. She has tutored many under-fives courses, has worked with children and parents together in a family play therapy group, and was a member of Jerome Bruner's Preschool Research Project.

The handbook of play therapy

Linnet McMahon

London and New York

First published 1992
by Routledge
11 New Fetter Lane, London EC4P 4EE

Simultaneously published in the USA and Canada
by Routledge
29 West 35th Street, New York, NY 10001

Routledge is an imprint of the Taylor & Francis Group

Reprinted 1993, 1995, 1997, 1999 and 2000

© 1992 Linnet McMahon

Typeset in Times
by Michael Mepham, Frome, Somerset
Printed and bound in Great Britain by
Mackays of Chatham PLC, Chatham, Kent

British Library Cataloguing in Publication Data
A catalogue record for this book is available from the British Library

Library of Congress Cataloguing in Publication Data
A catalogue record for this book is available from the Library of Congress

ISBN 0–415–07923–3 (hbk)
ISBN 0–415–05986–0 (pbk)

In memory of my father, the pain of whose childhood
cast long shadows forward

Contents

Tables and figures

Acknowledgements

This study owes much to the inspiration of two great and wise teachers. Marianne Wolman of Pacific Oaks College in Pasadena, California, who worked with Anna Freud in the Hampstead nurseries, first introduced me to the psychodynamic approaches to therapeutic work with children of Erikson and Bettelheim. Brenda Crowe, a Froebel teacher and later National Adviser to the Pre-school Playgroups Association, taught me how to understand and respond to the feelings of children and parents, and to recognize the healing power of play.

I am extremely grateful to the great number of people using play in their current work with children who have shared their ideas and experience with me. Many have been kind enough to let me use their unpublished working notes and papers. They also told me of the origins of their knowledge of therapeutic play and so put me on the trail of other workers, publications and courses.

Social worker Richard Woodfield showed me that the psychodynamic approach can still be an invaluable tool in understanding a problem. Child guidance worker Bernie Stringer introduced me to family therapy. Oxfordshire social workers Elizabeth Wright and Janet Turner explained the specialized methods of their work in sexual abuse and family placement respectively. I received valuable help and contributions from independent social workers Jo Carroll in Marlborough and Philip King's Independent Child Care Agency in Birmingham, from social worker and play therapist Janet West in Nottingham, from Leicestershire court welfare officer Jackie Kiggell, and from child guidance social worker Barry Bowen in Kettering. Madge Bray and SACCS (Sexual Abuse: Child Consultancy Service) gave freely both information and help.

Much exciting work is taking place in voluntary organizations. Chris Richards and his team at the Children's Society in the Wrekin were generous in sharing accounts of their aims and methods in practice. I greatly appreciated the opportunity to learn from Kate Burke about her superb work with children in preparation for family placement, in the Catholic Children's Society in Reading. I am extremely grateful to the National Children's Homes (NCH) who gave me access to some of the innovative work going on in its organization. Their workers included Anita Edwards and Mary Stone at the Nomony Centre in Plymouth, Christine Froude and Margaret Coles, with head teacher Gwyn Davies, at Bourne Place special residential school in Kent, Sandra Foster at North Hull Family Centre, John Diaper at Bodmin Family Centre, Rosemary Lilley at Greenham House Family Centre in Newbury, and Marion Burch at Hull Professional Foster Home. I very much appreciate all their contributions.

Christine Bradley, training officer for the Caldecott Community, showed me some of the exciting new developments in the use of play within the Community, as well as contributing examples of her own profound work with children. Susan Turner, independent art therapist, helped me to understand her work. Jean Gregg told me about her innovative work as hospital play specialist at Lord Mayor Treloar Hospital in Hampshire and put me in touch with members of the National Association of Hospital Play Staff, who were helpful in turn. I value the help and friendship over many years of Gill Howgego, formerly my colleague and now group leader at Dingley family play therapy group in Reading's Child Development Centre. Roy McConkey spent an unforgettable evening with parents and workers there, reminding us of childhood memories of play. Ann Henderson, editor of the the Pre-school Playgroups Association magazine *Contact*, helped put me in touch with workers and parents, Bernie Ross and Julia Prosser. Margaret Marshall, of Bristol Home Start, encouraged her volunteers to contribute examples of their work. Margaret Shephard kept me up to date on her work using music with families. Rachel Pinney, Sally Maxwell and Jenny Senior introduced me to the approach of the Children's Hours Trust. Rose Larter showed me her use of therapeutic play with children at the Resource Unit at Geoffrey Field Primary School in Reading. Fiona Garwood, of Family Conciliation Scotland, gave much information and help. Lesley Aberdein, of Aberdeen Voluntary Service, contributed an account of her work as a children's divorce counsellor.

Occupational therapists/play therapists Lyn Bennett, Bridget Leverton, Fiona Hawkridge and Anne Sené in Oxfordshire, Anna Sanders in London, Roz Huddleston in Lancaster and Pauline Little in Carlisle told me about their work with children and families. I am particularly grateful to Susan Monson for contributions from her and her colleagues at Marlborough Children's Hospital, and for helpful discussions about her work, for numerous invaluable suggestions, and for putting me in touch through the NAPOT newsletter with other workers in the field. Lily Jeffrey in Scotland provided information about training.

The British Association for Adoption and Fostering, the Catholic Children's Society, Barnardos and the National Foster Care Association gave further valuable information and booklists. Juliet Hopkins, child psychotherapist at the Tavistock Clinic, provided helpful bibliographies. The librarians at the NSPCC and information officers at the National Children's Bureau were enormously helpful in providing references and obtaining more obscure publications. Jackie Boffin, of Community Insight, kindly proved information about children's books. Berkshire's Education Library Service and Oxford's Children's Library were most helpful.

Thanks too to my husband, Tom, not least for teaching me about computers and word processing, and for help with drawings, to our daughters Kendra, for her encouragement, and Kate, for her constant invitations to play!

I should like to express my gratitude to the National Children's Bureau for the award of a Kellmer Pringle Fellowship which gave financial support as well as recognition of the need for the work. I value the help of critical readers and friends, including child psychiatrist Mary Snow, and Joyce Rimmer, formerly my social work tutor at Birmingham University, where this book started life as a Master's degree dissertation. Joyce's conviction that the work was important encouraged me to see it through. Other contributors in turn added their comments, suggestions and encouragement. To them all, many thanks. Any mistakes and misperceptions are, of course, my own.

Introduction
The state of play

Children and their families are living in a time of uncertainty and change which places great pressures on family life. Child-rearing skills are no longer passed from generation to generation, although, at a deeper level, ways of behaving and responding to situations are often transmitted. Past patterns of bringing up children are often irrelevant today, and some of them were emotionally damaging. Each set of parents must think afresh about how to bring up their children and many feel at a loss. At the same time the lack of support as relatives become unavailable is compounded as functioning neighbourhoods decline and the support of the welfare state diminishes. New pressures, including high expectations, the changing role of women, poverty and isolation, mean that family relationships may suffer and many families break down under the strain. Stress may be increased by disability, illness or bereavement. Parents may not always be able to understand or respond to their children's unhappiness without outside help. In some families there is a long legacy of damaging and abusive relationships and children's emotional needs have been ignored.

The emotional needs of children are becoming increasingly understood and there is a broad body of knowledge about how they can be met. Blaming parents is no solution; family systems theory is helpful in removing notions of blame. Training in therapeutic play can enable workers in a variety of settings and with a wide variety of initial training to offer help to children and families. The methods of play therapy are particularly suitable because they offer support or 'containment' of child or parent and at the same time do not disempower them. On the contrary, play therapy depends on releasing creativity so that the players, child or adult, become able to work out their own solutions to their difficulties. This does not negate the need for a just society. Without the framework of a fair society which meets its members' basic needs it may not be possible for the individual to become a creative autonomous being.

While working with children and families in a Child Development Centre a few years ago I wanted to learn more about play therapy. I could find little except Axline's inspiring *Dibs – In Search of Self* and her *Play Therapy*. Yet I knew from experience that children's play is healing and that as a worker with children I was sometimes in a position to help this healing process. Further, as a tutor in the

Pre-school Playgroups Association I had found out that play can also be healing for adults. This book is the result of a continued search to find out who is using play in work with children and families. I talked to people in different professions and agencies, and with varying background and training, who are using and developing play techniques. I heard about their different methods and became aware of how these are influenced by workers' differing roles and the context within which they operate, as well as by the theory on which they are based. Some have inherited skills from earlier generations of workers; some are developing highly innovative and creative approaches. Many are working in relative isolation, often unaware of similar kinds of work going on elsewhere yet eager for new ideas. Many are too busy to write about what they are doing. When they do write their work tends to appear in specialized journals and publications. I found that an exciting range of skills is now available. Perhaps the most significant development is the move to using therapeutic play in family work, with parents as well as with children.

Developments in theory include a renewed interest in the psychoanalytic work of Melanie Klein, the application in practice of Winnicott's and Bion's notions of holding and containment, and the refinement of understanding of Bowlby's great work on attachment, separation and loss, the underlying themes of human life. These theories form the essential foundation to the use of play in work with both individual children and families.

I am writing this in the early 1990s when the tragic results of several cases of child abuse and the storm of controversy over sexual abuse have led to a renewed focus on child protection. There is increasing awareness of the need for sound techniques for communicating with children. The 1989 Children Act requires that the wishes and feelings of children be taken into account when decisions that affect them are made. Above all, there is a desperate need for appropriate help for large numbers of children who have suffered some kind of emotional hurt.

This book aims to equip workers who lack specialized knowledge of play with the basic background and skills which they will need in order to begin using play to communicate with children and to carry out therapeutic work with children and families. It aims to provide a forum in which more experienced workers can glean ideas from others. It gives advice on training. The main fields explored are under-fives and family centre work, child protection involving investigation of abuse and subsequent therapy, work in schools, hospitals and child psychiatric units, divorce court welfare work and conciliation, court work, family placement and therapeutic work with children in care. Much work takes place in voluntary organizations as well as in statutory services. Workers include field and residential social workers, guardians *ad litem* and divorce court welfare officers, occupational therapists, hospital play specialists, teachers, workers and therapists in special and residential schools, and also home teachers, nursery nurses and playgroup workers, nurses, speech therapists, psychotherapists, art therapists, foster parents, counsellors, psychologists and psychiatrists. This book examines the published literature and uses information and case studies from workers in the field, presenting examples of good practice.

I have tried to relate practice to the theory of play and play therapy in order to provide a theoretical framework for different forms of work.

Chapter 1 is about the place of play in child development, particularly about the way in which play is linked to children's emotional development. This provides the essential foundation for understanding how play can be used to help children to develop emotionally and cope with emotional difficulties. However, workers who prefer to start from practice may want to read ahead to an area of work that interests them, returning later to fill in the gaps in their theoretical knowledge.

Chapter 2 is about the different theories of play therapy and their application in practice, past and present. These range from psychodynamic and non-directive approaches to focused approaches, some of which are highly structured. Some approaches deal with deeply unconscious levels of thought; others work with the child's conscious understanding of events.

Practical guidance for workers starting therapeutic play with children is given in Chapter 3.

Chapter 4 is about the use of play to help children under five and their families, and goes on to examine play in family work with older children as well. The use of play in family work is a thread that runs throughout the book; play therapy is not just for children.

Play therapy, both individual and group methods, to help children living in unhappy families is explored in Chapter 5. Sometimes these children have experienced physical abuse or neglect as well as emotional conflicts. Chapter 6 investigates the use of play to help children with developmental problems, and children with disabilities or illness, including stays in hospital, and also children for whom emotional and learning difficulties become intertwined.

Therapeutic play, including group work, to help children suffering separation and loss through bereavement or divorce is considered in Chapter 7.

Chapter 8 examines the use of play approaches in investigating child sexual abuse and in providing therapy for abused children.

Chapter 9 explores the use of play by guardians *ad litem* in assessments for the courts, and the range of play techniques in helping children in care deal with experiences of separation and loss of their families.

Some thoughts on training for play therapy are offered in Appendix 1. The few opportunities for training in therapeutic play are described here.

Appendices 2–4 list further sources of information and help, including books for children.

Many workers have contributed case studies. Most of these are their own accounts. Others have been told to me informally and written up with the agreement of the worker. In all cases, names of children and families have been changed to preserve confidentiality. Sometimes identifying details have been either omitted or changed.

I hope that the case studies I have included will give prospective workers some idea of what it feels like to be involved in the messy, complex and often confusing process of therapeutic play with children and families, and give them some help in getting their bearings. I hope too that they will be heartened by the courage of children in facing up to their own pain and growing through it. Children will forgive the mistakes a worker makes provided that they have confidence that their worker is really trying to understand and to see them through a difficult time. Their power to heal themselves through play can be astonishing. On hearing that her worker was going to give a talk, a girl who had survived the most horrific ritual abuse, said 'Tell them that we play but it's much much more than that'.

> Thirty spokes share the wheel's hub;
> It is the centre hole that makes it useful.
> Shape clay into a vessel;
> It is the space within that makes it useful.
> Therefore profit comes from what is there;
> Usefulness from what is not there.
>
> (from the Tao Te Ching of Lao Tsu
> translated by Gia-Fu Feng and Jane English
> (1972) Wildwood House Limited, London)

Chapter 1

The development of play

WHAT IS PLAY?

Most of us are familiar with the mental freezing which can accompany the pressure to achieve a particular goal, whether it is a self-imposed goal or set by somebody else. We long for the time and space to think, to let our minds wander around a problem, to explore different possibilities, to relax enough to let surprising thoughts occur, to be creative. Simply, we need to play. Play is not a mindless filling of time or a rest from work. It is a spontaneous and active process in which thinking, feeling and doing can flourish since they are separated from the fear of failure or disastrous consequences. The player is freed to be inventive and creative. Play is a way of assimilating new information and making it part of ourselves. In the process we change ourselves' and our view of the world. We dare to change because our autonomy is not challenged or threatened. On the contrary, the process of playing gives the glorious sensation of increased autonomy. Play can be deeply satisfying.

As it is with adults so it is with children. Yet children's needs to play are greater since their autonomy is less. The pleasure and excitement of playing, the intensity and concentration, the freedom to experiment, to explore and to create, to find out how things and people work and what you can do with them, to give the imagination free rein, and to fill the gap between reality and desire, all these derive from the fact that in play the child is in charge. Thus 'play under the control of the player gives to the child his first and the most crucial opportunity to have the courage to think, to talk and perhaps even to *be* himself' (Bruner 1983).

Although play can be a serious as well as a joyous activity, the crucial condition is that errors do not have serious consequences. A child's exploratory play within a familiar setting is a different kind of experience from unprotected exploration of an unfamiliar and potentially frightening world. Risks can be taken because the play itself matters more than the results of play. Play can only take place within a safe boundary, providing both a time and a place, so that the child knows where play begins, 'and where it ends and the rules change back to everyday life' (Skynner and Cleese 1983: 298). Huizinga puts it more formally:

All play moves and has its being within a playground marked off beforehand either materially or ideally, deliberately or as a matter of choice ... All are temporary worlds within the ordinary world, dedicated to the performance of an act apart. Inside the playground an absolute and peculiar order reigns ... the laws and customs of ordinary life no longer count.

(Huizinga 1949: 10–12)

For young children the boundary of their 'playground' is provided by parents or other adults who protect them from intrusion from the outside world. This may involve a special place, usually with familiar features or objects, or a special time, or both. When two or more children are playing together, or an adult is joining in as a player, they will normally indicate to one another that 'This is play'. This may be a look, a 'play face', a laugh, or perhaps a verbal recognition such as 'You *pretend* to be my mummy'. Play is paradoxical in that the interaction between players is real but the message between them is that what they are doing is not real (Bateson 1973). Inside the boundary the player can experiment with changing normal ways of categorizing things, often a source of humour as the child realizes this. Play can be a 'special way of violating fixity' (Bruner, in Garvey 1977: 104). For example, the child with a new baby in the family may take a delight in playing 'mother' whilst the real mother has to play the baby who, like Hansel and Gretel, gets sent off into the forest.

The beginning of play is in the safe space between the infant and mother, Winnicott's (1971) area of illusion, as the infant starts to realize that it has a separate existence from her and is not omnipotent. Play is the infant's way of coping with the anxiety that this produces, bridging the gap between its inner experience and the reality of the outside world. As the infant explores real objects and people and imbues them with its own magical phantasies[*] it achieves its first sense of autonomy and mastery. Here too, as we shall see, lies the power of the child's first creation, the 'transitional object', usually a soft cloth or toy.

Play is children's means of assimilating the world, making sense of their experience in order to make it part of themselves. The opposite process is accommodation in which children are learning to fit in with the demands of reality (Piaget 1951). The importance and excitement of play lie in its ability to link the real world and the inner mental world of the child. In play, children can transform the world according to their desires, especially a situation 'in which the individual finds his self, his body and his social role wanting and trailing'. The child both imagines and practises being in control, 'in an intermediate reality between phantasy and actuality' (Erikson 1965: 204).

Making sense of the world is an enormous task for young children. They are constantly at risk of being overwhelmed by events or feelings. Then 'solitary play remains an indispensable harbour for the overhauling of shattered emotions after periods of rough going in the social seas'. The child brings into his play 'whatever aspect of his ego has been ruffled most ... To "play it out" is the most natural self-healing method childhood affords' (Erikson 1965: 214–15). By re-enacting

---

[*]   Throughout the text the word 'phantasy' refers to unconscious processes of the mind as distinct from 'fantasy' which is a more conscious wish, day-dream or imagining.

and repeating events, often in a symbolic form, and by playing out their own feelings and phantasies, children come to terms with them and achieve a sense of mastery. They can safely express anger and aggression without harming other people, or without it rebounding to harm themselves. As anxiety is relieved and inner harmony restored the child becomes ready to cope with subsequent real events.

Social play with other children may have some of these healing qualities. The presence of others, however, means that play is often closer to the world of reality. Children may be involved in negotiating or coordinating their actions with one another. The demands of social interaction may sometimes inhibit the playing out of individual inner phantasies, unless the phantasies of several players coincide. The satisfaction of play may come from the enjoyment and excitement of play which reflects close relationships and mutual recognition. Yet where play involves a pecking order, those players with little power may find social play hurtful and even damaging.

The development of children's play follows a predictable pattern and is linked to aspects of physical, intellectual, social and emotional development. It is necessary to recognize the developmental level which a child is at if we are to use play appropriately to help. In particular we need to understand the process of emotional development from birth in order to appreciate the importance of play in contributing to and indicating development. Observations of spontaneous play are invaluable in diagnosis and assessment.

The rest of the chapter is an account of children's emotional and play development from birth to adulthood. This is summarized in Tables 1.1 and 1.2.

THE BEGINNING OF PLAY IN THE AGE OF ILLUSION

Maternal pre-occupation, attachment and containment

Play starts in the first weeks of a child's life. Donald Winnicott, celebrated paediatrician and psychoanalyst, used to advise parents who were fearful of the enormous responsibility of caring for their apparently helpless new baby that a baby is 'a going concern', with an immanent potential to live and develop. Yet he also observed that 'there is no such thing as a baby, only "a baby and someone"' (D.Winnicott 1964: 88). In the relationship between a baby and its mother, usually but not necessarily the biological mother (and there is no reason that mothering should not come from fathers), lies the foundations of a child's emotional development. A crucial part of that relationship involves play.

In its waking hours a baby experiences the distress and pain of hunger and physical discomfort inside or outside its body, the excitement and pleasure of feeding, and the relaxed comfort and pleasure of warmth and physical contact when urgent needs have been satisfied. In this tranquil state the baby responds to the mother's playfulness as she talks to and touches it, and starts to explore and play with its own and its mother's body. The infant is starting to find its physical edges.

Table 1.1 Stages in child development

Approx. age	Freud	Erikson	Peller	Klein	Winnicott	Dockar-Drysdale	Bruner	Piaget
0–12 months	Oral	Basic trust vs mistrust	Narcissistic (child by self, includes mother)	Paranoid-schizoid	Age of illusion (maternal pre-occupation)	Primary experience	Enactive thought	Sensory–motor
1 and 2 years	Anal	Autonomy vs shame and doubt	Pre-oedipal (child with mother)	Depressive	Transitional experience / Age of concern	Integration / Secondary experience (symbolization)	Ikonic thought / Symbolic thought	Pre-conceptual thought
3 and 4 years	Phallic	Initiative vs guilt	Oedipal (child with parents)					Intuitive thought (Fraiberg's magical thinking)
5–12 years	Latency	Industry vs inferiority	Post-oedipal (child with others)			(realization and conceptualization)		Concrete operational thought
Over 12 years	Genital	Identity vs role confusion						Abstract thought

Table 1.2 The development of play

Approx. age	Sensory / Creative play	Physical play	Exploratory play	Social play	Symbolic play
0–12 months	Using whole body and all senses – smelling, feeling, tasting, sight and sound. Using senses to experience world	Sensory-motor play. Practice play. Manipulative play, repetitive and ritual play	Own and mother's body. Pleasure at 'being a cause' – What is this object? What can I do with this object?	Baby and mother turn-taking games – Peep-bo. Pat-a-cake. Imitation of mother's actions and sounds. Solitary play	First 'words. Transitional object
1 and 2 years	Play with food and own waste products. Play with sounds and words. Using all senses	Large muscle play – walking and climbing. Small muscle skills – building	Exploring physical world: in/out, push/pull, hide/seek up/down	Baby and mother – hide and seek. Baby and father – rough and tumble. Baby and siblings. Solitary play, and watching parallel play with peers	Enactive naming, imitative play, self-pretend, doll pretend, role play, and situation or sequence pretend
3 and 4 years	Sand, water, play dough, painting, words, stories and music	Running, jumping trike riding dancing, ball skills drawing and cutting	Problem-solving, construction and puzzles	Associative play or cooperative parallel play. Cooperative play – domestic themes and chase games	Solitary elaborated symbolic play: complex and sustained themes increasing symbolism in use of objects in pretend, imaginary companions, 'talismans'
5–12 years	Creative art, music, books and stories, and pets	Games with rules, gym and sports, bike riding, sewing and construction, writing	Making things using domestic, technical and scientific skills	Cooperation, competition elaborate social organization. Formal games with rules	Cooperative socio-dramatic play: actions and roles coordinated (weddings, schools, camps, shows, hunter and hunted, continued from day to day). Elaborate solitary 'small world' play, books, stories and television
Over 12 years and adults	Creative arts, music, writing and books, sex and loving, cooking and eating, children and pets	Sports and games hobbies and skills	Science and technology		Playing with ideas, thinking, day-dreaming, writing and role playing in living

Emotional edges take longer to find. The baby's intense feelings of pleasure and pain, of love and anger, are bound up with its mother. The 'good enough' mother, whom Winnicott describes, initially meets her baby's needs totally. She is able to do this through her *maternal pre-occupation* in which she 'gives the infant the illusion that there is an external reality that corresponds to the infant's own capacity to create' (D.Winnicott 1971: 12). The mother's gradual and inevitable failure 'to perfectly accommodate herself to her infant's every need enables the infant eventually to relinquish the illusion of unity and omnipotence', to find its own 'edges' and to explore the reality of the outside world. A perfect mother who remained totally adapted to her infant's needs would not allow her baby to start to experience itself as a separate person.

Psychoanalyst Melanie Klein's ideas are helpful in understanding what happens between mother and infant (Klein, in Mitchell 1986). The infant's first experiences of the world involve the whole body. These sensory experiences may be pleasant or unpleasant. The infant's mental development requires it to sort and separate, or split, these sensory experiences into good and bad feelings. This gives a space in the baby's mind where good feelings can be stored to form the beginnings of the self. Because of the initial psychological merger of mother and child, the baby splits off or gets rid of the bad feelings by projecting them on to the mother, with a paranoid fear of them being returned. In the process it loses touch with that part of the self. Klein called this the *paranoid–schizoid position* and saw it as part of normal development. It remains to a greater or lesser extent an underlying part of everyone's personality. The tendency to blame and hurt others surfaces at times of stress.

The mother attends to her baby's feelings, good and bad, to such an extent that she experiences them as if they were her own. This is Bion's (1962) maternal *reverie*. (Most mothers will recall the compelling anxiety produced by the sound of their baby's crying.) The 'good enough' mother acts as a container, holding on to her baby's feelings, thinking about them and then giving them back to her child in a more bearable form. She gives back more good feelings than bad ones, more experiences of love than anger or hate, and the infant introjects these. This *containment* enables the child to integrate both good and bad feelings into the self. From the initial state of merger with the mother the edges of the infant's self become more defined. The predominance of loving feelings enables the child to bear and manage angry and anxious feelings. The child no longer has to get rid of them on to someone else. In addition, the child 'takes in the feeling of "being contained", of maternal space having been available for his anxieties to be born and thought about' (Copley and Forryan 1987: 241). Eventually the child in turn becomes a container for its feelings, able to hold on to them and think about them, a process helped by putting them into words. The child has reached Klein's *depressive position*. This does not mean that the child is depressed but that it is able to experience pain and sadness, guilt and grief. From the original state of merger with the mother the child has become an emotionally separate person.

Dockar-Drysdale (1968a, and in Tod 1968) describes this as the achievement of *integration*. She summarizes the processes which must be gone through in order to reach integration: *experience*, *realization*, *symbolization* and *conceptualization*. Children can only benefit from good experiences if they can feel that they have really happened to them, if they have a way of remembering and storing the good thing inside them, at first symbolically but eventually as a conscious intellectual process of putting it into words so that it can be communicated.

Unintegrated children

The aim of much play therapy is to repair or replicate the process of attachment and containment. Sometimes the mother is overwhelmed by the pain of the infant's angry projections. This may happen if she too is anxious or angry and does not have enough good feelings of her own to hold on to, or if she herself is not 'contained' by someone else. Copley and Forryan (1987) offer a catalogue of maternal responses of non-containment: 'sieve', where the communication goes straight through or the mother is overcome by anxiety, 'teatowel', where the infant's distress is wiped away, 'nappy' or 'sponge', soaking up distress but taking away some of its meaning, 'dustbin', where pain is dumped, or 'brickwall', a lack or mis-timing of response, as in the depressed mother described by Lynne Murray (1987).

Research based on attachment theory (Bowlby 1969 and 1982) has helped to identify children's responses to different kinds of non-containment. Young children have been observed in Ainsworth's 'strange situation' in which they are left briefly with an unfamiliar person and then reunited with their mother. Securely attached children are readily comforted by the parent's return. Others show insecure or *anxious attachment*. The attachment of children who show great distress, with much crying and clinging on mother's return, is described as *anxious/resistant*. Some children initially avoid their parents on return and refuse to be comforted; their attachment is described as *anxious/avoidant*. A third group show *disorganized* behaviour and attachment, perhaps to be equated with the completely uncontained child. Lynne Murray (1991) reports on findings of George, Kaplan and Main that link the child's insecure attachment to the mother's own attachments, as revealed in her memories of childhood and her present feelings about these. Mothers who had not resolved mourning a death or other loss had babies with disorganized attachment. Mothers who dismissed their childhood and reported it in a split-off way had 'anxious/avoidant' babies, whilst mothers enmeshed or preoccupied with early relationships had 'anxious/resistant' babies.

The uncontained child finds bad feelings unbearable and continues to project them on to other people in order to find relief. The child is stuck in the paranoid-schizoid position, with a diminished sense of self. As Dockar-Drysdale (1968) describes, such children remain *unintegrated* or *frozen*, broken off rather than grown away from the mother and unable to form a reciprocal relationship. Their greatest fear is of *annihilation*. They may try to preserve what is left of the self by annihilating others, mentally as much as physically. Another method is *adhesive identification*, holding or clinging to an object, such as a bright light, or a person treated as an object, or using sensuous feelings or body movements to hold the child together against the terror of falling apart. These are explained in Copley and Forryan (1987) which also provides a most lucid guide to understanding the process of containment.

As well as frozen children, Dockar-Drysdale describes two other forms of unintegrated children. *Archipelago* children have isolated islets of ego functioning which are not linked up into a coherent self. *False-self* children operate with a front which conceals and protects the turmoil within. Dockar-Drysdale's work in providing unintegrated children with the primary experiences which they have missed set the framework for much current work in therapeutic communities. Her use of play therapy will be discussed later.

Sensory-motor and narcissistic play

In the first weeks a baby's play is centred on its own body or on its mother's body as if it were its own. Peller (in Haworth 1964) calls this *narcissistic play*. Early experiences are sensual. The infant responds with its whole body to *sound*, such as a rhythmical heart-beat, or being spoken or sung to, to *smell* and *taste*, of mother's milk and her body, to *touching* and *movement*, the warmth of contact-comfort with mother's body, the texture of clothing, the sensation of being carried or rocked, the feel of feeding and eliminating, or of water in the bath, and to *seeing* light and dark, brightness, colour and pattern, faces and movement.

Piaget (1951) describes the development of *sensory–motor play* from these beginnings. The infant uses its mouth in early exploration, Freud's *oral stage*. It finds hands, then feet, and plays with them, finding out how to reach objects, make them move, grasp them and bring them to be further explored by the mouth or both hands. The infant takes delight in repeating a learned action, such as grasping a rattle. In this *practice play* the infant takes 'pleasure in being a cause', becoming more skilful and more familiar with the object. Sometimes play becomes ritualistic as an action is repeated many times with both concentration and delight – for example, peeping through a hole or rolling a ball. At this stage, play concerns only the present, since the infant has no words or symbols or even mental images to codify its experience. The child is using its senses and its body to *assimilate* experience. Bruner (1966) calls this *enactive thought*. The infant is actively finding out about the real world. This is possible only as long as the object of exploration is relatively new but not fearful. *Exploratory play* can only take place within safe boundaries. As the objects of play become more familiar, the infant moves from asking (not, of course, consciously at this stage) what does this object do, to what can I do with this object. (Millar (1968) calls this stage *manipulative play*.) The child who has established the physical edges of its own and the mother's body, and of objects in the real world, is on the way to Winnicott's stage of *transitional play*.

The mother's play helps her baby to find these edges, physical but also mental. Early play centres round feeding, bathing and dressing. Totally adapted to her baby, the mother imitates it, reflecting its sounds and facial movements. Donald Winnicott (1971) describes this as the mother making actual what the baby is ready to find. The infant, he says, finds this play immensely exciting because it is being given the experience of omnipotence or magical control. The infant begins to *imitate* the mother's actions – for example, as she introduces turn-taking games such as Pat-a-cake and Peep-bo. For the infant these involve a process of *accommodation* to the real world and the beginning of *social play*. At first the mother paces the game so that she catches the child's response and incorporates it, or she leaves spaces where the child can join in and have a turn. As the child's imitation becomes more practised the mother helps the child to take the initiative – for example, hiding its face in Peep-bo – until the play becomes truly reciprocal. This further helps *assimilation* so that the game becomes spontaneous and part of the child's play repertoire rather than the mother's. The mother then moves from fitting in with her child's actions to introducing her own ideas to enrich play. Mother and child are playing together but increasingly as separate people rather than as a unity.

Children's growing realization that they are not omnipotent and, like all humans, are ultimately alone, leads to anxiety. Play helps children to cope with this, giving them autonomy and a sense of being in control as they play in the safe space between self and mother. It is a way of bridging the gap between the child's inner world and the reality of the world outside. In 'play under the control of the player' the child's phantasies and imaginings become linked to real people or objects. Winnicott sees this as the beginning of all creativity. The first thing which a child creates is the *transitional object*, the soft cloth, ribbon or toy which serves as soother, comforter, protector and friend. It has its own vitality of warmth, movement, texture and smell which must never be changed except by the child, and which can survive excited loving and mutilation as well as affection and cuddling. Because it is something both inside and outside the child, the transitional object supports the child 'engaged in the perpetual human task of keeping inner and outer reality separate yet interrelated' (D.Winnicott 1971: 2). The integrated child who creates its own transitional object has made the first step in symbolic play.

The play needs of unintegrated children

Children who, for whatever reason, have not experienced the feeling of being contained or held in the first year of life have not reached integration. They lack the capacity for symbolic play and so cannot make use of this in therapy. Their play needs are more fundamental. They require *primary experience*. This may be provided by their mother if she receives appropriate support and help, of which play may form an important part. If the mother is to contain her child she herself must be contained. Failing this, children need a total therapeutic environment which replicates the process of containment.

Regressive play forms a crucial part of primary experience. It can help to restore missed sensory experiences. These children need blankets, cushions, soft sofas, bean bags and 'nesting material': they need small enclosed spaces, such as cardboard boxes, to curl up in, warm milk and feeding bottles, soft toys and teddy bears. Dockar-Drysdale (1968a: 141) also recommends sand, water, bubble-blowing and finger-painting materials, glove puppets, story books to read aloud, a mirror and a large jar of coloured sweets.

A child's senses can be re-vitalized through appropriate play experiences and programmes. Prescott and Jones (1975) offer a 'softness index' to assess the sensual-tactile responsiveness of a pre-school environment. The softer the environment, the more it includes of: play dough, water, finger paint, clay or mud, sand which children can be in, earth to dig in, grass to be on, laps (of people holding children), swings, rockers, cosy furniture, a rug or carpet, animals which can be held. Cooking and eating, thinking about the associations of smells, listening to and making rhythms and music, singing and being sung to, exploring colours and textures, painting and drawing, all these can also help to put children of all ages in touch with their senses so that they feel more really alive. *Sensory play* is discussed further in Chapters 2 and 9.

As well as regressive and sensory play, unintegrated children need the equivalent of the *reciprocal play and turn-taking* games of infancy. For older children these can be action songs, rhymes or finger plays involving body movement or contact. They can include all sorts of play, provided that the adult takes part and supports, rather than drowns, any initiation from the child. The adult needs the skills of the 'good enough' mother of an infant.

Unintegrated children are not ready to play and share with other children. They need to play within the safety of a containing relationship with a mother figure. The adult must be able to survive repeated annihilation by the child and to continue to act as a container, holding and thinking about the child's feelings and returning them in a more bearable form. As the child moves towards integration the adult provides the safe space in which the child can begin to find itself through play.

PLAY IN THE AGE OF CONCERN AND AUTONOMY

The development of children's thinking and understanding

Children normally reach integration towards the end of their first year of life. Because they have enough good feelings about themselves they no longer need to project and get rid of their bad feelings. They have been contained and so have become containers themselves, able to think about their feelings and experiences. Becoming a separate person means that they are able to experience feelings of anxiety and sadness, of grief and guilt.

Children's awareness of having a separate existence from the mother is inevitably linked to desperate anxiety about losing her. Powerful *attachment* feelings and *separation anxiety* increase from the age of about six months and remain acute usually until at least the age of three. This anxiety is reduced by familiar surroundings and people. Children often have secondary attachment figures, such as fathers, grandparents, older siblings or child minders, who can provide the security they need to enable them to explore and play. In situations of overwhelming anxiety only the primary attachment figure, the mother, will do. The work of Bowlby (1969 and 1982, 1973, 1980) and the Robertsons (1970, 1976, 1989) has been crucial to our knowledge and understanding of the processes of attachment. They have also shown how to prevent or mitigate the emotional damage caused by separation and loss, as children move through the stages of response, from *protest* to *despair* and *detachment*, with eventually some form of *reorganization* if all goes well.

While the child's attachment needs remain strong into and beyond the second year of life, the mother's level of attachment to her child tends to drop, often because of the birth of a new baby. This 'dethronement' affects many children profoundly. Those who cope best emotionally are generally those children whose fathers 'take on' the older child (Dunn and Kendrick 1982).

Children's ability to cope with the unfamiliar is helped by their growing intellectual capacities. They become able to hold images in the mind. This *ikonic thought* is a means of remembering the mother in her absence. It also enables the child to make use of delayed imitation in play. This and the development of language prepare the way for symbolic thought and play. Piaget (1951) describes the child's thought at this stage as *egocentric* and *pre-conceptual* or pre-oper-ational. As Donaldson (1978) has shown it is not that children cannot think logically but rather that they do not yet have enough information about the world. Therefore they go by the evidence of what they perceive and experience. Their sense of time is developing but is still weak. They do not know that other people see things from a different point of view, quite literally as well as emotionally. So they assume that they are the cause of others' behaviour. Fraiberg (1959) calls this egocentrism *magical thinking*.

In the second and third years of life most children learn to control the bodily function of elimination, Freud's *anal stage*. Erikson saw this in the broader context of children learning to hold on and let go, as they struggle with the conflicting needs of dependence and independence. Where this is successful the child establishes a sense of *autonomy* which gives the beginnings of self-control and will-power. Failure results in a sense of *shame* and self-*doubt*. Play continues in the safe space between child and mother or mother-substitute. Children are only free to play when they feel secure and contained in a familiar world. The quality of their play, seen in their abilty to relax and become absorbed, in their concentration and curiosity, and in their ability to develop play themes, indicates how far they have achieved a sense of autonomy.

Development of play

Sensory and physical play

Sensory play becomes linked to *physical play* as children continue to use the whole of their body in experiencing the world: warmth and cold, water in a bath or pool, the squelch of mud, sand trickling through fingers and toes, shuffling through fallen leaves, the wonder of paint and finger paint, the smell of food, of grass, of tarmac and petrol in a hot street, hard ground, soft beds and clothes, wind and rain, music and singing, picture books and stories. As children become able to walk, run, jump and climb, they gain great pleasure from practice play of new skills involving physical movement. Confidence and self-esteem are increased as children demonstrate control of themselves in their environment, a source of particular satisfaction when their small physical size often makes them incompetent in a world of giants.

Children around the age of two often play at building towers and knocking them down. Erikson sees this as children's expression of mastery of space, at an age when they have only recently learned to stand upright without wobbling. The triumph lies in the child controlling the destruction. If anyone else should destroy the tower the child is very upset as it then sees itself in the vulnerable tower (Erikson 1965: 212).

Exploratory and social play

Exploratory and *manipulative play* continue. The play themes of one- and two-year-olds often concern attachment and autonomy, separation and individuation – for example, putting objects into containers and, like Eeyore, taking them out again, or games of Hide and Seek. Brenda Crowe (1980) wonderfully describes play themes of in/out, up/down, push/pull, fill/empty, hide/seek, do/undo, look/show. Children often talk aloud as they play, Piaget's *monologue*. (In play therapy the worker may do this for the child.) Children also play with language, delighting in the sounds of words and new combinations of them.

Social play develops from turn-taking games with mother to active games such as Hide and Seek, often involving ambush, which is again a reflection of the separation–individuation process (Hoxter 1977). Many children enjoy rough-and-tumble play, increasingly with fathers or older siblings (Cohen 1987). Outside the family, children play alongside rather than with children of a similar age. In this parallel play the children may appear to be playing together but the origin of each child's play is in its own phantasy. 'Other children seemingly drawn into play are really puppets. Their response is not ploughed back into the play, it falls by the wayside.' (Peller, in Haworth 1964: 180). Children talk out loud as they play but it is a *collective monologue*, each talking about its own actions. They may be aware of what other children are doing or saying, and contact may occur through play with the same toy, but it is to their mothers that children turn when they want the other child to do something.

Symbolic or pretend play

The most important development in children's play at this stage, supported by developing language skills, is *symbolic* or *pretend play*. We have seen how the transitional object is the child's first real creation. It is a symbolic object, existing in the real world but with properties given to it from the child's inner world. It may directly stand for the mother and give comfort in her absence. It may also be the child's way of becoming the mother, internalizing her within the self – for example, as a child in play may tell its toy rabbit what to do (Skynner and Cleese 1983). This too eases separation anxiety. From this beginning, symbolic play develops in a recognizable pattern. In the following account of development, ages are based on those given in Sheridan (1975).

In their first year, children have already begun to use *imitation* in reciprocal play with the mother. They elaborate this play – for example, as they copy the performance of domestic tasks. These imitations become assimilated and remembered – that is, they become internal images. Early pretend play tends to involve the *remembered imitation* of familiar domestic situations. At about 15 months, children show definition by use, or *enactive naming*, of a familiar object – for example, putting an empty cup to their lips. Around 18 months, *self-pretend play* occurs. The child performs a pretend action such as pretending to drink or sleep. The next stage is *doll pretend*. Children start to carry round a doll or teddy bear, held the right way up, rather than by one leg, Christopher Robin fashion, as they have before. They may feed teddy or put it to bed. As teddy 'comes to life' they may make teddy feed itself.

Children start to take the roles of others, with a progression from actions to simple roles and then situations. For example, a child may pretend to drive using actions only, later going on to play 'I'm mum driving the car'. This stage of *role play* is sometimes called *decentred symbolic pretend* as the child becomes less egocentric. This is followed by *sequence pretend*. The child develops pretend situations, such as 'I'm Mum driving the car to go shopping'. Pretend sequences become longer and more elaborate. By three years, children may be playing out a complex sequence – for example, undressing teddy, bathing it and putting it to bed. In this spontaneous play the child is usually playing alone, although perhaps making frequent reference to an adult attachment figure.

Children may take pleasure in joining in with pretend and 'silly' games initiated by parents or older siblings. These games can create excitement and fear as well as laughter – for example, in games of chase such as Valentine's (1956) game of Roaring Lions with his infant son. They can involve flights of fancy, or role incongruities, as in Cohen's (1987) description of his one-year-old daughter's laughter when her mother sucked her dummy. A 'play face' often introduces social or *shared pretend* (Garvey 1977), in mutual recognition of pretending.

The imaginative or 'as if' quality of play develops in parallel. The first stage is pretend using real objects. Then comes pretending with toy objects, usually child-sized. This is followed by the use of miniature or scale-version toys, such as dolls' house people and animals. Pretend play using nothing, such as offering an invisible pretend meal, involves a still greater degree of symbolism. At the highest level it is the use of symbolic objects which bear little resemblance to the real thing – for example, pretending to telephone using an ice-cream scoop. The use of several symbolic objects in a complex play sequence indicates a high level of symbolic play.

Through symbolic play, children in the *age of concern* are working at making sense of the world they live in, understanding how it works and their own place in it, and so increasing their confidence and autonomy or sense of mastery. 'Play is the infantile form of the human ability to deal with experience by creating model situations and to master reality by experiment and planning' (Erikson 1965: 214). Children also use play to help them cope with difficult situations where they have experienced fear, anxiety or anger. For most children their own play experience is sufficient to provide self-healing.

A famous illustration of this self-healing is Freud's account of an 18-month-old boy who had a wooden reel tied to his cot with a string. When in his cot he constantly repeated a game of throwing out the reel, murmuring 'O-o-o-oh' and then hauling it back again with a delighted 'Da'. Freud noted that this game coincided with the mother being out of the house all day. He interpreted the game as the child's compulsion to re-enact painful experience (which would now be called separation anxiety), with the difference that the child became master of the situation by controlling the reel's reappearance. (Freud's account is quoted in Erikson (1965: 208–9).) Erikson noted that while this game had a specific meaning for this child, about coping with loss, for most children a reel on a string may simply symbolize an animal on a lead, but for children reaching the stage of autonomy it may signify a new mastery of holding on and letting go.

A contemporary illustration of a similar use of play is Julia Prosser's account of how her rising three-year-old dealt with his father's necessary absence from home for two nights a week. She writes:

> He was clearly very angry and confused about his father's departure He wept when he left in the morning and refused to speak to him on his return. He came to terms with this by doing jigsaws almost exclusively for a month. It seemed to me at the time that he was ordering a world in play that he felt he could not cope with in reality. This was confirmed six months later when his small sister developed chicken pox and consequently required rather more attention from us. The jigsaws which had not really been used since the earlier period came out again, his favourite on both occasions being a fairly complicated fifty piece one. This seemed to be a spontaneous decision on his part, although he has always been interested in jigsaws. It was the intensity and consistency with which he played that suggested to me that it was some form of coping strategy.

Children who need play help

Children whose lives have been disrupted through experiences of separation and loss at this stage of their development may benefit from play help. They may be unable to cope alone with severe grief and anxiety. Others may be suffering from emotional neglect or abuse, or other emotional damage, which produce the painful feelings of shame and doubt which result from failure to achieve a sense of autonomy. Perhaps they are unable to play because they lack the security of a familiar environment and the containment provided by the mother. They may suffer play disruption, being unable to play because of the strong emotions of anger or acute anxiety which are aroused.

The use of play, together with other forms of support, to repair mother–child attachment can help many children and their families. Some children may benefit from play in which they can re-enact events and play out their inner feelings in symbolic form in the presence of a safe adult. In former times, as Erikson points out, this adult might be a grandmother or favourite aunt. Today it is more likely to be a professional worker. At this stage, children are usually quite unconscious of the symbolism in their play and their use of it to make sense of their experience and to cope with anxiety. They have not reached Dockar-Drysdale's stage of conceptualization, so it is unlikely that the adult can help by interpreting or making explicit the symbolism, although it may be possible to work usefully within the symbolism. The sense of mastery which symbolic play provides, together with the containment offered by the adult, may help the child to restore inner harmony and to be better prepared to cope with the complicated relationships of the next stage.

PLAY IN THE OEDIPAL STAGE

Development of children's thinking and understanding

With the child's growing sense of autonomy and identity comes a need to understand roles and relationships in the family and their link to the roles of the world beyond. The child at this *genital stage*, normally between the ages of three and five, may be struggling with the strong feelings of the *Oedipus complex* in which the boundaries between the generations are made clear. Feelings of love and desire for the parent of the opposite sex, and thus of rivalry with the parent of the same sex, become transmuted into a socially acceptable identification with the parent of the same sex. Children become interested in sexual differences and aware of the maleness or femaleness of their bodies. Boys take the additional psychological step of transferring attachment to the mother to identification with the father. Children learn that future sexual attachments must be made outside the family, giving the impetus to grow up and develop a wider network of relationships. They are unconsciously absorbing the values of their families and of others in their immediate world. Their *racial* and *cultural identity* is already being determined.

Children at this stage are intellectually curious and continually ask questions, about how things work, why people feel as they do, reflecting their growing understanding of space and time as they ask what happens in other times and places and about other people that they know. Their curiosity starts from their own experience of reality. They must have a personal connection. One thoughtful three-year-old's questions to her mother, Elaine Howells, included: Why can't boys wear dresses? What makes the wind blow? Why do men have nipples, they don't feed babies? Can a lady with seeds in her tummy have a baby if she doesn't want to get married? Where will you sit when I'm driving the car? Why do fireman kill people in fires? Why do we have to die? Why haven't I got a Teasmade in my bedroom? When we have counted to a hundred is that the end? Why can't I see myself grow?

It is hardly surprising that a child of less than 50 months sometimes makes a wrong inference based on incomplete information – for example, in asking why firemen kill people in fires. They are still at Piaget's stage of *intuitive thought*. A child asked, for example, *why* Mrs Smith is John's mother 'just knows'. Children still go by the evidence of what they see and experience. A child who goes into foster care may not 'know' that their original home and parent still exist. Magical egocentric thinking is still strong. Children think that they are the cause of other people's behaviour or of events which affect them, believing, for instance, that father left home because they were naughty. Social worker Madge Bray worked with a child who thought he was in care because he 'pinched the biscuits' the morning his mother went into hospital.

When children feel that their sexual and intellectual curiosity is accepted and valued by their family they develop a sense of *initiative*, a feeling of direction and purpose. The world is their oyster. If they meet with constant discouragement and disapproval then instead they develop a sense of worthlessness and *guilt*, a conscience which can become a crippling burden, especially when fuelled by mistaken interpretations of a situation.

Development of play

Sensory, physical and exploratory play

Play in the age of initiative continues and develops many earlier themes. *Sensory* and *creative play* occur in play with natural materials such as sand and water, mud and clay, in painting and finger painting, in singing and music, and in play with words and sounds. *Physical play* involves exercising new skills, as children become able to run, climb, hop, dance, swim, ride a trike, and throw, kick and catch a ball. Physical play is often incorporated into energetic social pretend play and informal games. In *exploratory play* children investigate and make use of objects and solve play problems. Through their play, children build up their knowledge of the physical world, developing concepts of space, time and number, conservation of quantity and volume, of cause and effect, increasing their sense of confidence and mastery.

Erikson noted that body identity and sexual differences are reflected in play constructions. Boys tended to build towers and to make models involving much activity; girls created quieter scenes, typically an enclosure with an entrance. He recognized too that children's choice of play material depended on what is available in the child's culture as well as on the skills a child has developed.

Symbolic or pretend play

In *pretend play*, new themes emerge concerned with the various roles which people play outside as well as inside the family. These themes occur in solitary play and in increasingly frequent social play with parents, siblings and other children outside the family, nowadays often of a similar age in playgroup or nursery. Peller writes:

> In oedipal play, the fantasy may be social in its origin (several children putting their heads together). It is usually social by way of content, dealing with several people in various roles, and the execution may be either solitary (e.g., a child plays alone with dolls or toy soldiers) or social (several children playing together). However, contact between coplayers is loose. It can be lost, and the players may never know the difference.
>
> (Peller, in Haworth 1964: 180)

The symbolism in pretend play becomes elaborated as invented people and objects become involved in the child's development of a complex imaginary theme. A theme may be sustained, but children often change themes rapidly as their thoughts go off at a tangent as they play. For example, a child says she is mum bathing baby, holding a doll in a box full of imaginary water and using a brick for soap. Moments later the box is a table and the brick is food for her family.

By playing the roles of others, children not only start to understand how others may feel but also can acquire a better idea of themselves and their own role and identity in the family. In both solitary and shared pretend play, children can safely express their feelings and anxieties. Some children have imaginary friends who are important as companions or scapegoats to represent their split-off bad selves as the age of guilt dawns.

Piaget (1951) came surprisingly close to psychoanalytic thinking in his models of play. In his *compensatory play* the child plays at doing things normally forbidden, or pretends that something has happened that has not really occurred. Such play may be a cathartic neutralization of fear or anger, or it may be a wish fulfillment. For example, a child jealous of the baby may hit its doll, or, in role reversal, play at being the baby itself. In *liquidating compensatory play*, children facing difficult or unpleasant situations may relive and come to accept them. The child who is ill or injured may play that its doll is also ill or injured. In *anticipatory play*, children play out fears of the consequences of refusing to do what is expected of them. The child constantly told to be careful may have dolls that 'forgot' and come to harm.

Erikson asked a number of four- and five-year-old children to make something with blocks and toys. From observing their play he concluded that the themes presented in these play constructions may be the repetitive

> working through of a traumatic experience: but they may also express a playful renewal. If they seem to be governed by some need to communicate, or even to confess they certainly also seem to serve the joy of self-expression ... If they seem dedicated to the exercise of growing faculties they also seem to serve the

mastery of a complex life situation. As I would not settle for any one of these explanations alone, I would not wish to do without any of them.

(Erikson, in Bruner, Jolly and Sylva 1976: 691)

These different possibilities warn the observer that although a child's play *may* be a direct imitation of something that has happened, this is far from always being the case. For example, if the child is playing the role of the mother and smacking the doll baby, it does not follow that the child's own mother does this, although it is a possibility. It is equally likely that the child playing mother is putting in its own immature response as to how to cope with a fractious baby. Another strong possibility is that the child is expressing its own anger and jealousy of a younger sibling.

Children at this stage are often struggling with the difficulty of separating fantasy from reality. Television, videotapes and stories in books may be experienced as real events. Sometimes too the stories which children invent, or their imaginary companions, take on a mistaken reality. Even then the content of children's fantasies reflects their own experience or their feelings. 'Children cannot fantasize about events which lie completely outside of their experience' (Pithers 1990a: 20). For example, although young children have sexual feelings they cannot enact sexual behaviour in play unless they have either seen or experienced it, whether directly or on a videotape, photograph or other medium. The detail of the child's enactment or description will often indicate which is more likely.

Fantasy and reality are rarely blurred in every part of a child's mind, even at this young age. For example, a child with an imaginary companion, who feels quite real to the child, is as likely as any other child to be able to give an accurate description of what members of the family did this morning. However, because adults are such powerful figures, under-fives may sometimes agree with a suggestion an adult makes, although they are usually able to resist suggestions which go completely against their experience. On the other hand, they have not learned to 'hedge' and are likely to answer an open question with the truth as they perceive it.

Social pretend play

Dramatic play with other children develops at this stage. At first it is *associative play* (Isaacs 1933), with each child involved in its own imaginative theme and engaged in collective monologue, although there may be a play object in common which results in some joint activity. The beginnings of coordination are illustrated in Brenda Crowe's famous account of two children from different social backgrounds playing in a home corner at playgroup. The boy announces, 'I'm making the stoo for dinner' and the girl responds, 'All right, while you do that I'll just pop to Harrods for the canapés' (Crowe 1983: 109). Dressing-up is popular for a long time for itself, without being followed by any enactment in role play. Some children show a keen need to wear a particular hat or cape, perhaps as a sort of magic talisman to keep them safe in stressful situations such as playgroup and nursery.

Cooperative pretend play usually begins with *domestic themes*, such as meals, shopping, going to bed and being ill, in which the players take different roles, such as mother, father and baby. Packing, going on a trip or holiday, repairing and telephoning are common, and Garvey (1977) also noted that *treating* and *healing* was a constantly recurring theme. Play is assimilative as children make sense of the events in their lives. For example, two boys who had recently moved house spent all morning shifting the whole contents of the playgroup home corner to the far side of the room. Children often construct dens with any available materials, disappearing inside to pretend or giggle together. Both boys and girls become involved in domestic play, and either may play the familiar mothering roles. Playing the father's role is often harder, because it is less known, demonstrated by the boy who, announcing he was dad going to work, went out of the door and looked non-plussed as he wondered what to do next.

Roles are less differentiated in informal games of running and chasing or hiding, although there may be a leader and followers. These games are mostly played by boys and often have symbolic themes such as monsters, Cowboys and Indians, Batman, Superman, the A Team, Mutant Turtles, or whatever is the current fad. The underlying game is the same, a mutual phantasy, often to do with *averting threat* – for example, killing the monster or putting out a fire. It may be to do with the need for feelings of autonomy and control at an age when boys are establishing sex role identification but lack power in their own families.

Children who need play help

Because of the still limited language skills of pre-school children observation of play is valuable in diagnosis and assessment. It may indicate how the child feels about itself and others. Sometimes the adult has information which needs to be communicated to the child – for example, explaining what is going to happen. Although children may hear the words, they may understand more fully if the adult also uses play methods of communication. Play also helps the adult to grasp how much the child has really understood.

Children who have suffered emotional damage during the oedipal stage, rather than earlier, may be able to make good use of the provision of a therapeutic play situation. They are usually able to use symbolic play to express their feelings and to help them to make sense of them and come to terms with them. The child's communication to the adult is often through the symbolism used in play. The adult who can make a space for the child in the mind is able to attend to this communication even if it is not fully understood. This helps the child to start to progress from using symbolism alone, to thinking about the feelings which the symbolic play expresses, and, as feelings become more conscious, to putting them into words.

As at earlier stages, play for child and parent together, in pairs or in groups, can help to repair damaged attachments and give parents increased confidence and skills, enabling them to 'contain' their child.

Older children who experienced damage at the oedipal stage may benefit from help which allows them to go back to playing out the symbolic themes of these years. The adult will carry some transference from the child's parents which may be used to help the child to come to a more satisfactory resolution of the developmental tasks of this age.

PLAY IN THE AGE OF INDUSTRY

The development of children's thinking and understanding

Freud described the years between five or six and adolescence as the *latency period*. Sex roles and family relationships have settled into established patterns. Strong drives are relatively dormant. Children's developmental task is to make their way in the world outside the family, specifically in the domain of school and the peer group. This is Erikson's *age of industry* in which children learn the skills of their culture. If they are made to feel inadequate compared with other children, they may develop feelings of *inferiority*, which in turn affect the development of skills. Social play with peers may contribute to these feelings as well as the degree of success in school work or experience in the home and neighbourhood. Adults other than parents may be greatly admired and their opinion of the child may affect self-esteem.

Children's racial and cultural identity may be decisively affected. Children learn how others perceive the colour of their skin, the background of their parents, the language or accent with which they speak. Maximé (1986) views the child's *racial identity* as a separate aspect of personal identity. She uses Melanie Klein's object relations theory to understand the black child's difficulty in establishing a satisfactory self-identity in a white majority culture. Black children may introject society's negative images of blackness and use projective identification to 'be' white. They then need help in achieving a positive black identity.

Intellectual and linguistic skills at this stage include literacy. Understanding and expression may appear quite sophisticated, clouding the fact that concepts underlying language may not be understood in adult ways. In so far as the world is familiar and what they are doing makes sense to them, children will be using *concrete operational thought*, understanding cause and effect through their observations of the world. They are rarely capable of abstract thinking. Intuitive thinking will persist where cause and effect cannot be clearly understood, and children's egocentricity will mean that they often perceive themselves as the cause of events. For example, they may blame themselves for the death of a parent or the break-up of a family in divorce. They can be reassured by simple concrete explanations of the reasons for events. For example, adopted children can understand that their birth parents were 'too busy', 'very ill', 'died', 'did not have enough money' or 'had too many children' (Brodzinsky, in Burnell 1990).

Around the age of eight many children start to be aware of the complexities of relationships and need more rounded explanations. Brodzinsky observes that children begin to see that relationships are not absolute but conditional. They also begin to understand the possible feelings and emotions of other people. If situations and feelings can change then they can also be reversed. (Piaget noted that appreciation of reversibility marked a child's transition from intuitive to concrete thought.) Children who have suffered loss need to enter the process of 'adaptive grieving' (Brodzinsky, in Burnell 1990). This may involve a period of disturbed behaviour at home or school, as children go through the stages of shock and denial, protest and despair, to reach a new integration. Their understanding remains related to concrete events and situations. It is not until the approach of adolescence that abstract concepts can be fully grasped.

Development of play

Sensory, physical and exploratory play

Sensory and *creative play* become closer to the creative arts and music. *Exploratory play* comes under stronger social influence with girls and boys diverging in their interests, which focus on the technical and technological skills required in post-industrial society. Computers, constructional games and hobbies such as model-making, cooking or sewing take children closer to adult occupations. *Physical play* involves the enjoyment and practice of new skills, from hop-scotch, skate-boarding, bike and horse riding, to dancing, gym and football.

Solitary and social pretend play, and games with rules

Socio-dramatic play increases in sophistication with the growth of social skills, which allow cooperation and the coordination of roles. Close rapport between players is essential. Each child stays within its allotted role and supports others in their roles. Games may involve more realistic detail than formerly as well as flights of imagination (Garvey 1977). Building camps, adventure games or secret societies go alongside more domestic games of weddings, schools and hospitals. Earlier themes of hiding and seeking, chasing and ambushing, continue with the addition of a new theme, the hunter and the hunted (Hoxter 1977), of the good guys versus the bad. Games may be very elaborate and continued from day to day, although play is still spontaneous and may take off in unplanned directions. Often the planning and preparation for a game take all the time and the intended game may not happen. For example, planning parts and costumes, or puppets, for a show become the real play, rather than the final enactment which may be cursory or non-existent.

While group pretend play may be very satisfying to a child there is also the possibility of frustration and conflict, of exercising power and feeling oppressed, which arises out of the social nature of play. There is another danger. With older children the boundaries around play that keep it safe are more easily breached; the adult presence may be distant or missing. Group play can lose its space between phantasy and the real world and become, as in *Lord of the Flies*, both a group phantasy, often with scapegoats, and an awful reality.

Games with rules become common at this stage, chasing games such as tag, singing and ring games such as In and Out the Dusty Bluebells, counting and hiding games, skipping games, marbles, and numerous card and board games. Piaget thought that from the age of seven games with rules largely replace imaginative games, although others, such as Opie (1969), have noted that both continue side by side or in combination. Some rules are handed down and given; others are spontaneous. This kind of play fits in with the child's need to learn and practice the rules of social life outside the immediate family in order to become eventually a full member of society. Peller (1964) asserts that the emphasis on belonging to the group and on fairness, the strict rules, and the urge to re-play or start again, which typify *post-oedipal play*, are children's way of coping with their anxiety as they doubt their abilities for the first time. It remains play as long as it is an end in itself and players are bound only by the need to cooperate for the success of the game. Once an element of compulsion or the need to win replaces this it ceases to be play, as many a school-child who loathes sports would agree.

Solitary play survives and continues, providing a last haven for purely assimilative play. Children may play complex imaginative games with dolls and animals. Small world play with miniatures, such as dolls' houses, animals, Lego, play people, cars, space ships, and numerous other vehicles and machines, bricks, blocks and construction materials, can become very elaborate and sustained from day to day. In this play where children are directors of all that happens in these small worlds, inner calm may be restored after, in Erikson's phrase, 'periods of rough going in the social seas'. Books and stories, and also television, are a vital means of respite for many children. They also provide a way into pretend worlds. These can help children to make sense of their real situations and to try out different solutions in safety. Through identification with powerful children in stories their sense of autonomy and competence can be restored.

Children who need play help

While most children find solitary play sufficient for self-healing, those whose lives are severely disrupted may need the help of an adult presence as they play. Their play may have stopped, or become 'stuck', repetitive and defensive, covering up rather than dealing with painful feelings. The therapeutic adult provides containment, a space where the child's feelings can be borne and thought about. As at earlier stages the adult may be enabling symbolic play, helping the process of self-healing. Children whose intellectual and language skills are sufficient to the task may be able to think about the feelings they have expressed symbolically, and put them into words. This stage of conceptualization enables a conscious retrospective reflection on their experience. However, if children's experience of damage and deprivation goes back over many years they may need at first to go back to much earlier stages of play help.

Play may be especially helpful to children with language difficulties and delays or with other mental or physical disabilities which restrict their ability to talk about their feelings and experiences.

Play may simply be used to ease communication with children. Clare Winnicott (1964) observed that children more easily become relaxed and spontaneous when both they and the adult are concentrating on a 'third object'.

The growth of social skills and the social influence of the peer group make therapeutic group work possible at this stage. Drama therapy may be helpful. Play techniques may make a group more enjoyable so that children are more relaxed and spontaneous. Carefully thought out structured games may help children to deal with difficult emotions with the support of peers who have had similar experiences. These groups anchor play firmly to reality. Very occasionally group work may take the form of a group phantasy, where the only link to reality is provided by the group leader, who has the enormous responsibility of ensuring that the phantasy takes a therapeutic rather than a damaging direction.

PLAY IN ADOLESCENCE

The strong emotions of early childhood surface again in adolescence. The ways in which earlier developmental tasks were dealt with is reflected in behaviour. Issues of trust, attachment and separation, containment and non-containment, autonomy and shame and doubt, initiative and guilt, all these re-emerge in the adolescent's developmental task of establishing a sense of *identity*. Failure to achieve this results in role confusion (Erikson 1965). Intellectually adolescents are more like adults, with a developing ability for abstract or disembedded thought. Even so, much everyday thought continues to be rooted in concrete explanations of events.

Play continues but is expressed in more adult forms, in the creative arts, sports and physical activity, in intellectual curiosity, within new sexual relationships and in peer group social activity. Because of their need to demonstrate to themselves and their peers that they have become members of the adult world, adolescents often strongly reject what they perceive as more childish forms of play which threaten to return them to a stage which they are struggling to leave behind. Playful fantasies and day-dreaming may take emotional energy. Deeper feelings are often more accessible through counselling and talking therapies than through play. Art therapy, however, can be very helpful. Sometimes the use of structured games can open and ease communication between the young person and adult. Playful methods in group work, such as drama therapy, may be very powerful.

Play may be a route to help young people with immature minds who find themselves inhabiting strange physically maturing bodies. They include adolescents with learning difficulties or mental disabilities or illnesses, or language disorders. They may be children so emotionally damaged earlier in life that regression to previous stages is needed to help them to re-build their sense of self.

THE PLAY NEEDS OF ADULTS

Many adults believe that play is childish and would agree with Piaget that play fades away towards the end of childhood, to be replaced by real work and recreation. Yet adults have play needs beyond recreation from work. We do well to recognize this and to understand that play is not just a filling in of time before real work and learning begin but an essential element of growing and being fully human. As we have seen, play is spontaneous and creative, free from the inhibition produced by fear of failure.

Many aspects of children's play can be seen in adult creativity. *Sensory play* is reflected in art and music, in caring for pets, and in sensual and sexual touching and loving. As parents we can share again many of the sensual delights of childhood. I remember making blissful drippy sand castles on a warm beach with my husband and small daughters, only to realize that the children were doing something else and my husband and I were playing contentedly together. Playing and laughing with our children satisfied our own play needs as well as our children's.

Physical play becomes translated into sporting and physical activities. *Imaginative* and *pretend play* become day-dreaming, thinking and perhaps creative writing. *Exploratory play* may become thinking and playing with ideas in science and technology. The great physicist, Richard Feynman, tells of the freezing of his ability to do research when appointed to a post where he felt great results were expected of him. It was only when he was told that it was the university which took all the risks when he was appointed that he became able to play with ideas again, starting from a moment watching the university crest wobbling on a spinning plate.

> I used to do whatever I felt like doing – it didn't have to do with whether it was important for the development of nuclear physics, but whether it was interesting and amusing to play with ... So I got this new attitude. Now that I am burned out ... I'm going to *play* with physics, whenever I want to, without worrying about any importance whatsoever ... just doing it for the fun of it. And before I knew it ... I was 'playing' – working really – and with the same old problem that I loved so much ... It was effortless. It was easy to play with these things. It was like uncorking a bottle. There was no importance to what I was doing, but ultimately there was. The diagrams and the whole business that I got the Nobel prize for came from that piddling around with the wobbling plate.
>
> (Feynman 1985: 173–8)

Transactional analysis provides a useful succinct description of adult mental structure, dividing it into *Parent*, *Adult* and *Child* parts. The *Parent* contains attitudes, values, opinions and learned concepts, as well as the ability to look after oneself and others. It may be 'critical', leading to controlling and judgmental behaviour, or 'nurturing', caring for others. The *Adult* is concerned with rational thinking and decision making. The *Child* is made up of 'emotional responses to situations, as well as creativity, spontaneity, intuitive thinking and early, learned behaviours' (Pitman 1984: 141). It also contains the 'needy child' (Eichenbaum and Orbach 1983), representing adults' continuing emotional needs for love and care. As adults we retain the *Child* part of our make-up, including room for spontaneous creative behaviour or play. As Brenda Crowe (1983) observed, 'At any age play is not so much what we do as how we feel about what we are doing; play is not even always a doing. Play is a feeling'. If play needs can be met in adult life, in ways which are helpful to the self and not destructive or irresponsible towards others, adults' happiness and self-esteem may grow, and if they are parents their children will benefit from this too.

Parents who are least able to recognize and meet the play and other needs of their children are often those whose own needs were never adequately met in their own childhood. They learned to adapt, conform and be good, or to rebel against oppressive demands; they learned to bury feelings of pain and loss, constructing elaborate defences to deny to themselves and others that they have been hurt. In the process they cut themselves off from others, preventing themselves from further hurt but diminishing their ability to give to their own children the care and the love they themselves had so sorely lacked. Sometimes the spontaneity of play remains but is used irresponsibly, in the interest of the adults and not their children. Nover (1985) describes a parents' game with their baby of 'now I'm going to get you'. Parents may tease their children in an abuse of power. They may play with their children as if they were sibling rivals. Parents' own 'child' needs and feelings require containment. Where this cannot be offered by family or friends it may come from professional help. Containment may also be offered in less formal situations. Play can be an important way to help parents to find the spontaneous child within themselves and to use it to meet both their own and their children's needs.

CONCLUSION – WHO NEEDS PLAY HELP? PLAY OBSERVATION AND DIAGNOSIS

All children need play but not all children need play therapy. Most children do not need extra help in dealing with the ups and downs in their lives. Their own spontaneous play combined with the containment of 'good enough' mothering is sufficient to enable them 'to weather small storms'. Yet some children have too much happening in their lives, separations, losses, abuse, repeated disruptions, changes of family membership and abode, changes of caretakers and attachment figures. Such events can be too great to cope with unaided. Some children, while anxious and angry, can cope adequately if they have an opportunity to share their feelings with an understanding adult who can help them to make sense of what has happened and clear up the frequent misapprehension that the child was to blame. Play techniques can be a good way of helping these conversations along. Other children, often those experiencing continual deprivation or abuse, or suffering from very profound loss, need more help in exploring and communicating their strong feelings, which have possibly been long repressed or expressed inappropriately.

Children who have suffered a profound but isolated upheaval in their lives may respond quickly to play therapy, speeding the process of recovery which might otherwise take a long time and interfere with other aspects of development. Where experience over a long period of time has been damaging, children are often too disturbed to be able initially to use spontaneous play therapeutically. For them a longer experience of play therapy may be helpful. Children whose infancy did not provide 'good enough' mothering remain unintegrated unless they receive containment and primary care, of which play forms a part.

Other children who can benefit from play approaches and play therapy are young children with emotional problems whose language skills are not well developed, older children with difficulties in the use of language, and elective mute children (those who choose not to speak). Similarly, children with developmental delays and learning difficulties, even in adolescence, may be helped through play therapy.

In making decisions about what sort of help a child needs the worker's observation skills are crucial. Through observation of the child's play, alone with the worker, or with the mother figure or with peers, the worker can begin to assess the child's state of attachment and containment, and to establish the child's levels of development. The least damaged children may play spontaneously at a developmental level appropriate to their age. Others may be playing at a much earlier stage of development or may have missed out on certain types of play experiences. It is often important to determine whether the child can use symbolic play. Diagnostic accuracy depends on the worker's knowledge of how children of a given age, community and culture usually play (see Tables 1 and 2).

From the child's use of recurring themes in play, workers can learn which aspects of life are causing the child most difficulty. From the intensity of the emotion expressed in play it becomes possible to identify areas of acute distress. (For example, all children are likely to be jealous of a new baby and may show this by squeezing a doll baby; acutely hurt children may squeeze or hit the doll harder, more often, and with more display of anger.) Some children may play defensively, hiding rather than revealing their true feelings. Others may suffer from play disruption. The extent of disruption and the play events which lead up to it may give the worker some idea of areas of difficulty. More severely damaged children may initially not be able to play at all.

This discussion has focused on assessment of children. The next chapter explores different approaches to using play in helping children and families.

Chapter 2

Approaches to therapeutic play

COMMUNICATION THROUGH PLAY – A 'THIRD THING'

Many people working with children can recall a time when they have sat with a child on a chair opposite them and they have attempted to find out how the child was feeling. The adult, as uncomfortable as the child, resorts to questions. 'How are you getting on at school?' 'All right.' 'What's your favourite subject?' 'Games.' 'How do you feel about your dad being away?' 'Don't know.' 'How are things at home?' 'All right.' 'How do you get on with mum and Paul?' 'All right.' Communication has not even started. Clare Winnicott explains how to bridge the communication gap. She writes:

> We spend a good deal of time creating the conditions which make communication possible. We try to establish between ourselves and the children a neutral area in which communication is indirect. In other words we participate in shared experiences, about which both we and the children feel something *about something else*, a third thing, which unites us, but which at the same time keeps us safely apart because it does not involve direct exchange between us.
>
> (C. Winnicott, in Tod 1968: 70)

The 'third thing' may be an outing or journey, a pet, a hobby or interest, but equally it may be a toy or game, or simply play. An informal shared play experience is not threatening and takes out the strain of communication, enabling the worker to build a relationship with a child which is 'personal but yet structured' (Winnicott, in Tod 1968: 57).

The ultimate aim of communication is to help children to sort out the muddle in their lives 'so that things add up and make some sort of sense', preventing and relieving some of their distress. It is concerned with linking real events and people in children's lives with their feelings about them. Clare Winnicott writes:

> We have to be able to reach them and respond to them at any given moment and be willing to follow them as best we can. Of course we shall not always understand what is going on or what they are trying to convey to us, and often this does not matter. What matters most is that we respond in a way which

conveys our *willingness to try to understand*. And it must be obvious that we really are trying all the time. This in itself can provide a therapeutic experience. Having reached the child we try to look at his world with him, and to help him sort out his feelings about it, to face the painful things and discover the good things. Then we try to consolidate the positive things in the child and in his world, and to help him make the most of his life.

(C.Winnicott 1964: 46 and 57)

This chapter explores the different ways in which workers use play 'to try to understand' and to help children to face the painful things in their lives, to find the strength to grow and develop, and to make the most of their future. It starts with Axline's non-directive play therapy and goes on to examine the use of play in child psychotherapy, looking at diverse ways in which these approaches may be applied by other workers. It considers the range of focused or structured play techniques and their application. It examines developmental and behavioural play techniques. Finally it considers play methods in group work with children and in the growing area of family work.

NON-DIRECTIVE PLAY THERAPY

Perhaps most people who become interested in play therapy were initially inspired by reading Virginia Axline's (1964a) *Dibs – In Search of Self*, a moving account of how she enabled a disturbed and withdrawn boy to heal himself and to reveal his incredible intellectual gifts. She further describes her approach in *Play Therapy* (1947, republished in 1989). Her non-directive approach is based on the belief that children contain within themselves both the ability to solve their own problems and the 'growth impulse that makes mature behaviour more satisfying than immature behaviour'. She writes:

The therapeutic value of this kind of psychotherapy is based upon the child experiencing himself as a capable, responsible person in a relationship that tries to communicate to him two basic truths: that no one ever really knows as much about any human being's inner world as does the individual himself; and that responsible freedom grows and develops from inside the person.

(Axline 1964a: 57–8)

Axline equipped her playroom with a wide variety of play materials, including sand, water, paint and drawing materials, finger paint, a dolls' house and family, miniature cars and people, a nursing bottle and perhaps an inflatable rubber figure. Within this protected setting the child was free to choose what to do. The child's relationship with the therapist was crucial. Axline, who worked in the United States, was influenced by the philosophical approach of Carl Rogers's (1951) active non-directive counselling. She used the technique of reflective listening, based on the counselling principles of empathy, warmth, acceptance and genuineness, (described in Truax and Carkhuff 1967). Play therapy adds to this counselling method by using the child's play as a means of communication to the therapist (Dorfman, in Rogers 1951). The therapist's task is to recognize the feelings which the child is expressing in speech and play and to reflect these back so that the child can get some insight into its behaviour. There is no attempt to direct play or to hurry the child. The only limits are those necessary to keep the therapy anchored to the real world and to make children aware of their responsibilities to the therapy.

Axline (1947 and 1989) sets out eight principles for non-directive play therapy.

1 'The therapist must develop a warm, friendly relationship with the child, in which good rapport is established as soon as possible.'
   She explains to a new child that it may play with any of the things in the playroom or use them in any way it wishes. She does not suggest anything particular that the child might do. If the child sits in silence, the therapist accepts it and sits quietly too.
2 'The therapist accepts the child exactly as he is.'
   The therapist must be neutral. Praise and encouragement are as inappropriate as criticism and disapproval, since both imply judgment. If the child does a beautiful painting she will not praise it because it is the child's opinion that matters, not hers.
3 'The therapist establishes a feeling of permissiveness in the relationship so that the child feels free to express his feelings completely.'
   The child needs to feel free – for instance, to 'beat up the mother doll or bury the baby in the sand, or lie down on the floor and drink from a nursing bottle ... without shame or guilt' (Axline, in Haworth 1964: 264). Axline illustrates her approach. She went into the playroom with Oscar who had reluctantly left his mother. He screamed 'Don't shut the door'. She replied: 'You don't want me to shut the door. You're afraid to stay with me if we shut the door. Very well – we'll leave the door open and you can close it when you feel like it' (Axline, in Haworth: 98–9).
4 'The therapist is alert to recognize the feelings the child is expressing and reflects those feelings back to him in such a manner that he gains insight into his behaviour.'
   For example, Oscar looked round the room and said 'I'll bust up everything in here!' Axline responded, 'You're feeling tough now'. She warns against falling in to the trap of responding to the *contents* of his words by saying 'You can play with the toys any way you want to but you can't bust them up'.
5 'The therapist maintains a deep respect for the child's ability to solve his own problems if given an opportunity to do so. The responsibility to make choices and to institute changes is the child's.'
6 'The therapist does not attempt to direct the child's actions or conversation in any manner. The child leads the way; the therapist follows.'
   If the child needs or asks for help in play, she gives only the limited amount needed at the time.
7 'The therapist does not attempt to hurry the therapy along. It is a gradual process

and recognized as such by the therapist.'

Axline illustrates this in her description of a six-year-old's play with a doll family and sand tray.

> He took the boy doll out of the house and said to the therapist: 'She is sending the boy out where the quicksand is ... He cries and tells his mother that he is afraid but she makes him go anyway. And see. He is sinking down and down and down into the quicksand.' The boy, showing much fear and anxiety, buries the doll in the sand. This child is certainly dramatizing his fear and his feeling of insecurity and lack of understanding ... If she follows the child she will say: 'The boy is being sent out of the house and he is afraid ... He tells his mother he is afraid, but she makes him go out anyway and he gets buried in the sand.' If she had said, 'You are afraid and your mother doesn't pay any attention to your fears and that scares you still more', she is getting ahead of the child and interpreting ... Perhaps the interpretation is correct, but there is a danger of thrusting something at the child before he is ready for it.
>
> (Axline (1964b), in Haworth: 262–3).

8 'The therapist establishes only those limitations that are necessary to anchor the therapy to the world of reality and to make the child aware of his responsibility in the relationship.'

The notion of the child assuming responsibilty for itself is crucial in Axline's approach. It underlies her expectation of the child taking the initiative and choosing how to use time in the playroom. As in all play, freedom is possible only because of the safe limits of the situation. The boundaries consist of time, one hour, usually weekly, and space, the playroom and materials within it. The child is not permitted to hurt itself or the therapist and some limits may be placed on the destruction of materials. These limits are not laid down at the outset but explained to the child as the need arises. The child is helped to understand that the playroom hour is only part of its life and that the real world imposes other constraints and limits to which it must adapt, whatever it feels. For example, Axline told Dibs he had only three minutes more before it was time to go home.

> Dibs suddenly stood up. 'No!' he shouted. 'Dibs no go out of here. Dibs no go home. Not never!'
>
> 'I know you don't want to go, Dibs. But you and I only have one hour every week to spend together here in the playroom. And when that hour is over, no matter how you feel about it, no matter how I feel about it, no matter how anybody feels about it, it is over for that day and we both leave the playroom'.
>
> 'Cannot paint another picture?' Dibs asked me, tears streaming down his face.
>
> 'Not today', I told him.
>
> He sat down muttering 'No go home. No want to go home. No *feel* like going home.'

'I know how you *feel*', I told him.

(Axline 1964a: 448–9)

Non-directive play therapy based on Axline's principles can be effective in reaching feelings of which the child is unaware and bringing them into consciousness where they can be dealt with. However, as the example of doll play in the sand shows, the therapist does not make direct interpretations of play but stays within the symbolism expressed in play, until the child is ready to move on. Since therapy goes at the child's pace and direction it is unlikely to damage further a child by uncovering unmanageable feelings which neither child nor perhaps the therapist are ready to handle. The adult, however, needs to be alert to areas the child is avoiding. This method is invaluable in diagnosis when the worker has limited information as to how the child is feeling and what is the problem for the child. Non-directive play therapy is particularly suitable for use by workers who do not have a psychodynamic training. Its drawback is that it can be a very slow process and there may be few workers who have time to offer it. It offers, however, great hope of recovery to some deeply disturbed children.

Children's Hours

The Children's Hours Trust, founded by Rachel Pinney, a medical doctor who had earlier worked with Margaret Lowenfeld, offers 'Children's Hours' in south-east England. These use non-directive principles similar to Axline's, including reflective listening techniques which Pinney has simplified so that very inexperienced workers may safely employ them. She uses (1983) and teaches 're-capping', in which the adult describes aloud the child's actions in play, a sort of running commentary. She believes that 'children, whatever their circumstances, benefit from having a time and space in which to play out their thought and feelings with an attentive adult who receives all that is said and done without passing judgment' (Pinney 1990: 4).

A Children's Hour takes place in a playroom containing robust unstructured material which feeds the imagination, 'such as sand, water, clay and paint; music or soundmaking equipment; giant-sized cardboard boxes; sagbags, blankets and mattress; bricks of all shapes and sizes and other building equipment; soft-balls, small models of people and animals, puppets, kitchen equipment, pipecleaners, hammer toys and all kinds of miscellaneous objects' (Pinney 1990: 5). The child is also allowed to go out. The adult takes responsibility for limits. Each Children's Hour begins with an introduction, for a five-year-old along the lines of:

Hello James. You've come here for a special playtime. You can do anything you like, and we can go outside if you want to. I'll make sure nothing is dangerous and nothing gets damaged ... We've got till the big hand says four o'clock. And I'll be with you.

(Pinney 1990: 6)

The adult makes itself totally available to the child, and makes the child aware of this by 're-capping' the child's activity, or lack of it – for example, 'You're looking around – looking in the box – you've found a lion'. Closer to Axline, feelings as well as actions are re-capped – for example, 'You're kicking that chair over – you're really angry', or 'You're crying – you're really hurting'. The adult may mirror the child's body language. With one child who sat still for 50 minutes the adult copied his body movements and facial expressions; much later he recalled this session as helpful. Very occasionally contact is made with a reluctant child by the taker starting to play itself (hostessing); the taker ceases to take the initiative as soon as the child joins in. If the child puts the taker into a role, such as prisoner or monster, the taker takes that role but is ready to drop it as the child indicates. At all times the adult avoids making suggestions, interpretations or assessments. A session ends with a ritual form of words, 'It's nearly the end of your special time, and I'm going to count you down slowly from ten to one ... And now it's the end of your special time for today' (Pinney 1990: 8). These mark the child's re-entry into the world outside. Jenny Senior's account (see Chapter 5) of Children's Hours with Keith illustrates this approach, also used by Anna Sanders in work with both children and adults (see Chapter 4).

PSYCHOANALYTIC PLAY THERAPY

Play therapy has been taking place in Britain for over 50 years. Students of Freudian psychoanalysis, such as Anna Freud, Melanie Klein, Donald Winnicott and Margaret Lowenfeld, each in their own very different ways, have developed the theory and practice of psychoanalytic work with children.

Anna Freud's child psychoanalysis

Anna Freud worked with her father Sigmund Freud in Vienna and moved with him to London where she founded the Hampstead War Nurseries, later to become the Anna Freud Centre for the Psychoanalytic Study and Treatment of Children. Before starting therapy she aimed to create a loving and caring relationship with the child so that the child would like her and feel dependent on her. Play was one of the main ways of achieving this. Also by observing play she was better able to understand the child's problem. Unlike Melanie Klein who thought that all play was symbolic, Anna Freud believed that it could be a re-playing of real events or even pure exploration. For instance, a child who looks in her therapist's handbag is not necessarily looking to see if her mother's womb is holding another baby. After initial assessment she used play methods less than 'free association', asking children to 'see pictures', tell stories, draw, or describe their dreams.

Anna Freud saw playing in therapy as a means of permitting children to talk about conscious feelings and thoughts and to act out unconscious conflicts and phantasies. Interpretation to the child of the symbolism of its play might follow, but only if it was suggested by a good deal of material. The positive tie created earlier helped the child 'face up to the often very painful revelation of repressed material' (A. Freud 1965). The immature self of the child used the analyst as a model for identification. Anna Freud's analytic work was often with latency age children, those who had developed strong psychological defences and therefore resistances to therapy. She always kept sight of the child's real world and worked only slowly down from reality and conscious feelings towards deeper levels of the child's unconscious. She did not think a quick, deep interpretation could be lastingly therapeutic.

Melanie Klein's psychoanalytic play therapy

Melanie Klein started her psychoanalytic work in Berlin and, like Anna Freud, moved to London as the Second World War loomed. In sharp contrast to Anna Freud, Melanie Klein made profound interpretations to children of the unconscious meanings of their play from the outset. If the child strongly rejected her interpretation she felt that this indicated that it was correct. When a child accepted an interpretation its anxiety and guilt would lessen, enabling the symbolic exploration of feelings, free of the fear of damaging real people. Her interpretations often involved sexual meanings which she did not hesitate to offer to the child. It is perhaps this which led many people to reject her ideas, although with the current concern about sexual abuse a re-appraisal may well be due.

Klein's most significant contributions have been her explanation of the origin of the child's emotions, tracing them back to infancy, (as Chapter 1 has described), and her specific use of play in therapy. She believed that children's play could be used as the equivalent of free association in adult psychoanalysis, revealing unconscious anxieties and phantasies. She concluded that it was possible to work with very young children. Many of her patients were under five years old and some were as young as two. Klein thought it was important to analyse the child's transference – that is, the child's feelings towards the therapist which had their origin in the earlier mother–child experiences. Anna Freud, in contrast, felt that transference was less significant since children were still developing their relationship to their parents; parents were still real and present as love objects, which also meant work with the parents could directly benefit the child.

Klein was probably the first therapist to use a carefully planned playroom. Her materials included a large number and variety of miniature toys with many human figures, drawing and painting materials, materials for cutting out, and water. Each child's materials were kept in its own special drawer. Children directed their own play. If they gave the therapist a part in role play she would play the part allotted. They might play shops, doctor and patient, schools, or mother and child. Klein comments,

In such games the child frequently takes the part of the adult, thereby not only expressing his wish to reverse the roles but also demonstrating how he feels that his parents or other people in authority behave towards him – or *should* behave.

> Sometimes he gives vent to his aggressiveness and resentment by being, in the role of parent, sadistic towards the child, represented by the analyst.
>
> (Klein, in Mitchell 1986: 41)

The therapist neither encourages nor disapproves of expressions of aggression but interprets their meaning to the child.

Klein set the model for much subsequent child psychotherapy and play therapy. More recent work in this field, such as Hoxter (in Boston and Daws 1977), and Boston and Szur (1983), as well as Copley and Forryan (1987), draws on her explanation of the mental development of babies, and on developments of these ideas in theories of 'holding' and 'containment'. Like the 'good enough' mother the therapist provides containment of the child, providing a mental space in which she attends to and reflects on the child's communication. This communication may be received through the symbolism of the child's play. For example, Copley and Forryan describe Edward's game of a cops and robbers chase in which he showed anxiety about the outcome. When he changed the robber's van into a refuse collection lorry they suggest he 'may have portrayed an underlying hope that the worker would be able to collect together and hold some of his conflict' (Copley and Forryan 1987: 231). The child's communication may also be received through becoming aware of the transference – that is, the feelings which the child arouses in the therapist, which may be the child's own feelings projected on to the therapist. For example, play therapist Jo Carroll started to feel irritated and angry when a child kept barking like a dog, until she realised that this anger was the child's own feeling about a parent, projected on to the therapist. Interpretation of play continues to form a major part of current therapy, although a more cautious approach is adopted in which the timing of the interpretation becomes important.

An understanding of the workings of the mechanisms of projection and introjection and the use of containment, and the recognition and use of the transference, are invaluable methods which can be learned and applied by workers who are not trained in child psychotherapy. The use of direct interpretation to the child needs to be used much more cautiously and only with skilled supervision.

Donald Winnicott and Erik Erikson – play as therapy

Donald Winnicott has not only provided a theory of play but has also informed the practice of play therapy. He observed that the pre-occupation of a child playing is akin to adult concentration. In play, children use objects from the real world in service of some aspect of their inner world, and this precarious interplay makes play an exciting and even potentially frightening creative experience (see Chapter 1). Since play is a 'being honest with oneself' then 'playing is itself a therapy' (D.Winnicott 1971: 50). Erik Erikson, a child psychoanalyst who started as a teacher in Anna Freud's school in Vienna before going to the United States, also thought that children heal themselves through play.

Modern play therapy is based on the observation that a child made insecure by a secret hate or fear of the natural protectors of his play in family and neighbourhood seems able to use the protective sanction of an understanding adult to regain some play peace. Grandmothers and favourite aunts may have played that role in the past; its professional elaboration of today is the play therapist. The most obvious condition is that the child has the toys and adult for himself, and that sibling rivalry, parental nagging, or any kind of sudden interruption does not disturb the unfolding of his play intentions.

(Erikson 1965: 215)

Although Winnicott used interpretation, illustrated in case studies in *Playing and Reality* (1971) and *The Piggle* (1980), he believed that fundamental psychotherapy could take place without it. '*The significant moment is that when the child surprises himself or herself.* It is not the moment of my clever interpretation that is significant' (D.Winnicott 1971: 51). In this he differed sharply from Melanie Klein, observing that she was only interested in the content of play as a way of receiving communication from the child and that she had not recognized the value of the child 'playing'. Winnicott makes 'a plea to every therapist to allow for the patient's capacity to play, that is, to be creative in the analytic work. The patient's creativity can be only too easily stolen by a therapist who knows too much' and does not hide his knowing (D.Winnicott 1971: 57). This was as true for adults, he felt, as for children.

Erikson recognized that an excess of emotion, excitement or anxiety could disrupt play. It could happen suddenly or it could slowly inhibit play. The process is similar to 'resistance' to transference in adult therapy. It occurs when painful repressed material is getting too near the surface. The therapist's task is to try to understand the meaning of the play which led up to disruption. The therapist may interpret this to the child, trying to put its experience into words to increase its insight. Erikson used quite deep interpretations – for example, a child who built a rectangle of inward-facing dominoes was helped by the interpretation that it was his coffin. However, the level and timing of interpretation was crucial. Winnicott saw that playing might reach its own saturation point at which the child could not contain any more experience.

Erikson recognized that play therapy does not take place in a vacuum but that social context is crucial. A child's identity ultimately depends on finding a reflection within the child's own culture. Play therapy could only be successful where there were social and cultural reinforcements, both in the family and beyond. This could be denied, for example, to a black child in a white culture.

Margaret Lowenfeld's Make-a-World technique

At her Institute of Child Psychology in London, now defunct, Margaret Lowenfeld (1979) encouraged children to construct a series of miniature worlds in a sand tray, choosing from the enormous collection of miniature world material, stored in tiny drawers. Items included figures of people, soldiers, wild, domestic and farm animals, houses, cars, boats, fences and trees. She would tell children to use pictures in their heads to construct their world. When completed she asked the child to explain it to her. She thought that the therapist's role was to encourage and help, and that this was more useful than making interpretations, which she used only sparingly. Her own understanding of the child's play, however, still largely used sexual symbolism. Lowenfeld noted some recurring themes in children's worlds, such as a dam holding back water (feelings) to be eventually released. A child often built a volcano, representing internal turmoil, at the point where it had stopped getting rid of its bad feelings by projection.

The make-a-world technique has been borrowed and adapted for wider use. Sally Maxwell provided a sand tray with miniature toys, in a separate small room, in a Camden Family Centre. Children were offered regular opportunities to play there on their own with an attentive adult. The role of the adult was reflective listening, re-capping what the child was doing as it played (Pinney 1990). Elizabeth Newson, at Nottingham's Child Development Research Unit, recommends the technique for use in helping a wide variety of children, including children in care, slow learners and terminally ill children. She feels that it enables children to communicate with themselves and to look at their own predicaments which those involved with them may not be wholly aware of or tend to 'pat down'. Modifying the technique for non-psychoanalysts she warns against making any value judgments, such as saying 'This is a nice world', and suggests simply asking the child 'Whether he wants to tell you about the world. The first two times the child makes a world it is left at that. The third time he is asked if he is in his world' (Newson 1983: 17). Children may use a symbol, such as a monkey or an elephant, to represent themselves. No interpretation is offered. Newson suggests following a make-a-world session with drama play (described later).

ART THERAPY

Art therapy recognizes the creativity of children's play. It focuses on the creative processes of drawing, painting and three-dimensional work. Children may be exploring and playing with art materials as well as using them to create an image. Art therapist Susan Turner finds that painting and play offer the child

> A way to objectify and express thoughts and feelings, to experiment with relationships, to find new approaches, or to absorb and grow through past experiences by making a symbolic form in which the experiences can be safely contained and re-experienced and in time healed. Furthermore, strong statements can be made in an acceptable form, for example, aggressive, non-acceptable behaviour can be expressed in a painting where it can be worked through. The need to act out is reduced and this may bring about a positive change in the child's development and behaviour. It is also true to say that if the child needs to be destructive in his painting he also has the opportunity to take action and to restore in the art work what he needed to destroy for a time. This

can be very helpful in enabling the child to overcome his fears of being overwhelmed by negative emotion.

(Turner 1988)

The role of the therapist follows Axline's non-directive principles, including those on limits. Susan Turner aims to provide a relaxed and safe setting, which as far as possible is always physically the same, in which the child feels 'contained'. Like many peripatetic workers she may not have the use of a room specifically designed for her work. She sets out art materials for the child at the edge of a large plastic sheet on the floor and sits herself on a low chair close by. She continues:

The art therapist is trained to be alert and sensitive in recognizing the emotional nature of the painting/play processes. In the session her intervention and active involvement will vary depending on the needs and circumstances of the child. It may be enough that the child feels safe to reveal powerful feelings symbolically and works through them internally at an unconscious or conscious level without the therapist's intervention or discussion. The therapist maintains a respect for the child's ability to solve his own problems. In painting, the child takes the responsibility to make choices and to institute change. However, sometimes in therapy the child may need more active acknowledgment and interaction with the therapist concerning the communication within the painting/play. It may then be appropriate for the therapist to name and to reflect the feelings/anxieties back to the child so that he is not overwhelmed but will gain insight and, with the support of the therapist, be able to overcome his particular difficulties.

(Turner 1988)

This approach is exemplified in art therapist Ann Gillespie's account of work with Sonia, an 11-year-old black child trying to cope with life in a foster family after a childhood of uncertainty and violence. From a beginning of inertia and hopelessness, with Sonia's only burst of energy going into drawing a sad little black dog (herself?), her relationship with the therapist grew as 'Sonia drew and talked about countless cradles, babies and mothers', including babies who looked 'too old' (herself again). Much of their communication was unspoken, operating through the medium of drawing, painting and modelling, 'entrusted as I am with elements of her that are so deep and hurtful that they have to be hidden in fairy tale pictures and thick crude paint'. Gillespie continues:

After she discovered I had conferred with her family, she drew a fortified castle, warning me to keep our special relationship defended from outsiders. Twin-towered it stands, surrounded by its moat, door securely barred, alone in a large hilly countryside. Outside stand two riderless horses, one brown, one white (like us), saddled and waiting until we are able to continue our journey.

(Jefferies and Gillespie 1981: 14)

Art therapy helped Sonia to cope with deep levels of emotional pain, freeing her to benefit from relationships offered by her foster parents and her social worker.

Art therapy is perhaps closest to Winnicott's approach to play therapy, in that the child's self-healing through art or play is as important as the 'containment' offered by the worker. It can be helpful to children, and adults, of all ages, and is often acceptable to older children who feel too grown-up to play but may not be able to cope with talking therapies. It is used in work with children in a variety of contexts, including under-fives family centres, child psychiatry, black children, children in hospitals, assessment centres, residential special schools, described in Case and Dalley (1990), and family placement (Gillespie 1986). A more general introduction to art therapy is Dalley (1985). While it is a specialized field and art therapists expect to nurture and be fed by their own creative art process its basic approach can be used by others.

For example, social worker Chris Braithwaite (1986) notes what aspects of a child's drawing take most effort and concentration, what is missing as well as what is there, and how each person is placed relative to others. She may comment quietly 'Two houses' (pause) 'I wonder who lives there?' but remains tentative and does not probe beyond the child's painful avoidance of issues. She describes how 15-year-old Mark, about to return home from care, drew a picture of pointing fingers, illustrating his feeling that dad had always called him a thief and his fear that his step-mum did not want him, and an exploding bottle. He admitted that he had been close to smashing a window but instead was able to talk 'about his anger at being caught "in the middle" in his family and between his social worker and the resident staff' (Braithwaite 1986: 17). The worker did not need to speak. The therapy of drawing had enabled the child to put his feelings into words where they could be thought about. Chris Braithwaite sums up the adult's role.

> When working with a child's drawing, the intention is not to interpret and hence impose an 'adult' or 'professional' meaning on it, but rather to explore it alongside the child, while he makes sense of it and himself to himself ... The art is to be non-directive but to 'actively listen', confident that the process in itself is sufficiently therapeutic to redress imbalances and provide the impetus for progress ... Drawings can simultaneously supply the means of communicating and alleviating a client's 'dis-ease'.
>
> (Braithwaite 1986: 16–17)

FOCUSED PLAY TECHNIQUES

Early forms of focused play techniques, such as release therapy, concentrated on specific anxieties. Relevant play materials were offered at frequent intervals so that the children could overcome their fears by repeatedly playing out the situation provoking them. For example, a child afraid of using the potty would be offered dolls and potties to play with. Today the use of focused play is more varied. Where the worker has some knowledge of what has happened in a child's life the child may be provided with specific play materials, such as doll families, which enable the child to re-enact events or to indicate what it would like to happen. Jewett (1984) suggests an open-mouthed dinosaur, a van with sliding doors that can take people and furniture, a hulk-like figure and a police car, to help children to play out angry feelings and re-play their experience of loss and separation. Alternatively the worker may be more active in directing play, either openly or more subtly. The worker may introduce play themes through participation in pretend play, or may ask children to talk to the figures or puppets they are playing with or drawing and ask them to speak as the figure, or write letters to them. Such Gestalt methods are described by Oaklander (1978) and their use is spreading – for example, in Madge Bray's (1991) work. The theory behind them is that it is more useful to help children to deal with their present feelings than to go back to early traumatic experiences.

Oaklander suggests many fantasy and projective techniques. For example, children might be asked to draw their family as symbols or animals, to go on a fantasy journey, perhaps in a guided fantasy, and draw their room or the place they get to, to create their own world, or a particular feeling, on paper, just using shapes, lines, curves and colours, or to draw themselves as a rosebush or a boat in a storm. Older children might be asked to choose a toy in the room and then to imagine that they are it, describing how they are used, what they do and what they look like, and what they want to do. The worker might set up a structured situation such as a family scene in a dolls' house, and the child told, for example, that they are all arguing and asked what happens next. In another projective technique a child might be asked to draw a house (symbolizing the mother), a person (the father) and a tree (the child) (Sluckin 1989). Donald Winnicott used his famous 'squiggle' technique as a way of quickly establishing communication between child and adult on the level of unconscious processes. He would draw a random squiggle and ask the child to turn it into something, then in turn ask the child to draw a squiggle which he would then complete.

The use of a 'third thing' is a strategy used by many social workers, especially those involved in long-term work with children in care. Many play techniques are now used to enable worker and child to get to know one another, to help uncover a child's feelings and to permit their expression. Ecomaps, picture genograms or illustrated family trees, picture flow charts and time drawings are widely used (Figures 2.1–2.3). Card and board games, often invented by the worker to meet a particular need, are popular. A child may be encouraged to draw or paint its family or some aspect of its life. Cathartic techniques, including water techniques, candle ceremonies for grief work, and planned anger work are used by workers prepared to handle strong feelings (Jewett 1984, Owen and Curtis 1988, Redgrave 1987). Life-story books are familiar to most social workers, but there are also numerous games with rules, playful tasks and play situations which have been devised to help children to make sense of their past, present and future. Many of these approaches concentrate on children's difficulties in the real world and are less concerned with their inner conflicts, although they help children to distinguish between reality and phantasy. They deal with conscious or near-conscious feelings rather than deeply unconscious ones. These focused play techniques will be discussed further in later chapters.

Some focused approaches border on non-directive play. In one form of drama play the worker tells the child 'Anything that happens now will be because you want it to happen. I will play with you as much as you want, but you must tell me what to do' (Newson 1983: 17). The worker sits on the floor and waits to be asked to join the game. Toy telephones are provided to ease communication. If the worker is not invited after ten minutes the worker may pick up a telephone and ask the

Figure 2.1 Family tree or genogram

child to 'come to tea' or 'come to the shop'. Otherwise the child is free to direct play and people within safe limits. Newson's aim is to offer the child total attention

Figure 2.2 Ecomap

and an experience of being in control, as well as relevant new experiences and the opportunity to symbolize and communicate feelings and problems through play.

Figure 2.3 Picture flow chart (1)

Responding to the child's communication

When using focused play techniques the worker's role is to respond to the child's communication but not to make hasty interpretations of play. Clare Winnicott warns against going ahead of children and verbalizing or interpreting feelings before children have shown that they are ready to think about them. She reassures us that children work things out in their own way. The adult's role is to wait alongside the child, especially with suspicious, withdrawn, depressed or even extrovert children. With angry and hostile children, whether anger is expressed overtly or by passive indifference, adults must meet and survive their hostility, even when feeling out of their depth and not understanding. Later the worker can help them to put their feelings into words. A brief acknowledgment of a painful or frightening experience may touch deeply and there is no need to 'wallow' in feelings.

Workers' responses vary according to their training and background. Some deal solely with the child's conscious feelings and views expressed through play. Others recognize less conscious feelings in the child's symbolic play and may choose to convey this recognition to the child, usually working within the symbolism, saying, for example, 'This boy doll looks as if he's very cross with the big brother doll', avoiding the direct interpretation of 'Perhaps you are feeling very angry with your big brother'. Such an approach can be effective, especially with younger children. Going at the child's pace makes the therapy more bearable to the child at any age.

In Violet Oaklander's approach, while the worker does not interpret the child's play the child may be asked to do so, and in this way is helped to own its own feelings and projections. The worker may, if it feels right, direct the child's awareness to the content or the process of play, saying, for example, 'You like to do that slowly', 'You are burying the tiger', 'This plane is all alone', or even 'You sound angry'. If a pattern repeats itself, the child might be asked about its life, 'Do you like things tidy at home?'. This may be asked during play or afterwards. Children may be asked to repeat a situation yet again or exaggerate an action, such as a fire engine doing lots of rescuing, and asked 'Does that remind you of anything in your life?'. The child with the fire engine replied that since his dad had been away his mother expected him to do everything! Children are often asked to speak as the people, animals or objects in their fantasy or drawing – for example, 'You be that fire engine. What does it say?', 'What might that snake say about itself?', 'What would the fire engine say to the truck if it could talk?', or 'Do you ever feel like that monkey?' (Oaklander 1978: 162). Where they are ready for it children are helped to go beyond symbolization to conceptualization of their feelings, becoming able to reflect on them, developing a stronger self-awareness and self-esteem, and helping them to reach integration.

Sensory and regressive play

Some focused methods work at profoundly unconscious levels. Chief among these are sensory and regressive play. These can help children who have suffered severe deprivation and loss, as well as children in hospital and children with learning difficulties. Sensory work with emotionally damaged children is based on the belief that a child's senses are dulled by the many traumas that have been suffered. Children have often either withdrawn and isolated themselves from contact with their environment, or else, particularly in the case of abused children, submerged their self to accommodate adult expectations (Thom 1984). They

> have blocked off the feeling part of them and hence do not have the means to know what they feel or the tools to express these feelings. Development of the senses – of the 'contact function' – looking, talking, touching, listening, moving, smelling and tasting has therefore become an important part of work with children and a significant part of the development of the sense of self.
>
> (Simmonds, in Aldgate and Simmonds 1988: 14)

Children can re-learn to become aware of their bodies and their contact with the world around them. Violet Oaklander (1978) has been the source of inspiration for much recent sensory work, especially by social workers for children in care.

Kate Burke, a family placement worker with the Catholic Children's Society, often uses sensory work as part of a programme of intensive work in preparing children for new families (see Chapter 9). She aims 'to renew and strengthen the basic senses that an infant discovers and flourishes in', within a relationship which gives the child individual time and attention and builds trust. Sensory work gets in touch with and validates a child's feelings on two levels, the external and the internal. She gives the example of the girl who cannot tell hot from cold; on a hot day she sweats in heavy clothing and does not think of taking any off. Her senses are blunted, a sign of her low self-esteem. Sensory work can 'unfreeze' her, putting her in touch with her senses so that she can use them again. Work might start by asking about the kinds of textures she likes and dislikes feeling. She expands a child's vocabulary of 'feeling' words, which helps in later life work and abuse work. Each week she concentrates on one of the senses – touch, sight, sound, smell and taste . Every session begins with relaxation and breathing exercises, and an explanation of what will happen in the session. Sessions end with a summary of what they have done and checking out the child's understanding of this, praising the child for any particular cooperation or ability. Day-to-day opportunities for sensory experiences are seized, and foster parents or carers are asked to follow up each session in an enjoyable way with similar experiences. Her programme includes the following ideas:

Touch – Relaxation and breathing exercises, paying attention to different sensations. Explain what we will be doing. Begin by exploring our own bodies, touching ears, toes, hair. What can we feel? How do we feel? Touch a collection of objects made of wood, rubber, rock, sponge, fur, silk, tissue, cotton wool and face cream, talking about how they feel and using words such as bumpy, fluffy, sticky, warm, prickly, spongy, hairy, freezing, tingly.

Use clay, sand and water trays, taking time, and touching with hands, feet or noses. Use finger paints and talk about touching and feeling. From a bag of hidden objects, ask the child to find things that feel soft, hard, silky, etc.

End the session by discussing what we have done. Ask carers to continue exploring touch during the week, in the house and outside, with grass, trees and earth.

Sight – Begin by looking around the room, then look at each other, and then look in the mirror, describing what we can see. Choose an object in the room to look at and draw from memory. Talk about colours, shades, light and dark, colours we like and don't like. Look at objects through a magnifying glass, Cellophane and water. Dim the lights and then have bright light. Look at objects close to, far away and upside down. Look at pictures in a book, and try to remember them in detail. Play I Spy.

Sound – Begin by listening to soft background music, then loud, fast and slow music. Encourage child to move to music and to talk about how it sounds and how it makes you feel, how you feel like moving. Ask the child to describe and guess sounds on a tape, such as a car, dog, eating crisps, a food mixer, running water, using words like gentle, smooth, grating, harsh. Use musical instruments to introduce rhythm, and to make gentle, loud, scarey or happy music.

Have a blank tape on which we explore tones of voice, angry, sad or excited. Talk about liked and disliked everyday sounds, and imitate them. Talk in gibberish for fun. Replay the tape.

Be aware throughout of the memories that may be recalled and give space to explore these.

Smell – Talk about how we smell. Experiment with breathing through nostrils and feel exhaled air. Smell substances such as coffee, flowers, peppermint, soap powder, onions, curry powder, nutmeg, pepper, garlic, oranges, lemon, perfume, as well as some things that do not smell, such as flour, rice, water, sugar and salt. Pretend to have a cold and to talk about what it is like not to be able to smell. Draw pictures of things with a strong smell, and talk about smells we like and those we don't. Think about outdoor smells such as a bonfire, warm tarmac, petrol, hospitals, flowers. Play a game closing eyes and guessing smells.

Taste – Share a meal, perhaps inviting carer, which includes crisps (salty), a grapefruit (bitter), natural yoghurt (sour), Milky Way (sweet), and talk about the texture and taste of each food.

Experiment with tongue, lips, teeth and cheeks, and describe what each does. Pretend to be a cat and lick up a saucer of milk, and talk about how it feels to lick things. Play a game tasting and guessing foods with eyes closed. Write down or draw foods liked and not liked.

Redgrave (1987) suggests ways of providing sensory experiences for self-healing and enrichment where a child has suffered nurturing deprivation. He believes activities should be freely chosen; play is not directed by the worker except through the provision made. This can include all sorts of water play, play with sand, clay and play dough, outdoor experiences, finger and foot painting, cookery, junk modelling, sounds and music. Brenda Crowe (1974) discusses the value of these kinds of play activities, and their provision and management in pre-school groups. In therapy these activities can fill gaps in experience for older children as well. Play activities may need to be provided in a form which is acceptable to older children, perhaps as cookery rather than dough play, for example, but without the pressure of having to produce an acceptable end product. Similarly, puppets and papier mâché may appeal. Some illustrations of sensory play activities in group work with children, by Susan Monson, are found in Chapter 5.

Children in hospital or in other stressful environments may be calmed by listening to soothing sounds and music, such as birdsong or 'womb music' tapes, watching moving patterns of coloured light, receiving gentle massage, or lying in a 'soft play' ball pool or on a transparent waterbed with lights playing through it. Snoezelen centres (Walters 1991) originated in Holland (Hulsegge and Verheul 1987). Light projectors, sound equipment, and things to touch and smell provide a whole body sensory experience that can be either relaxing or stimulating according to individual need. These ideas are described further in Chapter 6.

Sensory work allows a child to regress to earlier stages of development, either to compensate for missed experiences or to repair emotional damage. Some children are helped to become stronger in the end by regressing even further, to play with baby toys, to experience contact and comfort through the sensory responsiveness of people and things – laps, cushions, pillows, blankets, soft toys, rocking, to oral comfort through using a baby's bottle or dummy, and to the safe containment of being wrapped up in bedding or a cardboard box. While this often happens in non-directive play therapy it may also take place within focused work. Owen and Curtis (1988) use baby play to give deprived children some understanding of the needs of babies and their own unmet needs at the time, showing why they were not properly cared for as a baby and making it clear that they were not born 'bad'. They suggest providing soft cushions or a mattress to represent the infant's cot, baby equipment such as nappies, bottle, powder, rattle, a teddy or doll to represent a baby, play people, and telephones for communication. The worker puts these among the other toys and leads the child into finding them, and explains that they are things used for caring for a baby. As they play at feeding, changing and rocking a baby, with a teddy or doll or the child itself as the baby, they talk about why it is important for a baby to be held. The worker may say something like 'It was very sad. When you were a tiny baby your mummy had a lot of muddled up feelings inside her which made her tense and she couldn't hold you close' (Owen and Curtis 1988: 31). The child has space to talk and express feelings, and to ask questions (to which the worker must know the answers when they concern the child's past). Sessions may end with cuddling, although some children can only bear a light touch or sitting quietly together, perhaps listening to soft music.

At their best, focused methods can involve a carefully planned series of therapeutic interventions with a child – for example, Sandra Foster's work described in Chapter 5, and Kate Burke's work in Chapter 9. Focused methods are helpful in saving time and shortening therapy, as well as making sure that vital areas of assessment and therapy are covered. Yet they risk rushing children into painful confrontations which they are not ready to handle. Their use needs a trained and sensitive worker who can judge which technique is appropriate to a particular child at a given time. An assessment of the child's developmental level is an essential part of this process.

DEVELOPMENTAL AND BEHAVIOURAL MANAGEMENT PLAY METHODS

All those doing therapeutic work with children need to make an assessment of a child's developmental level in order to decide how to proceed. One approach to therapeutic work with children who are judged to be behind in some or all of their developmental milestones is to use play to help them progress. The main distinction between focused play techniques and developmental play lies less in the actual methods used, which may be the same, but in the rationale behind them. The aim is not so much directly to help children to cope with painful feelings but rather to help children's achievement of appropriate developmental play which will in turn enable them to cope better with the demands of the outside world. There may be a number of possible reasons for children's delayed development, including deprivation, neglect and lack of stimulation, inappropriate parental expectations (whether too high or too low), lack of opportunity or of permission to play, anxiety and emotional disturbance, or physical and mental disabilities, such as autism, or language or learning difficulties. Often it is a combination of these and it may take time to unravel them.

Developmental therapeutic play starts from the stage the child has reached and provides the play experiences needed to help the child to reach the next stage. These play experiences may be broken down into very small steps. For example, a developmentally delayed two-year-old may pick up a cup and pretend to drink but continue to hold teddy upside down by one leg. The adult lets the child see her hold teddy and gives him a drink, saying 'Teddy wants a drink'. She then helps the child to do this, using physical and verbal prompts or backwards and forwards chaining, doing all of the actions except the last or first bit herself and gradually doing less of the sequence as the child does more (Jeffree, McConkey and Hewson 1985, Newson and Hipgrave 1982). By giving help only at the point that it is needed children are enabled to do as much as possible themselves.

Spontaneous play is encouraged. The role of the adult is to be alert to and respond to the child's play, enjoying play at the child's level but sometimes offering a play response at a level one step on. The adult is not just an observer but plays with the child. Although the worker is helping the child to achieve apparently physical and cognitive skills, by joining in and responding to spontaneous play, she is also fostering children's view of themselves as active participants with control in play, so developing a positive self-image. A total concentration on teaching the next skill, even when done with the use of praise, risks stunting emotional growth as children become dependent and passive. Children may need help to learn that play has no serious consequences, that it is all right to make mistakes, that play can be fun. For example, play therapist Bridget Leverton has a teddy who won't stay where he is tidied, or she will pretend to make a mistake, which she and the child can both laugh about. The development of symbolic or pretend play is often a prime need of children with developmental delays. Turn-taking games, such as Peep-bo, help to develop a child's ability to communicate and respond to others. The starting point for these games is often the worker's imitation of the child's action, which leads to the child's imitation of the worker, and eventually to reciprocal play. Parents of young children, where mother and baby play has been unsatisfactory or involved difficulties, can be involved in play, as Chapter 4 on family work will show. Where parents are supported, rather than undermined by 'experts', the benefits to their children's development can be very great.

Behavioural methods

Behavioural methods are sometimes used in developmental play and also in work with emotionally disturbed children. They seem to be particularly favoured by psychologists and some child guidance clinics. Nicol (1988) describes the use of a classical behavioural approach by a clinical psychologist in play therapy with children from abusing families – the 'coercive' family type. Some children's initial responses to the limits of the therapy session were temper tantrums, screaming, destruction, aggression, 'manipulative behaviour' and threats. Their behaviour was ignored or 'when necessary restrained until it died down' (Nicol 1988: 706). Constructive and friendly behaviour was rewarded with praise and attention. During the sessions the children, with ages up to 14 years, chose their own play activities from a wide selection of materials: dolls' house, paint, sand, water, trains, cooking, games and puzzles, drawing materials and books. Older children tended to choose drawing, talking or structured games. Symbolic play was encouraged if the child initiated it but interpretation was avoided. Some unobtrusive behaviour modification was used for socially unacceptable behaviour. Where obvious developmental gaps occurred, children were given help in concentrating on a task rather than 'flitting', as well as experience of collaboration, including winning, losing and sharing.

This deliberate use of behavioural methods within play therapy seems to be an unusual intervention and a clear departure from classical play therapy. It accords with Jeffrey's (1981) doubt about the value of aggressive-cathartic play; she felt that perhaps a child needed to learn self-control. However, whilst behavioural methods may be employed to help children to achieve the self-control to make use of play therapy, their continued use puts the worker in an ambivalent and sometimes conflicting position. Axline's non-directive approach is not compatible with an approach where the worker has a hidden agenda. The worker contemplating behavioural approaches has some hard decisions to take.

PLAY TECHNIQUES IN GROUP WORK WITH CHILDREN

There is no single approach to using play with children in groups. Jeffrey (1981) identifies a bewildering variety of play therapies for groups of children: playgroup therapy (for young children) and activity group therapy (for older ones), therapeutic playgroups, group play therapy, non-directive group therapy, group analytical therapy, transitional groups and activity–interview group psychotherapy.

Structured or focused group play techniques are commonly used when it seems likely that children will benefit from sharing difficult experiences with one another and find that they are not alone. These groups might include, for example, children whose parents are divorcing, a sibling group in a family with problems, sexually abused children, children with a sibling with physical or learning disabilities, or children who have been bereaved. The use of therapeutic play in some of these groups is discussed in later chapters. Playful tasks and games to help children to feel relaxed and comfortable in a group are used initially, followed by specific games to deal with areas which are causing difficulties for the children. Because there is often little spontaneous play the therapeutic value more often comes from the recognition and communication of feelings rather than directly from the play experience itself. The use of play, however, brings a lightness of touch, a playfulness, which fosters open communication.

Activity group therapy tends to involve the provision of play activities in which children's participation is voluntary and relatively unstructured. The aim is usually to help children who have a poor self-image and difficulties in making relationships with other children but who have some give-and-take skills. Through play activities they can channel aggression constructively, perhaps producing a satisfying end product, such as a boat to sail in the bath, and become more able to manage relationships with other children. For example, an eight-year-old boy who found joining a group difficult was encouraged to set up a pretend shop and to play on his own until the worker came in 'shopping' with the rest of the group; he was the centre of attention and interaction was made easy for him (Leverton, unpublished). Activity playgroups are often provided by occupational therapists and nurses in child psychiatric units, or by teachers in classes for maladjusted children. Kolvin (1981) gave an indication of the potential value of playgroup therapy in infant schools with deprived children at risk of emotional disturbance. Hospital play specialists may provide group play activities but with emphasis on helping children to cope with a stay in hospital and the treatments involved.

In Dockar-Drysdale's (1968b) classic account of therapeutic playgroups at the Mulberry Bush, a residential school for emotionally disturbed children between the ages of five and twelve, she described how she provided separate groups for children according to whether they were integrated or not. Integrated children have had enough primary experience to become containers themselves, and can realize and symbolize what happens to them; they have had a 'good enough' start even if subsequently deprived (see Chapter 1). She provided a group of integrated children with materials for symbolic play, such as dolls and puppets, and play involving communication and games with rules which they could manage and enjoyed. For a group of unintegrated children who needed to be contained, sometimes even physically held, Dockar-Drysdale provided narcissistic and transitional play, with play materials to encourage sensory and regressive play. She responded to children's needs, to be tucked up in a 'nest', to be wrapped up, to be fed, simply allowing them to 'be' if they wished. Although the children were physically in a group there was no expectation that they would behave as members of a group. Their needs were individual and were individually met. In both groups the role of the adult was crucial, involving the use of Axline's eight principles of non-directive therapy.

Dockar-Drysdale describes a game of Desert Islands which she initiated in a mixed group. The children turned a table upside down for a boat and set sail. They were shipwrecked in a storm and all except one managed to reach the island (a mat), where they stayed until rescued by a passing ship. She writes:

> During this adventure I perched on a table with some of the audience. I said very little except when someone involved me in the drama. There were calls for help from the captain, 'Are you going to let us drown?' I replied that he must feel that no one was helping him. The captain replied, 'We've got to do it ourselves!' One of the crew asked me, 'Shall I stay for ever on the island?' I said that it must be difficult to decide whether to go or to stay. One of the audience shouted: 'You've got to decide!'
>
> (Dockar-Drysdale 1968b: 149)

In this profound form of play, children's deep problems were safely acted out in symbolic terms, without adult direction. 'Their lives had been stormy voyages; often there had been family shipwrecks: the island had something in common with the therapeutic school which they would one day leave' (Dockar-Drysdale 1968b: 149–50). The Mulberry Bush, which Dockar-Drysdale founded, continues to provide a therapeutic environment for integrated and non-integrated children, dividing them into 'Bigs' and 'Smalls'.

> For 'Smalls' the Mulberry Bush offers a security and containment which is almost womblike. Staff put toothpaste onto their brushes, serve them at meal-times, brush their hair, bath them and put them to bed ... Therapy goes on all the time, everywhere ... There are 'nesting boxes' which could double up as space ships, and cupboards with ladders up the sides, for improvised and imaginative games.
>
> (Zwart 1988: 8)

Axline, who herself worked with small groups of children, or sometimes pairs of children, noted that one of the difficulties for the therapist is that showing acceptance of one child may be taken as a negative comparison and implied criticism by another child. She suggests that this problem can be avoided if the therapist concentrates on reflecting children's feelings rather than what they are doing. Jenny Senior, taker of Children's Hours, uses children's names to show that each child is reflected equally. She might say, 'Jamie wants the horse all to himself, Kate wants to get on; he *still* wants the horse, she *still* wants to get on'.

Group play therapy on the Axline and Dockar-Drysdale models seems to be uncommon in current practice, even in residential schools and homes where it could be more easily organized. Christine Bradley set up a playgroup for children in a residential school for children with physical handicaps. She found that two grown-ups were needed, one for the integrated children and another to keep in constant emotional contact with two non-integrated children, neither of whom could sustain any activity beyond a few minutes. She decided it was not possible to cater for more than two non-integrated children in a mixed group. The basic materials were paints, sand, water, dressing-up materials and puppets, although the two sorts of children used them differently. Integrated children acted out internal conflicts and phan-tasies in pretend play with dolls' families and playing houses, shops and hospitals. The unintegrated children played with simple toys such as soft animals or teddies, curled up in a blanket, listened to stories, or enjoyed blowing bubbles or trickling sand through their fingers. Christine Bradley is currently supporting the work of nurture groups at the Caldecott Community which provide these kinds of primary care activities for severely emotionally damaged children.

Similar psychodynamic principles underlie art therapy which may be provided for groups of children. Emotionally deprived children may find group art therapy a rich and stimulating creative and social experience, a means of sharing and acknowledging one another's creative impulses and feelings. Drama and drama therapy have a similar value. They make use of techniques such as mime, masks, improvization, puppetry, myths and stories, movement and dance, combining therapy with ritual and theatre.

PLAY IN FAMILY WORK

In all the approaches to play discussed so far the focus has been on direct work with children. Often other interventions take place in parallel – for example, counselling or conciliation with parents, planning and preparation for fostering or other placement. The strengths and weaknesses of children's physical and social environments may have been explored and some attempt made to improve them. Most of this work does not involve play. Family work can.

Play in family work has two main strands. One is concerned with supporting the mother–child relationship, promoting attachment and providing 'containment' of the mother (or mother-substitute), meeting her 'child' needs. This kind of work is based on the psychodynamic description of mother–infant relationships, following Bowlby, Klein, Winnicott and Bion. Play work may take place with a mother and child (for example, play for the child in which the mother is involved), with groups of mothers and children together (for example, music with mum groups, or play sessions for several children in which parents are involved), or with groups of mothers (for example, informal play workshops).

Parents may lack sufficient knowledge of how children develop and may have unrealistic expectations, or they may lack skills in managing children's behaviour. Where play methods are used to help parents to acquire knowledge and skills there is a greater possibility of maintaining parents' autonomy and so support their parenting role, rather than when disempowering and undermining didactic methods of instruction are used. Again, play work may take place with individual families (for example, Home Start visiting), with parents and children together (for example, family centre work), or with groups of parents learning together in informal groups (for example, playgroup courses). The use of play in family work is probably greatest in under-fives work.

A different strand of family work involves all the members of a family where there is a problem. Play and games may be used in apparently informal work involving the whole family (for example, in Family Service Units). In more formal family therapy, children's play may be seen as part of the communication occurring between family members in the therapy session. Often it makes an important contribution to diagnosis of the family problem. Such work is usually based on family systems theory. A child's emotional problem is seen as one indication that some aspects of the way the family works is dysfunctional. There may be faulty communication or a lack of communication between family members, or communication between them may be based on misperceptions or unhelpful family 'rules'. The balance of the family may be out of kilter; parents may be too far apart, or the boundaries between generations may not be sufficiently established, perhaps with inappropriate alliances across generation boundaries. In a combination of family systems and psychodynamic theory a child with an emotional problem, who is 'the identified patient', may be seen as carrying the unbearable projected feelings of another family member – that is, the child is scapegoated. Therapy will then try to help each member to take back their projections and to own their own feelings. Introductions to the family systems approach and its variations are found in Gorell Barnes (1984), Jordan (1972), Minuchin (1974 and 1981), Burnham (1986), Walrond-Skinner (1976), Satir (1964), Skynner and Cleese (1983), and Carpenter and Treacher (1989).

Child guidance and child psychiatric units are most likely to use a family systems approach. Conciliation work with families in divorce is a newer area of this work in which the family's break-up is recognized and parents are helped to understand their children's feelings and to make the best possible arrangements for the future. Play is used to help children both to express and communicate their feelings. Because family work differs in important respects from much direct work with children it will be discussed separately in Chapter 4.

CONCLUSION

This chapter has shown that there are differing approaches to using therapeutic play in work with children and families. Yet there are some essential qualities which distinguish play therapy from other kinds of help. Play therapy works because play is children's natural means of expressing, communicating and coping with feelings. It depends on the healing power of spontaneous creative play in which the child 'surprises himself or herself'. The therapist or worker provides the play setting within safe boundaries which makes this healing play possible, offering the child a 'containing' relationship, a mental space in which the child's anxieties can be borne and thought about. Attentiveness and reflective listening are the worker's most powerful tools.

To determine whether individual play therapy is an appropriate intervention there needs to be a thorough assessment involving all relevant agencies. Family work and family therapy, or group work, may be more appropriate. Therapeutic play may be an important part of these other interventions, as Chapter 4 will show. Often play therapy with a child is carried out alongside some other form of work with the family. The necessity for this is suggested in Nicol's (1988) research which indicated that play therapy alone was little help to children in 'coercive' abusing families where attitudes to the child remained unchanged.

While there is little research into the effectiveness of play therapy, numerous case studies bear witness to the power of play in healing the hurt child. The next chapter is designed to help the worker to prepare to use play therapy in individual work with children.

Chapter 3

Preparing to use therapeutic play with children

Workers may use therapeutic play in different ways, according to both their perceptions of a child's needs and the demands or constraints of the context in which they work. At the simplest level, play is used to facilitate communication between child and adult, about matters of which the child is aware but which are hard to discuss, whether because the subject is painful or embarrassing or because the child lacks the ability to use other forms of expression. All workers who need to communicate with children from time to time can helpfully use play in this way. Even so, all need a basic understanding of child development, including knowledge of the stages of emotional and intellectual development. In particular every worker requires a thorough understanding of the theory of attachment and of children's reactions to separation and loss.

Yet play usually reveals much deeper meanings of which the child may be unaware. If play takes place in the area of illusion between the child's inner reality and the outside world, helping the child to mediate between the two, and is spontaneous, exciting and capable of surprising the child with its own discoveries, then its potential power is immense. The worker who helps the child to explore deeper feelings by provision of a safe and accepting play situation, and by a willingness to join in spontaneous play, may unleash strong feelings, often of anger and fear. This can be frightening and, as workers, we may fear being overwhelmed. Knowing about transference helps us to recognize that the feelings we are experiencing are usually also those of the child towards its parent. The task is to hold on to these feelings and to think about them, eventually passing them back to the child in a more manageable form. This 'containment' of the child is crucial and involves more than 'a good relationship'.

We must be aware of our normal desire to rescue children rather than to help them to confront their pain. We must be aware too of feelings which arise out of our own unresolved past experiences. Another fear is being out of our depth and not understanding. It does not matter that we do not understand all that a child's play may mean. The task in play therapy is not to interpret it to the child but to stay with children as they find it out for themselves. In the words of *The Prophet*, 'No man can reveal to you aught but that which already lies half asleep in the dawning of your knowledge' (Gibran 1972: 50).

The skills of reflective listening are a minimum requirement. Some focused methods, especially Gestalt methods, enable the child to go deeper more quickly. They need skill in their use, so that the child is not so overwhelmed by feelings that it is unable to play. When this happens we need to know how to respond so that, rather than leaving pain conscious but unresolved, the child can play again and continue with its own healing process.

It is rarely easy to provide a well-equipped playroom free from distractions and interruptions, and we have to consider how this can be most nearly achieved. We need to take account of the context in which play is provided and the meaning to the child of the place where it meets. Some thought needs to be given to the other occupants of the building and how to manage the child in relation to them.

As workers we need to be aware of the full range of our roles in relation to the child and family. Are we solely play therapist to the child or do we have a place in the child's real world, such as working with the parents, finding a new home, or making a report to the court? Where a worker is one of a number of workers with the child and family there is a need to coordinate efforts. For example, as a child's feelings come to the surface in play therapy they may sometimes spill over into behaviour in other places; the child's carers need to be prepared to handle this. Failure to coordinate may result in the child's premature withdrawal from therapy.

If the worker is to 'contain' the child, workers themselves must be contained. Their work needs management support; managers must understand and value the therapeutic work, and provide the structure and facilities within which it is possible for effective work to be carried out. This is in addition to workers' need for effective supervision from someone who understands the psychodynamic approach, including the implications of transference as well as the normal painful feelings which the work involves.

WHO DOES PLAY THERAPY?

There is no single professional preparation for play therapy in Britain. Play therapists arrive at their knowledge by a variety of idiosyncratic routes. (Further information about training is given in Appendix 1.)

Child psychotherapists and art therapists use a profound understanding of therapeutic play in their work with highly disturbed children. Their work is focused on the therapy session only; they may even take pains to avoid seeing the child in other contexts so as not to confuse the relationship. The therapist can then remain a completely subjective figure to the child, concerned with the child's inner conflicts above all else. However, a therapist may work closely with others in the child's world, including parents – for example, if based in a child guidance clinic or offering consultation to day centres, residential homes or schools.

In contrast, the social worker has a role in relation to the child in the real world, as well as roles in relation to other members of the child's real world. This gives the social worker the advantage of being able to act as a bridge between the outside world and the child's feelings, as Clare Winnicott (1964) describes. The disadvantage is that workers can be distracted by other aspects of their role, such as work with parents, or statutory obligations, assessments and reports to the court, or they may suffer from divided loyalties. Their role is as an objective part of the child's reality, although this may help them to reach the child's inner world too.

Social workers may specialize in assessment or therapeutic work with children. In social services departments, field and residential social workers are likely to be working with children who may have been neglected, or physically or sexually abused, or with children who have suffered severe loss, disruption or deprivation in family life, and are in care, whether fostered or in residential homes, or being prepared for adoption. Social workers in voluntary organizations may be carrying out assessments and therapeutic work with similar children, although workers' freedom from statutory obligations may enable more time for direct work with a child. Divorce court welfare officers and guardians *ad litem* work with children in order to make assessments for the courts and may have limited time for therapeutic work, in contrast to conciliation workers in voluntary organizations who may have more opportunity for therapy with children. Field social workers tend to use focused methods of assessment and therapeutic play. Social workers in under-fives family centre work, with co-workers who may include nursery nurses or teachers, may provide informal as well as structured therapeutic play for children and their families. Residential workers may provide play as part of a therapeutic environment.

There is a long tradition of psychiatric social workers' use of play therapy in child guidance clinics, exemplified by Prestage's (1972) account of her work with Kim. Today the use of behavioural methods in work with children in child guidance seems more common. Even stronger has been the influence of family therapy, based on a systems approach to understanding family dynamics, leading to an emphasis on family work. Family work is widely used in child psychiatric units. Social workers in child psychiatry, as elsewhere, are likely to be working with aspects of the child's real world, including parent and other agencies, as well as directly with the child. However, they have often developed special skills in communicating with children.

Play therapy in child psychiatric units tends to be offered by occupational therapists. Lily Jeffrey (1981) analysed the work undertaken by occupational therapists in 20 child psychiatric units in Britain. They offered developmental and behavioural play-based assessments and programmes for children with behavioural difficulties and functional disorders such as autism, communication disorder, or sensory–motor impairment, as well as assessment and therapy for children with emotional problems. Jeffrey concluded that 80 per cent of play therapy was said to be non-directive, and often acknowledged the influence of psychodynamic ideas. Practice, however, tended to be eclectic, with workers choosing methods that were felt to be appropriate for a particular child.

In the field of education, therapeutic play is most likely to be offered by specialist teachers in classes and units for maladjusted children. Play therapy is sometimes available in residential special schools, sometimes from art therapists and psychotherapists but also from teachers and residential social workers who have acquired some skills in this work. Teacher-counsellors for pre-school children and other special needs teachers, and also some speech therapists and psychologists, may use play in helping developmentally delayed children and children with disabilities and learning difficulties. Nursery teachers and nursery nurses may use therapeutic play in nursery schools and classes. In the voluntary sector, playgroup leaders may offer therapeutic play opportunities in playgroups.

Hospital play specialists and child development centre workers use play in their work with sick, disabled and developmentally delayed children. Some nurses and teachers have acquired play skills in working with these children, and others have acquired them in working with children and families in child psychiatric units. Occasionally psychiatrists and clinical psychologists will use play methods in work with children and families.

DEVELOPING SKILLS IN THERAPEUTIC PLAY

Getting in touch with the 'child' within

Workers who are contemplating using therapeutic play with children need above all to be in touch with the child within themselves. Workers who have valued their own creativity and playfulness will be well placed to allow the child to use the freedom and creativity of spontaneous play, and to provide the conditions which make it possible. Knowledge of the child within the self is a most effective way of becoming aware of how a child may be feeling. It is important, however, to distinguish between the 'child' feelings which refer back to one's own experience and those which are felt through the child projecting them on to the worker. The more workers have thought about their own 'child' feelings the less likely is this confusion. This is why psychotherapists undergo personal psychoanalysis as part of their training. This analysis, of course, is not possible for most workers using therapeutic play, and they must find other means of getting in touch with their child self. Recalling childhood memories is a potent method which is often used on training courses. Because of its potency it is not to be used lightly, especially in group work where members may be surprised into revelations, startling as much to themselves as to others, and which they might not otherwise have chosen to share. Members need to have support available, or permission to opt out.

It can be helpful to start with good memories, which even the most deprived childhood may hold, making it possible to acknowledge more painful ones later. Crowe (1983) tells of a mother's memory of playing blissfully with a stick and a worm in a muddy puddle and her surprise that there were any good memories from her appalling childhood. Family placement worker, Janet Turner, asks people to draw the house they lived in when they were about eight years old and to then tell someone else about it. Social worker, Elizabeth Wright, uses an exercise she calls 'Through a glass darkly' in which someone tells a painful memory to a neighbour in the group who then tells the whole group. They then explore the emotions raised.

This contains the additional message about how hard it can be for a child to tell about its pain, especially when it has been abused. It is important to have an empathic understanding of the impact we have on children when we start to explore their emotions and memories. Imagining you are having an argument with someone in your family and then someone coming and taking one of you away is a potent exercise in revealing feelings.

Weinstein (1987) gives workers an opportunity to experience a wide variety of play materials. She invites people to imagine themselves at the age of the child with whom they are working and to play accordingly. She finds that workers are surprised by the extent to which this exercise brings them closer to children and enables them to pick up non-verbal cues. Some tutors similarly use familiar children's books and stories. In another exercise, used by Elizabeth Wright, people are asked to think about present-day habits that they can relate back to childhood. As they realise it is not easy to change oneself they also learn that it is not easy for a damaged child to change.

We might agree with Moore's (1985) list of the qualities needed for communication with children, – some passivity and thus patience, a belief in magic, some infantile traits, and a comfortable sense of ourselves as adults.

Learning to observe

The ability to observe children objectively is a crucial skill. Child psychotherapy training starts with observations of babies, and the Central Council for Education and Training in Social Work (CCETSW) has recommended that social workers should do this too, as part of a series of observations of young children. An understanding of infant emotions contributes to workers' understanding of the psychodynamic approach and the process of containment. Workers come to recognize the parallels between the child's expressions of emotions in later childhood and those expressed in infancy.

Under-fives workers, such as nursery nurses and playgroup leaders normally receive a thorough training in observing children, and other workers could benefit from a similar training – for example, using methods described in Sylva, Roy and Painter (1980), and Holmes and McMahon (1978). While a knowledge of child development, including the development of play, is essential, only good observation skills can ensure that it may be applied appropriately.

Reflective listening

One of the hardest and most essential skills to acquire is the ability to reflect the child's play. This skill is in complete contrast to normal behaviour where adults ask a stream of questions or make comments which reveal personal opinions or judgments. It can be helpful for triads of workers to practise on one another. While one is playing, perhaps with miniature toys, or involved in an activity, ideally in a playroom, another describes aloud what the first is doing, giving a running commentary, but forbidden to ask any questions at all. The third observes and gives the 'adult' feedback on how they were doing. With a child, one might say, for example, 'You're taking the crocodile to the sand. You're digging a hole. You're burying it deep down. You've got rid of it!' This is akin to the 're-capping' technique used in Children's Hours. It takes practice to make neutral comments. Even praise – for example, 'What a lovely painting' or 'What a pretty dress' – implies value judgments and needs to be avoided. It both distracts the worker from receiving the child's communication and discourages the child from further communication. Criticism is, of course, to be shunned. Yet it may involve a radical shift of approach for, say, the under-fives worker who is used to saying, 'That's not very nice' when a child is thumping a doll baby, and instead observes quietly 'You're hitting that baby doll very hard'. The discipline of not asking any questions is also difficult at first and requires practice.

The next stage is to practise becoming aware of the feelings which the other is communicating and then reflecting these accurately. To continue the earlier examples, 'You don't like the crocodile, it's a bit scary. You're angry with it (as child digs furiously). You're very pleased now you've got rid of it', and 'You look as if you're very angry with that baby'. It is not easy to empty one's mind of one's own thoughts and to make an internal space to focus on and to think about the child, and to receive their communication. Tentative reflections of feelings leave the child able to correct the worker when wrong – for example, 'It looks as though the boy doll is feeling quite sad'.

The more experienced worker may also use some questions. These should be open questions where the child is not constrained by the limits of a 'yes–no' or 'either–or' answer. Such questions often begin with 'what', 'who', 'when', 'where', 'how' or 'why'. A question used by many workers when the child has enacted a situation in play is 'Does that remind you of anything?' Leading questions such as 'Is that mummy? Did she do that?' should be avoided since children will often give the answer which they think the adult expects to hear.

Coping with the worker's feelings

To become aware of children's painful feelings is a most painful experience for the worker and it is natural to create defences against feeling this pain. People in close contact with children over long periods, such as in residential homes, can find the pain intolerable. Unless they themselves have support they may tend to distance themselves and become unable to contain the child, or they may leave altogether.

Other common reactions from any worker in contact with a hurt child are to want to rescue the child, feeling guilty that they are providing 'only' therapy, and to reassure children that they are not 'bad'. They may want to explain intellectually the reasons for the child's current predicament in terms of past events and other people's difficulties, or to blame other people. These are all unhelpful responses which avoid confronting the child's present unhappiness, and which do not offer containment. Shirley Hoxter (1983) notes that workers' fantasies of fostering the child are a useful warning that they are at risk of 'rescuing' rather than 'containing'. The notion of being a perfect parent matches the child's idealization, but is doomed to disillusion at the first minor frustration. The child instead needs help in developing more realistic expectations.

Workers may become afraid of their own angry and punitive feelings towards the child as they receive the full force of the child's anger in play sessions and may want to retaliate. Or they may be so busy defending themselves and the environment from the child's anger that they have no opportunity to create the mental space to reflect on and to respond to the child's communication. The victim has become a persecutor. Some children treat their workers with contemptuous indifference, a communication of the rejection they themselves feel. The worker feels useless and helpless, even contaminated. In these situations the worker feels inclined to give up. If this happens it confirms children's view that their feelings cannot be tolerated and are best dealt with by flight or projection on to other people. It can be helpful for workers to continually remind themselves that the attack is not personal but a re-enactment of the children's feelings towards parents whom they feel have let them down.

Children may create mess and confusion, and communicate this feeling to workers who can feel overwhelmed by confusion and their apparent failure to understand the child's communication. The child is forcing the worker to experience its muddled feelings. Shirley Hoxter (1983) offers these and other thoughts in an invaluable discussion of how to cope with feelings aroused in working with severely deprived children. Above all she suggests that workers have somehow to bear experiencing both the child's feelings and their own until they have been 'modulated' enough to respond in terms of the child's communication.

Supervision of workers is crucial if they are to continue helping children to cope with their pain. The supervision can provide containment of the worker who is then able to go on containing the child. Where the worker is not able to think about the child's communication during sessions it may be possible to do so away from the child. Supervision can help to sort out the child's projections from other reactions and feelings of the worker. Sometimes colleagues supervise and support one another. In some teams, workers take a videotape of work with a child for discussion and consultation with colleagues. Others look for supervision from a suitable and congenial worker, such as a psychiatrist or child psychotherapist, either within or outside their agency.

PREPARATION AND PLANNING

Some workers may be using therapeutic play as a spontaneous part of their everyday work with children. This 'on the hoof' therapeutic play is most likely in residential work and in under-fives work, where provision for play is normally made. Some nurses and teachers may also use play as the opportunity arises. Other workers may need to plan carefully before undertaking therapeutic play. Teamwork can help in creative planning as well as offering support in the course of work.

The context of therapeutic play

Workers need to think about their own role and the role of their agency, and how it is likely to be perceived by the child and its family. If they have other roles, perhaps statutory ones, workers need to consider if these may be affected by any revelations in the course of work, as well as affecting the family's perceptions of the possible outcome of work. They may need to consider whether there is support for the therapy from the family. A family which is using the child as a scapegoat may not want them 'cured', and may unconsciously sabotage therapy. Some may be jealous of the attention a child is getting or may resent a child becoming more assertive. Other interventions, such as counselling or family therapy, may need to be carried out instead of, or at least parallel to, play therapy.

The network of agencies which may be involved with a child and family can helpfully be involved in an initial consultation process so that play therapy fits into the context of other work. Also, other parts of the system can be prepared for possible overflow of feelings from play therapy into other situations. For example, a child whose anger or pain has not been sufficiently contained in a particular play session may later behave badly at school or with foster parents. Short-term distressed behaviour can be better tolerated by others if they are aware of the long-term goal. Others, such as foster parents and residential workers, may them-selves be able to make a major contribution to helping the child through therapeutic play if they are involved.

Professional jealousies can affect work. Workers with statutory responsibilities or other heavy loads may see the play therapy session as being 'the nice bits', while failing to take account of the fact that the worker in play therapy has to bear the child's unbearable feelings. The therapist may be jealous of or angry with those who are looking after the child, especially if the therapist has fantasies of parenting the child. In the latter case it is vital for the therapist to become aware of and take back this projection, so that the therapist can help the child (whose projection it is initially) in turn to take it back too. Thinking in terms of a systems approach can help to disentangle communication between workers.

Planning play sessions

Matching goals to methods

The aim of work may vary from assessments of or brief therapy of a child's feelings about a particular situation, or communication about specific events or plans, to 'deep' play therapy or a long piece of work helping a child to make sense of its past and to cope with its future. The previous chapter offered a range of approaches from which workers may choose those most suited to their aims, as well as those with which they feel most comfortable. Subsequent chapters present some of the approaches used by workers in different settings, illustrating their differing aims and styles of work. Some aspects of planning for therapeutic play are common to most workers and these are discussed here. Although the main focus is on individual work with a child many points also apply to family and group work.

Who?

The first decision is whether work should be with an individual child alone, or with siblings, with parent or parents, including foster parents, or with a group of children. This depends on the goals of work. Other work may be carried out in parallel to therapeutic play, with other members of the child's world.

Where?

Since a child's, and its family's, feelings are linked to places, an important decision is where the play sessions are to take place. The child's home ground is familiar to the child and may be used if the child feels safe there. A foster home may also be used, often with foster parents involved in continuing play. Some settings which themselves may cause stress, such as hospitals, provide therapeutic play to help the child to cope. Often a school is a convenient place for child and worker, but the child's feelings about school and the particular room to be used need to be considered first. A school may be the least stigmatizing setting, as compared with, for example, a social services department or a psychiatric unit. A neutral setting or 'sanctuary' gives a child, especially an older child, more 'breathing space', away from the constraints of the real world. A worker has to weigh up the relative benefits of taking therapy to the child or taking the child to the therapy. Is the child more relaxed in a familiar setting or in a 'sanctuary'?

Practical points must also be considered such as who is to bring the child and how feasible the journey is. The parent or 'chaperone' is usually an important figure to the child and this person may need a comfortable place to wait, where the child can have access to this person if necessary. Some thought needs to be given to dealing with the reactions of other occupants of the building to a possibly angry and noisy child.

When?

A weekly session is often the most feasible for both child and worker, but children with acute or severe chronic disturbances may need more frequent help if they are to feel contained enough to manage from one session to the next. Most workers offer sessions lasting from 40 minutes to one hour. Very young children and children with attachment difficulties may need much less, unless parents are present.

The time of day and the transitions, emotional as well as physical, involved for the child require some thought and may need to be planned with others. A child may need to be released regularly from school. Reliable transport may be necessary. Sessions should be at the same times each week, to provide predictability in the child's life. It is important for the worker to be reliable, and to be scrupulous about being on time and regularly keeping that time clear for the child. The child should, of course, see the same worker or workers from session to session. In group or family work, co-workers should be the same people each time.

The length of therapeutic work varies according to the aims of work and the child's progress. Some workers find it helpful to negotiate an initial block of sessions and to decide with others at the end of the period whether further work might be needed.

Confidentiality

The child needs to know how far the worker will tell other people about what happens in play sessions. The worker needs to be honest about this, perhaps explaining that 'she will talk about him to Dr Smith but that she will only tell his parents or carers very generally how he is getting on, and that she will not talk to anyone without telling him first'. The child may choose whether or not to talk about the sessions outside. It is a mistake to promise to keep secrets. A child can be told, as Madge Bray does in sexual abuse work, that some secrets are too big to keep. As far as possible, however, a child needs to feel that what it does and says in the play session is a private matter. A worker can help by asking the child's carers not to question the child about what took place. Some workers allow a child to take drawings and paintings home but the implications of this need consideration. Sometimes it may be better if they are kept for the child by the worker. Confidentiality is a difficult area, especially in child abuse, and many workers are aware that they 'are treading on egg-shells'.

Play provision

Some workers are based in beautifully equipped playrooms. Others stagger from place to place carrying everything in boxes or bags! Play equipment needs to be appropriate to the child's developmental level and needs (see Chapter 1). Equipment should offer opportunities for creative and imaginative or symbolic play. Play with miniatures is most easily provided but some children are not ready to use this degree of symbolism and may need to play with larger dolls and toys. Material such as clay, sand and water cannot be damaged and so can provide safe outlets for confused and angry feelings in messy and destructive play. These materials can be restored, which can help a child to learn that anger can be controlled and managed. (It may be a good idea to ask that the child comes in clothes that do not matter.) Messy play cannot be provided in all settings and sometimes play dough or Plasticine can be used instead. Baby bottles and toys, and sensory responsive items such as cushions, boxes and blankets enable regressive play. A drink and something to eat are often provided. A toilet should be near at hand.

Play materials should match a child's culture and race. Brummer (1986) notes that 'play materials for black children must include the kinds of dolls, paints, masks and books which enable both child and worker to reflect on sameness and difference of colour'.

Some workers provide a carefully chosen but limited range of play materials in the playroom, finding that some children cannot readily concentrate in a rich environment. One of the Caldecott Community's playrooms, designed and used by Sarah Hemsby, has a sand tray, with small baskets of miniatures, domestic and wild animals, dinosaurs and play people beside it. There are painting and drawing materials, and play dough at a table. Elsewhere there are dolls, teddies and puppets, and domestic play equipment such as cups and plates, a small sink with water available, a dolls' house, a large piece of orange material for dressing up, and a baby doll in a Moses basket near cushions in a corner for curling up in comfort. The floor is carpeted. The room feels spacious and uncluttered, offering clear invitations to play. The door is painted with a picture of a mother and baby. A wall painting of a wood in winter, which is the first thing a child sees as it enters, other pictures including a large Raymond Briggs 'Snowman' and a life-size painting in an alcove of a witch, lend the playroom an aura of magic, of being in a world apart.

Other workers have an extensive range of materials but may make more use of the adult's role in helping a child to understand their possible uses. A typical playroom of this all-embracing sort might include water play, wet and dry sand, Plasticine, play dough and clay, painting and drawing materials, finger painting, cutting and sticking materials for collage and model-making, miniature play with dolls' house and people, Lego and play people, wild and domestic animals, cars and trains, soldiers and a fort, bricks and blocks, a model village, doll families and domestic play including beds and telephones in a 'home corner', dressing-up clothes, books, puppets, equipment for drama and music, and for cooking, and also cushions and baby bottles for regressive play.

Peripatetic workers are more constrained in the variety of equipment they can provide. They tend to sort materials into bags within bags (or boxes). One bag may contain painting and drawing materials, and perhaps clay or play dough. Another bag may contain puppets (perhaps a witch), dolls and soft toys, both gentle animals and monsters, and other items, such as face paints, a collapsible plastic knife or a magic wand (as Lyn Bennett has). (A child can put the monsters back in a bag and pull up the draw string tightly!) A third bag usually contains miniature toys, an appropriate doll family, domestic and wild animals and monsters, small blocks or fences. A baby's feeding bottle, with a small plastic bottle of squash, enables regression play. Madge Bray describes the contents of a playbox used with Simon in his foster home.

> The playbox contains many tools to help build up a picture of Simon's perception of his life – what has happened to him and what he might wish to happen in future. There are happy and sad-faced dolls, small play people, ... dolls' furniture, a fuzzy hedgehog puppet, a rabbit who needs to be told lots of times before he can understand and wonders what it is like to live in human houses. There are face and animal masks, magic pencils which draw secrets, doll's house

with transfers, cars, telephones, snuggly blanket, baby dummy and other small toys.

(Bray 1986: 19)

Workers who are using focused play methods need the appropriate materials, such as pictures for the child to complete, or specially designed cards and games, or equipment for sensory work. (Other chapters give more details of these.) Some workers, such as hospital play specialists, have to become inventive about providing play for disabled or bed-bound children.

STARTING PLAY SESSIONS

The first session – aims and introductions

The aim of the first session is for the worker and child to make contact, for the child to start exploring the play possibilities of the situation, and for the child to have enjoyed or appreciated it enough to want more. The worker uses the session to start to get to know the child. It can be an anxious time for both worker and child. It can help if they have met previously, preferably on the child's home ground, whatever that may be. While a younger child may be content to be told that this is a place where children come to play, older children are entitled to an explanation of why they are there. One worker may say that 'other people are concerned that you have worries that are difficult to talk about'. She explains that sometimes children like to play or draw about their feelings and that words do not have to be used. A worker with young children may say something like 'I know you are unhappy and mum knows you are, so let's play'. A family placement worker might say 'These are special times to play and have fun, and to do work on preparing for your new family'.

Playing

Often a child starts playing spontaneously as it is shown the toys and the things there are to do. The worker may say something like 'You can do whatever you want with the toys and I'll make sure you don't do anything that wouldn't be OK ... I'll just be with you and share what you are doing' (Bray 1986: 19). The worker needs to be sitting on the floor with the child, although respecting the child's personal space. Occasionally a child will sit silent and immobile, when the worker must decide whether this is an indication of how the child is, which may need reflection in the worker's own body language and silence, or whether it is a feeling of pressure and powerlessness in the situation. If the worker judges it to be the latter, the most effective way to help the child to feel free to play is for the worker to start playing, returning initiative to the child as it joins in.

The prime task is to be aware of and to reflect the child's play, resisting any temptation to ask questions or to advise and direct the child. The worker uses the reflective techniques described earlier. An inexperienced worker may find the best way to start is with a gentle running commentary on what the child is doing. With experience, the worker can go on to reflect the feelings the child expresses in play.

The worker may gently join in play, perhaps demonstrating the frightened mouse who hides in a pocket, useful with a quiet or shy child. A nervous child can also be helped to relax if the worker has a puppet or teddy that keeps making mistakes, which they can laugh about together so that it becomes clear to the child that play has no serious consequences. It can help if the worker forgets something or needs help which the child can give spontaneously. The worker can introduce the teddy who finds it hard to say things, or the rabbit who only understands when told something several times, so they need the child's help. If a child suddenly speaks after a period of silence it is very important that the adult should respond as if it were perfectly normal and unsurprising.

Many children find puppets helpful, sometimes with the worker as the puppet's voice, sometimes themselves. Some children relax after the worker has conversations with a puppet in which the worker talks to it and answers for it. Similarly a worker may speak for the child, in the same way as a mother talking to her baby treats them as competent and answers for them. This is a form of reflective listening; what the worker says must be based on observation and understanding of how the child might be feeling. Obviously the worker keenly watches the child's reaction and is very willing to be laughed at and put right. (This latter technique is only to be used in connection with the child's perception of the worker and the play situation – for example, 'I wonder what she's got in her other bag', or 'Why is that silly woman playing with a rabbit with me?' It should not be used to ask the child about previous events, because it could become a form of leading questioning.)

The worker's role is to elicit play, not to direct it. If the child invites the worker to join in play or to take a role, then the worker follows the child's directions. If the child gives a role but does not tell the worker what to do, then it can be helpful to play it in a stereotyped way, such as a nagging or fussy mother or a disciplining father. The worker must be ready to drop the role at any moment, in tune with the child's play. With young children who are liable to confuse reality and fantasy it can be helpful to state, for example, 'I'm *pretending* to be your mum'.

Even for workers who plan to use focused play methods it can be a good idea to be non-directive in the first session. The child has an opportunity to be itself and to have recognition of this state of 'being'. If the child has enjoyed play and contact with the worker it will want more. The worker has an opportunity to observe and listen, to give caring attention. The worker can assess how the child seems to be feeling. Sometimes a child's own view of a problem may not be the same as an adult's. The worker can find out what the child's likes and dislikes are, for example, for drawing or playing with soft toys, and what it is able to do, such as writing. This can inform subsequent work and help in planning it. At the end of the first session when the worker is telling the child about the next session, the worker may say that the child can play next time too but that the worker would also like some 'time for me', and that the worker may be bringing some special pictures for drawing or some games.

Sometimes children, often older ones, cannot cope with initial free play and find a structured approach more comfortable. Tuning in to the child can guide the worker to the right methods for the child at that time. In all focused work it is important to give children the time that they need, and to avoid pressurizing them to use a session in a particular way if they are not ready. Some children may take months before they feel safe to reveal feelings.

Control and limits

Some workers tell the child at the beginning that they will be there to make sure that nothing is dangerous and nothing gets damaged. Many set limits as they go along, making it clear to the child that they will not let the child or the worker be physically hurt, and preventing excessive destruction of materials. Workers need to decide how much destruction and mess they can personally tolerate and how much is acceptable in a given setting. Playing in a foster parent's living-room obviously poses different constraints from work in a specifically designated play-room. Work usually takes place in one room and the session may be ended if the child leaves it, although the worker may wait until the end of the allotted time for the child to return.

The worker tries to understand the feelings a child is conveying in messy and destructive play, perhaps feelings of being a mess, or of being very angry, or of being frightened by angry feelings, of others or itself. If the worker's perception and reflection of this understanding is 'heard' by the child this play may be therapeutic. If the child is so out of control that it cannot 'hear' the worker, and the worker becomes anxious and feels that the situation is getting out of hand, then the worker can intervene and stop the child, change the activity, or ultimately end the session. When the child is at the stage of testing the limits the worker needs to be ready to make it clear what they are and then stick to them, so that the child feels contained. These limits may not be the same for every child. Part of the worker's skill lies in matching them to a child's needs, as well as what the worker feels able to cope with. The time limits of the session are an important part of the child's containment and should be kept to, even when the child is begging for longer. The child needs to be told when the session is nearing the end so that it can complete some aspect of play if it so wishes. A period of calm play at the end of a session, even helping to clear up, can help to ease the child's transition back to the real world and make feelings less likely to overflow elsewhere.

Recording observations and planning further sessions

Some workers find that they are able to jot down notes and observations in the course of a play session. It is always helpful to make notes as soon after the session as possible, as it is easy to forget or unconsciously alter what happened. The process as well as the content of play needs to be recorded. Violet Oaklander describes how she observes:

> I observe the process of the child as she plays. How does she play, how does she approach the materials, what does she choose, what does she avoid? What is her general style? Is there difficulty in shifting from one thing to another? Is she disorganized or well organized? What is her play pattern? How she plays tells a lot about how she is in her life.
>
> I watch the content of the play itself. Does she play out themes of loneliness? Aggression? Nurturance? Are there lots of accidents and crashes with planes and cars?
>
> I watch for the child's contact skills. Do I feel in contact with her as she plays? Is she so absorbed in her play that I see she makes good contact with her play and herself as she plays? Is she continually at the edge of contact, unable to commit herself to anything?
>
> What is the contact like within the play itself? Does she allow for contact between the objects of play? Do people or animals or cars contact each other, see each other, talk to each other?
>
> (Oaklander 1978: 160–1)

Planning for further sessions is based on the information gained from observation. It depends too on the time available for work – for example, the constraints of a court report or an impending family placement. The worker's skills and preferred mode of work, whether non-directive or focused play, also affect planning. Workers who use focused play may have a very clear programme for a series of sessions. Kate Burke's work in helping children to prepare for new families, described in Chapter 9, is an example of high quality focused play, in which her programme is meticulously planned to meet the needs of each individual child, yet allowing for 'eddies' in the flow of work. In contrast is the non-directive play therapy used by Lyn Bennett with Andrew, described in Chapter 5, in which the planning is equally thoughtful and important.

In choosing methods of work, particularly focused methods, it is important to use only those you feel comfortable with and have tried out previously – for example, with members of your own family.

Dealing with the painful bits

The aim of work with a child is to help it to confront and live with its emotional pain. It is important that this happens at a pace that the child can bear. This has been described as tiptoeing up to the child's pain. Non-directive methods which go at the child's pace are safer in this respect than focused methods. In either approach, play disruption tends to happen when the child starts to be overwhelmed by painful feelings. Then the worker might say 'That's hard for you to think about' or 'It's sometimes difficult to talk about it'. While not forcing the pace it is important not to abandon the subject but to help the child to come back to it again, not necessarily immediately, perhaps saying, 'We'll talk about it some more next time'. If children are upset or cry their pain needs to be recognized. Even a brief recognition may touch quite deeply – for example, 'You're really hurting', or 'You're very sad about it'. It may not be helpful to distract them at once to something more pleasant. Sometimes physical comfort may be offered, or with children who cannot bear to be touched the worker may need to sit quietly with the child, perhaps listening to music.

The worker has an equal need to be able to face painful areas and may be surprised by how hard it can be, for example, to tell a child that it was born of rape, or was found in a dustbin, or was hit by its father when it was a baby. Body language, such as not looking at the child or turning away, tell the child that what happened was not acceptable or bearable. Certainly judging the timing of information is essential but in the end the worker must believe in the child's right to 'be' and to have the information it needs to make sense of its life.

If a session has been painful it can be a good idea to try to end the session on a positive note, perhaps with a game or a good memory. How the child is at the end of a session is a good indicator of how helpful the child has found it.

The stages of therapy

As the tumult of a child's feelings pour forth in therapy it is very easy to become confused and disoriented as to what is happening. The worker may come to doubt whether there is any benefit to the child. Understanding of the stages through which the therapy is moving can help workers to get their bearings. Moustakas (in Haworth 1964: 417–19) describes these stages as follows. In the first stage the child's feelings of anxiety and anger are diffuse and pervasive, affecting every-thing. They are expressed in general ways such as apparently purposeless attacks on the materials or fear of everything. As the child experiences the worker's containment its feelings become more focused. In this second stage anger is directed at specific people, including the worker, or through symbolic play. Fears become fears of particular people and things. As the worker accepts these feelings the child's self-esteem starts to grow. At this third stage the child expresses positive as well as negative feelings of fear or anger, mixed up together. For instance, at one moment the child may be feeding a baby doll and the next moment thumping it hard. These feelings are expressed with great intensity at first, gradually becom-ing expressed in milder ways. In the fourth stage, the child has sorted and separated out positive and negative feelings about people and situations, in line with how things are in reality.

Breaks and ending

A child can feel abandoned when the worker is away, and earlier feelings of loss and non-containment are often aroused. The child therefore needs warning and preparation for the worker's holidays. One worker gives a child something small of her own to look after, or a 'thinking book' in which the child can draw pictures to show the worker on her return. A child may regress and the worker may need to deal with its anger at the worker's 'desertion'.

The termination of therapeutic work needs even more preparation. Ending ideally comes about because the child is in some way better. The aims of work, whether extensive or limited, may have been achieved, and the child is better able to handle what comes next in life. The length of therapy may vary from a few weeks up to one or two years. The longer the therapy has been the longer the preparation for ending needs to be. Play therapist, Janet West, describes the process of termination as mediating reality into the play situation. In the bridging phase the worker becomes a real-life person in the child's world rather than the neutral all-accepting therapist. They may leave the playroom to go on visits together, as well as important symbolic pretend visiting. The gap between sessions can be extended gradually. The child's sadness at ending needs to be recognized but the child who wants to stay in the playroom may be reassured, 'You've got the playroom inside you; you've got the biscuits, you've got me, you've got your memories of what we've done together' (West 1984: 81). Together they prepare for ending, perhaps planning a 'party', an exchange of photographs and a present for the child on the last session. Janet West suggests that there is no need for the relationship to end absolutely with the end of play sessions, with a further unnecessary separation for the child. With time the child will outgrow the relationship in the normal way. In the meantime she gives the child her address and telephone number so that it can make contact if it wishes. Occasional visits, letters and birthday cards with friendly rather than 'deep' comments keep alive a real rather than a therapeutic relationship.

Chapter 4

Play in under-fives and family work

There is a growing interest in the therapeutic use of play in family work. Play techniques are used by a number of services which work to repair damaged relationships in families and to prevent family breakdown. Family work which uses play takes place in two main settings. Work with children under five and their families is usually based in the community, in organizations such as family centres. Pre-school centres are increasingly involving parents and moving to family work, based on the recognition that parents whose own needs have not been met cannot offer adequate nurturing to their children. Attachment theory and related research provide a way of understanding what is happening between parent and child, as well as suggesting how help can be given to repair damaged and damaging relationships. Work with families with older children is most likely in child guidance and child psychiatric units, and is often based on a family systems approach to understanding and intervening in a family, and uses family therapy techniques, some of which may involve play.

WORK WITH FAMILIES WITH CHILDREN UNDER FIVE

Family work with under-fives has been quietly growing in recent years. Voluntary organizations such as the Pre-school Playgroups Association recognized long ago the benefits to many children and families of the involvement of parents in their children's playgroups (Pre-school Playgroups Association 1982). Offshoots of the playgroup movement were drop-in and family centres, such as the pioneering Hartley-Wintney Family Centre and the thriving Donnington Doorstep in Oxford, where parents and children play together. Local authority education and social service departments recognized the potential benefits to families and sometimes set up their own centres or re-examined the brief of existing centres, so that some education nursery schools and social service day nurseries changed into more family-oriented places. Non-statutory organizations such as Family Service Units, NSPCC and the National Children's Home set up family centres, usually in association with local social services. The 1989 Children Act means that provision of family centres is a statutory requirement, although lack of funding suggests that progress may be slow.

In the voluntary sector there are exciting innovative schemes such as the effective NEWPIN in south London, set up by Ann Jenkins (1989), where parents support parents within a psychodynamic framework. Home Start offers a home visiting service in a number of areas, befriending young families under stress and using play to help them to repair damaged relationships.

Under-fives workers generally recognize the importance of providing good play opportunities for children. They often perceive the benefits of play in terms of children's development of intellectual or cognitive skills, and of social skills – the ability to manage relationships with other adults and children. They tend to measure emotional development in terms of children's self-confidence and self-esteem, to be developed by positive experiences in a group or at home, or in terms of the acceptability and manageability of a child's behaviour, rather than in terms of the help needed to cope with specific difficulties and anxieties in a child's life.

Where children have opportunities for play in a non-directed but safe group setting they may play out and master difficult or painful experiences, either by playing alone or by social play with other children. The adults may never know that this has happened. However, observant workers who are aware of likely causes of stress may be able to show their recognition and acceptance of the feelings a child expresses in play, such as anxiety over a house move, anger over a new baby or grief at the loss of a family member. For example, soon after Peter's mother died he came into his playgroup and went to the sewing table and worked intently. 'I'm making a blue dress for my mummy to wear in heaven', he said. The worker helped Peter with his sewing. A child's play may also reveal how things are at home. In a family centre a child pretending to wash up in the home corner threw the bowl of dishes across the room, saying 'My mummy did it this morning'. This led to the workers finding out that the mother was under a lot of pressure as she was on the run from shop-lifting. In the same centre a worker was reading Ahlbergs' story of *Burglar Bill* to a group of children, with its moral ending where the burglars return the stolen goods, when one child piped up, 'We don't do that, we keeps it'. In this setting the workers felt that their aim for the children was to help them to feel strong and safe enough to survive.

Sometimes a worker may not know what is wrong but will start from a child's inability to play. Playgroup course tutor, Bernie Ross, describes how she helped Helen on her regular visits to help in the group:

Helen was a three-year-old girl who had been attending the playgroup for six weeks but still just stood and watched and could not play. Stories in the book corner were a safe way for me to win her over. She sat close to me and said nothing, her thumb in her mouth. My only guide to her enjoyment was the frequent whines and pointings to more books. Sometimes her attention was drawn to the play of other children. Sometimes more children would join us in the book corner, listen and talk, and go again. Helen said nothing. I announced that I was going to do a jigsaw. Helen sat on my lap again. We found a simple play tray, a picture of a horse. Her thumb came out of her mouth, she took one of the pieces and put it directly where it belonged. I continued to talk to her the whole time. She said nothing but stayed within inches of my knees, even when I needed to do other things. The following week Helen attended on the Tuesday as usual when I was not there and spent most of the morning watching. On Thursday she came straight to me and asked for a story, at least a single word between thumb sucks coupled with motioning towards the book corner. She selected one of the books we had enjoyed before and listened passively to several stories while watching the other children playing. I told her we would read just one more and then do something else. She agreed and joined in a little more with the jigsaws. After several sessions like this Helen would sit and play in parallel with others at the table toys or join a group with a helper doing some collage.

At break-time, when all 12 children had a drink and a plain biscuit, Helen would always have a special snack from home. It was allowed as a possible help to settling her into the group. Once, right out of the blue, when the children were chatting over the milk break, she piped up to talk about the horses she likes to ride. Her conversation was dotted with little giggles and frequent stammers. The real Helen had broken through.

When I was talking and playing at the dough table she would stand next to me but never touch the dough. She never wanted to do a painting, would not play with sand or water, and would use a glue spreader only very cautiously. She would watch intently but declined any invitation to try. One day I was kneading some smooth dough made with self-raising flour. She sat on my lap, just watching. 'Look Helen, here's my horses tail. You stroke it and feel how silky it is!' She touched it gently and began to stroke it. Later I persuaded her to shape a tiny piece in her fingers. I had to miss a couple of sessions at this stage but felt quite happy that Helen would not regress. On my return she was pleased to see me and wanted to cling. At milk-time she had no special snack. She chose a biscuit from the tin and ate it all up.

This effective piece of substitute mothering used play as the means of communication. As Helen's anxiety lessened she became free to start playing herself. Her acceptance of the playgroup's food indicated that she felt at home. At the same time, conversation with her mother had established that the family had recently moved to the area and that Helen was also attending a second nursery with a very different and structured programme. It was not surprising that she was confused and anxious. Friendly and non-judgmental support helped her anxious mother to understand Helen's anxieties and to decide to withdraw her from the second group. After a period of absence through illness Helen arrived at playgroup with her mother. Bernie Ross continues.

This time Helen immediately led her mum to the book corner, where out came the favourite books she always chose for me to read. Two hours and several quiet activities later Helen was contentedly playing with just her own mother. I assured her mother that she could go shopping if she wanted to but, although previously reluctant to stay, she declined, saying 'I'm quite enjoying it myself now!'

Some weeks later she told me how she had really enjoyed playing at play-group. She enrolled on a short course I was running, about the value of play. She was a shy student but eventually began to air her thoughts within the privacy of the student group. In the heat of discussion one day she blurted out, 'I'm terribly housepro...' and covered her mouth, bursting into giggles. 'I'm *not* terribly houseproud I meant to say!' 'Freudian slip!' laughed everyone. And I'm sure it was. Some time later Helen was happily settled at infant school and her mother became a regular helper at playgroup.

The similarities in the development of Helen and her mother are very striking. Both were held within a containing relationship and both were given opportunities for play within its safe boundaries. As a result both became less anxious and more spontaneous, able to play and to be more fully themselves. Helen no longer needed substitute mothering as her mother regained the capacity to 'contain' her. Although work with mother and child took place independently the benefits to the child were all the greater because of the support the mother received.

This kind of work is familiar in many under-fives settings. In Nomony NCH Family Centre, for example, project leader Anita Edwards helped a four-year-old child with a pregnant mother who found it difficult to relate to her. She worked with both, preparing the child for the baby by giving her her own doll to look after, and befriending the mother, to the extent of taking her a clean nightie every day when she was in hospital.

PLAY TO SUPPORT THE MOTHER–CHILD RELATIONSHIP

Work with Helen and her mother illustrates the use of play in one strand of family work in which the emphasis is on the mother–child relationship. (It is worth noting again that the term 'mother' is used to mean the person who is mothering the child and this may not be the biological mother. It does not even have to be a woman; it may be the father.) If mothers are to 'hold' or contain their children, in the sense that Winnicott described, they themselves must be contained. Many mothers feel consumed by their young children and begin to lose their sense of self, and with it their self-confidence and self-esteem. The realization of parents' own needs for nurturing stems in part from feminist recognition of the needy child within the mother, described by Eichenbaum and Orbach (1985). As Anne Jenkins (1989) recognizes at NEWPIN, if the hurt child within the mother can be healed, mothers can go on to heal their own children.

Through taking part in experiences which enable them to play, mothers can begin to accept and to value the 'child' within them. This helps them to accept both their children's dependence and their need for some autonomy. In play the player has mastery over the situation but feels contained within safe boundaries, which is the opposite of the experience of many mothers. Thus play can be a powerful way of restoring self-esteem and the ability to mother.

Play courses and workshops for parents

Informal courses and workshops in which parents learn about children's play by experiential methods – that is, by playing themselves – is one way in which play can be offered to parents. In 1987, 42,000 parents attended courses run by the Pre-school Playgroups Association (PPA), which describes its approach as follows:

> Creative play at an adult level might include using the raw materials of children's play, but more usually is just 'playing with ideas' in discussion, organization and planning and particularly in the planning of learning opportunities for adults, children or both together.
>
> PPA training aims to give first hand experience of creative play for adults by encouraging experiment, trial and error, exploration of materials and ideas and freedom of choice. The adult, by experiencing the joy of discovery at her own level, can be better attuned to the needs of the child.
>
> (Preschool Playgroups Association 1986: 38)

Helen's mother went on a PPA course. Family centres and other agencies may provide similar play experiences through group work and play workshops. I remember a group of young mothers, in a social services's run parents' group, trying out recipes for pink play dough for their children, who found themselves making male genitals and shaking with laughter as they expressed their feelings about the men in their lives. Spontaneous play had broken through their reserve and provided a healing experience.

Play for groups of parents and children together

Another approach involves play in groups with mothers and children together. Helping the mother to play with her child and to enjoy playing can meet the play needs of both mother and child simultaneously. It can be an effective way of strengthening the attachment between mother and child.

Margaret Shephard started 'music with mum' groups in Oxfordshire. Groups of mothers and babies, mothers and toddlers, or mothers and under-fives meet weekly for an hour, often in health centres, for a session of music, singing, and action songs and rhymes. Although deceptively simple, this can be a powerful method of promoting mother–child attachment. The programme is carefully devised to offer opportunities for body and eye contact between mother and child, particularly for the babies. A videotape illustrates this, showing lap songs for babies and knee-bouncing songs for toddlers. Margaret Shephard writes:

The traditional rhymes and songs can jog memories of the parents' own childhood and often lead to much more singing and playfulness within the family at home. Those parents without this childhood memory of songs and rhymes are enabled, nevertheless, to create the experience which will give their babies memories to look back on, as well as enjoying the togetherness now.

(Shephard, undated)

Dance therapy for mothers and children is based similarly on the belief that a relationship becomes apparent in the way that a parent and child move in relation to one another. It uses movement to create new patterns of relating. Bonnie Meekums' videotape (1988) of her work in a Leeds Family Service Unit shows how she uses 'mirroring' to put mothers and children back in touch as they copy one another's movements and crawl around the floor together. Reviewing this video-tape, psychotherapist David Pithers describes the value of dance therapy.

The dance enables stifled or inarticulate feelings to be expressed and to find an immediate response. It allows parents to let go of their inhibitions, their need to be like children and their fear of appearing childish, so that needs can be expressed and met in the same action. The dance is such a clear evocation of the rich ambiguities of the human condition, the struggle between physical limitation and the expression of the inexpressible, that it goes far beyond the primitive inadequacies of speech and patronising instruction.

(Pithers 1990a)

Some groups involve a carefully structured programme. A series of play workshops for mothers was repeated for the same group of mothers but with both mothers and children playing together, at Greenham House NCH Family Centre. A potential problem in this kind of situation, and even more so in free play sessions involving mothers and children, is that mothers may experience their children as sibling rivals. They may express strong fear of the 'power' of their children. These effects were recognized by the team at Cheswold House in Doncaster's Department of Family Psychiatry who were running groups for mothers and their young children aged four to six. The families were referred because the children had shown severe behaviour problems outside the home; both they and their mothers, mainly single parents, had often had traumatic and unhappy lives. The team found that a free playgroup had the effect of de-skilling mothers, who retreated to have coffee in the kitchen while the therapists played 'nicely' with the children (Wright 1991, Binney 1991).

Relationship play

In deciding how to tackle this problem the team, including clinical psychologist Val Binney, were influenced by Sue Jennings's drama therapy and by Veronica Sherborne's (1990) relationship play, in which the body is used as a play object. Their first experiments either led to explosions between mothers and children or, as in painting together, the activity was not intrusive enough. Attachment theory helped the team to understand that anxious, avoidant and ambivalent reactions from children could be protective and adaptive. The question was how to make the situation safe enough for both mothers and children to experiment with new behaviour. It was decided that mothers needed a place where they could work through their fears about play and touch. A discussion group was offered because it was recognized that these mothers disliked the intensive focus of individual work. A parallel playgroup was provided for the children. This lasted 45 minutes. A structured play session with mothers and children together then followed, for 15 to 20 minutes. The group was made up of five mother–child pairs. Experience showed that it was better if the worker with the children's playgroup did *not* take part in the joint group, avoiding the situation of mothers asking how their children had been and their jealousy on hearing that their children had been fine (Binney 1991).

The aim was to improve attachment by helping mothers and children to catch up on the early experiences that they had missed. Regression was seen to be helpful. For example, the relationship play session might start with toddler games and work back to baby games. The power of play was felt to lie in its physical contact, reciprocity and emotional content. The play format with its time limit and its opening and closing rituals helped mothers to feel contained. The content of sessions was graded carefully to provide 'desensitization' with 'graduated steps to intimacy' (Binney 1991). Without this it was found that the children became aggressive towards their mothers who tended to respond in kind with slaps.

The first four relationship play sessions consist of 'light' group work. Then there are three sessions of 'light' paired work. Four sessions of drama therapy exercises in pairs follow, with the final session being a party playing favourite games. First is a group warm-up exercise, such as Musical Knees, Pass the Parcel, followed by a game such as Ring-a-roses. The latter sometimes becomes the ritual game that families choose to play every week. This is followed by games, played mainly on the floor, to encourage positive physical touch. Then come back-to-back games, fingertip play, such as Incy Wincy Spider, and traditional games such as Grand-mother's Footsteps or What's the Time Mr Wolf?. (The first week the mothers are 'Grandmother', the second week the children take this role.) In later sessions paired touch games, based on the negotiation of power in an enjoyable way, include exercises such as mirroring, puppets or face painting. The child may be asked to draw round its mother on the floor, then mother draws round the child. Close body contact and eye-to-eye singing games, such as Rock-a-bye-baby and Row Row the Boat, are only introduced after the fourth week. They are played first as a group and then in pairs and may become 'homework'. Then everyone sits on the floor and takes turns in telling parts of a 'good' story and a 'bad' one; they must end on a good note. After this comes singing of Rock-a bye-baby, with the child sitting between mother's legs. Each session ends with a group 'yell' or an action story, such as Thunderstorm, designed to release the build-up of any tension and to prepare for leaving. (Many of these games are described in Masheder (1989).)

Three groups have been held and evaluation indicates that they have been effective in improving mother–child attachment, although children's internal fears and extreme phantasies seem to persist. The team emphasizes the necessity of the mothers' group, without which they feel that relationship play would fade out. The mothers discuss their 'terrible' children, their own childhood and the uselessness of men. They are helped to make connections between past and present – for example, how their being 'locked up' as children is reflected in their 'locking up' of their own children. The team emphasizes that the group leaders (nurses and an occupational therapist) need support if they are to avoid burn-out from the stress of mothers' disclosures and projections (Wright 1991, Binney 1991).

Work to support the parent–child relationship may also take place in less structured groups. Parents may be involved in play during an ordinary session in a family centre, playgroup or nursery. Parents' own child needs for play may be met as they join in play with their own or with other people's children. However, this can only happen successfully if the parent's self-esteem is supported. A parent needs to maintain autonomy and responsibility within the safe boundary of the play situation. As with children, if parents feel that their play is being directed or that they are being patronized or 'taught' then the spontaneity of creative play is lost, and with it the potential for growth. An example of informal group play to support the autonomy of both children and parents is the Dingley family play therapy group described in Chapter 6.

Play for a parent and child together

Play may be used on a one-to-one basis to help parents who have difficulty in forming an attachment and providing containment to their children, or who have other difficulties in managing their children's behaviour.

In Oxfordshire, Anne Sené, an occupational therapist, worked with parents and pre-school children referred to the psychiatric unit at Park Hospital for children. The focus of therapeutic work with these families was on establishing and strengthening attachment between parent and child. Not all parents can accept the intensity of one-to-one help. Anne Sené found that abusing parents who had shown some remorse were most willing to accept help in this way. Her aims were to:

assess the quality of parent–child interaction and attachment, increase positive interaction through enjoyable play experiences, help parents to develop more appropriate expectations for their child, and more appropriate ways of dealing with their child's behaviour, build on existing mothering skills and increase mothers' self-esteem.

The play session is used for a careful assessment of parent–child interaction. She observes parents' awareness of their child's needs, how they cope if the child cries, such as whether they comfort in a positive way, and how they manage their child's behaviour. She notes whether parents enjoy close proximity to their child, whether they respond to the child's overtures, if they take over play, and if they enjoy playing. She sees how much attention the child gets and whether parents are interested in their child's development. She observes the child's approach to play, how it copes with new situations and strange adults, and how it responds to brief separation and to the return of the parent. She finds Vera Fahlberg's (1988) checklists of attachment indicators for children at different ages extremely useful. (Bowlby's classification of the child's attachment as secure, anxious/avoidant, anxious/resistant or disorganized can be helpful.) Parents may also be involved during a developmental assessment of the child, which can be based on Sheridan's (1975) checklists (see also Chapter 1). This assessment can be used not only to assess any developmental delay but also to help parents to appreciate what it is realistic for them to expect from their child.

Anne Sené aims to create a relaxing and non-threatening environment in which parents can experience some positive interaction with their child. Before seeing a child she often asks parents about their own experiences of childhood and play. First sessions with parent and child are short, perhaps ten minutes, with the therapist taking complete control of the child and the parent adopting a passive role. She starts at a level at which the parent feels comfortable, avoiding putting on too much pressure. Parents may need to play themselves before learning how to play with their children. The therapist can model ways of playing, handling children's behaviour as it occurs – for example, in praising, rewarding, being consistent and setting limits. It is important for therapists to explain what they are doing and to help the parent in turn to do this too through discussing strategies for managing behaviour and giving practical advice on play. Videotapes of play sessions can be effective in helping the parents to gain insight into their behaviour and to build on existing mothering skills. Parents' attempts to play are encouraged and they are helped gradually to regain control. This may include choosing and presenting toys to the child, using new strategies to manage behaviour such as tantrums and being helped to persist. Success enhances parents' self-esteem, which is also built up through the nurturing they receive, such as the celebration of the mother's birthday as well as her child's. Some mothers may need to be involved in an activity, such as pottery, in their own right. Creative playful experience may help the mother to play more effectively with her own children once her own needs have been met.

Bridget Leverton, a play therapist who was involved in the early development of family work at Park Hospital and has since worked with parents and children in family centres, offers some further practical strategies. At first it is important to establish some trust with the mother rather than the child. Otherwise an abused child may be so receptive to an interested adult that this reinforces the mother's low self-esteem. A separate therapist for individual work with the child is preferable. The playing together time for mother and child should allow the child to be seen at its best and should help the mother to participate. Five minutes may be enough at first. Mothers tend to suggest structured activities such as puzzles since these show her in control of her 'good' child and so she feels safer. These may be permitted at first in order to make the mother feel comfortable. The worker goes on to encourage make-believe activities since these are directed by the child. If the child ignores mother, playing alone or with the worker, the worker might ask the child to show mother how the toy works. If the mother ignores the child's overtures the worker might say, for example, that teddy looks tired and is ready for bed, placing a toy cot near the mother. The mother finds it easier to play when actually presented with the activity. Placing a young baby in front of a mirror with mother behind often starts them laughing together. If the mother finds her child's behaviour difficult it helps to recognize her feelings, rather than say 'All children do this', before then demonstrating how to cope. As mother and child relax in play, the worker can teach play skills such as body language, for example, how to play on the floor rather than sitting on a chair above the child, how to smile and touch the child to show pleasure, or how to look firm when necessary, rather than anxious or uninterested. Mothers are often unaware of their own rejecting body language, such as crossing their arms over their chest as their child holds out its arms to be picked up. Once the mother is successfully playing with her child for the whole session, she may need help in planning how to maintain this relationship at home (Leverton, unpublished). Nover (1985) gives some examples of work based on a similar approach.

Anne Sené uses The Child's Game, in which parent and child spend 15–30 minutes in a regular special time together, based on the belief that children's behaviour improves when they have their parents' undivided attention. The game came from Peter Appleton, psychologist at Maelor Child Development Centre. It is similar to Pinney's re-capping technique used in Children's Hours, described in Chapter 2. (Pinney is more doubtful about parents using the technique with their own children as she feels a child might be confused by a parent adopting a totally different role from normal.)

Rules for The Child's Game

1 *Child's activity*: Allow your child to choose the activity. Do not introduce anything new into its play. If your child changes activities follow this but do not change the activity yourself.
2 *Follow*: Watch with interest what your child is doing. This could be described as 'shadowing' its movements or mood.
3 *Attend*: Describe enthusiastically what your child is doing. This attending to your child can be seen as giving a running commentary on your child's activity.
4 *Join in and copy*: Participate in your child's play, by handing it materials or by taking a turn. You may also join in by imitating your child's play. Be careful not to direct or structure play yourself. Remember that your child's play is to be the centre of your attention, so continue to describe its activity and not yours.
5 *No questions or commands*: Do not ask any questions or give any orders. (This is not as easy as it sounds.) These interrupt and structure your child's play.
6 *No teaching*: Do not use this time to teach your child or to test what it knows.

The worker tries the game alone with the child at first, then demonstrates it to the parent and asks the parent to try the game for ten minutes, at first with supervision and then later at home.

These approaches to family work use play to foster the attachment between mother and child and to 'contain' the mother and increase her self-esteem. Sara Deco (in Case and Dalley 1990), in her role as an art therapist in a family centre, uses family painting sessions to help mothers to control and manage their young children. Although Deco uses the language of Minuchin's structural family therapy, referring to the need to strengthen the boundaries between generations, her work could equally be explained in terms of containment, 'holding' the mother while helping her to manage her children.

Family Service Units, a voluntary organization which works intensively with entire families to prevent breakdown and promote healthier functioning, are known for innovative methods. Atkinson and Mead (in Martel 1981) describe an example of therapeutic play involving two workers. One worker was for an angry two-year-old, known in his day centre as 'Jaws' because he bit other children. The other was for his pregnant socially isolated mother whose lack of attachment to her son was causing concern. Mother and child came to a fortnightly play session, being visited at home on alternate weeks. The worker for the child gave him total attention, allowing him acceptable ways of expressing his angry feelings, such as kicking a ball and climbing. She used physical holding for aggression directed at mother or workers, and rough-and-tumble play and laughter to create a shared experience. The other worker supported the mother as she watched, at first quite detached, gradually drawing her into playing too, eventually to join in the rough-and-tumble play. This positive physical contact provided the basis for improved attachment between mother and child.

Occupational therapist Anna Sanders uses Pinney's Children's Hours approach, giving 'hours' to parents (or foster parents, or child care workers) on their own as well as with children. The adults have the opportunity to touch on their own inner child. The method is powerful in enhancing parent–child relationships because it is 'experienced' not 'told'. Working in a London day nursery she used this approach to develop an attachment between two-year-old Lee, an Afro-Caribbean boy who was being fostered, and his father and grandmother who were planning to adopt him, having had minimal contact till then. Lee had individual sessions two or three times a week. The grandmother visited the nursery each week to have a joint session with Lee, initially observing and then being drawn into play. Sand, water, dolls, play people (black and white), blocks, cars, tracks, coloured pens and paper, finger paint and Lego (popular with adults) were provided. Grandmother was then given her own 'hours', at one time reversing roles to give her worker some 'special time'. Anna Sanders comments:

As her sessions progressed the grandmother became a partner working towards a common goal while at the same time enjoying herself and apparently getting back to her own very early play experiences, helping her 'be' with Lee in a relaxed way without a forced sense of taking on the role of entertainer or perpetual questioner as she had at first. Lee's father came for a session which followed the same process of observer, individual session and joint time with a chance for him to practise. This enabled Lee to experience some continuity of this way of playing with both primary carers. Therapeutic play continued for three months, alongside good social work support for the family and efficient liaison and support all round. A loving grandmother had become a more sensitive primary carer for a little child. The father had been able to explore the importance of the emotional traumas of his son and his future needs. Lee had been helped to bridge a major life change with the help of constant 'special times' in which his pleasure and his pain were acknowledged. The nursery staff had learned to bear the pain of listening as well as carrying on the process outside my sessions.'

Susan Monson, occupational therapist at West Stowell Clinic, a child psychiatry unit at Marlborough Children's Hospital, feels that she has learned a great deal from others working in this field. A study-day talk by Bridget Leverton increased her awareness of the importance of the therapist taking a low-key role when the aim of treatment is to build up the mother–child relationship rather than the therapist–child relationship. Contact with Margaret Shephard, particularly watching her videotape, inspired her to use simple on-the-lap rhymes and singing games for mothers and children with problems. Her varied case-load includes work with mothers and children whose relationship difficulties have been caused by unhappy experiences in the child's early years or in the mother's own childhood. She works as part of a multi-disciplinary team, which she finds valuable. She writes:

> In a recent case a family had suffered the trauma of nursing the father who was at home through a terminal illness. The middle child was deeply affected at the time but too young to understand or talk about it very well. She responded to the situation long term by acting out her feelings in difficult behaviour. This was mainly directed at the mother, while everyone else saw a tense and far too well-behaved child. Careful discussion with the family and the team led to individual play therapy for the child, meetings for the family, and work for the mother and child together which I took on. My aim was to help improve their relationship so that some of the positives could be shared with mother and more of the negatives shown elsewhere. The mother had some time on her own with the therapists to help her understand what was happening.
>
> I often use parents' memories of their own childhood as a way of tuning in to their child's feelings and as something from their own lives to build on. An activity that has been enjoyed in childhood is usually a good one to choose. I also look for activities that involve physical closeness and those that provide an opportunity for fun; families with overwhelming problems have little experience of fun. In this case, activities included cooking, with mother and child working together making jam tarts and sharing the satisfaction of 'we made them together', paper plate puppets which led to much laughter, drawing round each others' hands, and making shakers when each had to listen carefully to the other's sounds – helping them to listen to one another. Despite the complexity of the issues this simple approach, in conjunction with the other help, brought

real progress. The family reported more balanced behaviour at home. They had been quick to follow suggestions on giving praise and using a firm cuddle to restrain any behaviour that got out of hand. They also began to understand how things like making a dreadful mess in the bedroom might link with the father's death. The most encouraging change was the open affection between mother and child that replaced avoidance and hostility. In discussions the mother had some opportunity to express her own feelings and then reassurance was given that the reason for the difficult behaviour was not poor mothering but the closeness of the relationship and the things that had happened.

The work then moved to the home and all the family enjoyed trying simple games and activities. They were able to suggest things themselves, like mime games, which enabled them to have fun together. The home-made play dough was popular with everyone! Special time with mum continued to be important but was balanced by family activities which helped with sharing. Individual play therapy continued during this period. Progress at home meant that the school had to start coping with some quite difficult behaviour. Partly because of regular liaison but also because the staff were so understanding the difficult behaviour was seen as improvement. This potentially awkward situation shows the importance of making time to talk with everyone involved.

Work with a parent and child in the home

The work described so far has been based in nursery and other centres, and in child psychiatric units. Work with a parent and child in the home has the potential for having a direct connection to daily life. Some family centres and Family Service Units also work this way, especially where families are not ready to attend a centre. Voluntary organizations, such as Scope in Hampshire, and Home Start whose work will be described later, see home visiting as the core of their support for families under stress. In some areas, educational home-visiting services work with families in their homes, sometimes using play methods. The following example shows the use of play to 'contain' the mother and to improve attachment, in my work in Birmingham's child guidance service.

Rachel, aged four, was referred by her mother because she would not speak. As I visited them at home and started playing with Rachel it became clear that her refusal to speak was a response to her mother's demand that she should talk to people, such as her rather strict grandparents, and that in a non-directive play situation she would quickly blossom. I had a tiny mouse in my pocket who would come out to see what was going on but was easily frightened and would run back to my pocket to hide if anyone came close or spoke to it. This matched what Rachel, on the other side of the room, was doing. I talked aloud about how the mouse was feeling but made no move to approach or question Rachel. She smiled with delight each time the mouse peeped out and when it ran away again. Soon she was quietly sitting by me, exploring the toys I was getting out. She was eager to draw with the felt-tip pens, although worried about making a mess. Later she was absorbed in play with a miniature village and people, arranging them on a tin tray covered with salt, for snow (it was winter). I sat on the floor with her and described what she was doing as she played. There was so much non-verbal communication between us that when she eventually spoke it seemed unsurprising and fitted into our pattern of communication quite naturally.

Rachel's mother was thin and drab, alternately sharp-tongued or complaining helplessly, Rachel could do nothing right. I realized that she felt that she had no control over Rachel or anything else in her life, and nothing seemed to give her any pleasure. As well as talking with her about herself and her own childhood I started to draw her into my play with Rachel, giving her a turn in card and board games such as Tummy Ache, and letting her win as often as Rachel. I would get Rachel's or my puppet to talk to her or tickle her, or need to take refuge on her lap. I read stories to which both listened. Gradually she thawed. She began to smile more often and sometimes the tone of her voice softened. I think the turning point came when I was showing them how to play clock patience. Her face lit up and she said that she remembered playing that when she was little. As we drew on her good play memories of childhood – there were not many but there were enough – the hurt child within her healed a little and became less demanding. Her creative child had more space. She became more able to assume parental responsibility. She agreed to read to Rachel for five minutes a day and I think both enjoyed this time. By the end of eight weekly play sessions Rachel and her mother were much happier together, showing improved attachment.

The approaches described so far have focused on the need to 'hold' the mother so that she can 'hold' her child. Yet some are also concerned with parents' lack of knowledge of child development and their lack of skills in responding to and managing their children. Some parents need help to develop appropriate expectations of their children, rather than under-or over-estimating their abilities and understanding. They may also need help to recognize what it is that their children are communicating, in language or behaviour, and to respond appropriately. Through play, workers can help parents to acquire new skills and an understanding of their children's behaviour while maintaining parents' self-esteem, rather than through the use of didactic approaches which can disempower and undermine. For example, a single father of a two-year-old had used so much pressure in toilet training that his son now refused the potty totally. A family centre used play to help both to resolve the conflict. The use of play is illustrated in the following two accounts by home visitors to young families under stress in Bristol Home Start.

As a volunteer working with parents of under-fives experiencing difficulties or stress, I had been visiting the family for sometime. The mother had a very strong-willed little girl of about 18 months. It soon became clear that there was a feeding problem. Every time I visited she had a bottle of milk in her mouth and would have it replaced as soon as she had finished it. The mother could not establish any meal-time routine since the child was not interested in solid food as she was continuously being satisfied by the bottle. Once the mother had recognized the problem and was willing to discuss it we started to tackle the situation. At first any advice I gave she rejected. I suggested replacing bottles of milk with juice but after a couple of days she gave up, unable to cope with the screaming protests. Realizing that I was unable to get through to the mother I started talking to her little girl about food as it was approaching lunch-time. There were Ladybird books scattered over the floor. I picked one up and we looked at the food pictures together. She pointed to the food she recognized and started taking me to the kitchen to find the food. We found some of the items and played feeding Daisy, her doll. By lunch-time she was full of enthusiasm and ate a hearty lunch. The mother and I agreed a contract for a week. No bottles of milk should be given between meals and only juice offered. They would share books and pictures about food. On my next visit I was told that the situation had improved and that her eating habits had become more regular. As far as I know the improvement is continuing.

In the second example the visitor uses play with dough to manage a two-year-old's behaviour, giving an implicit rather than explicit message to the mother about the value of play.

I never thought the introduction of a mixture of flour, water and salt, with a dash of oil and cream of tartar, would bring such contentment to a small boy. I had been visiting Michael and his mother and couldn't find anything to keep his attention for more than a couple of minutes. As he shouted and screamed for at least half the time I was there it was imperative for me to find something towards which he could direct some of his aggression. I showed his mum the dough which I had coloured red and blue and asked her permission to use it. She readily agreed and found some kitchen implements to add to a small rolling pin and cutters which I had brought. The morning seemed to fly by as Michael poked and prodded at the dough, and eventually he smiled as he was able to use the various cutters. The next week he took my bag from me and looked for the dough. He seemed to be a different child when we sat down at his table to play with it, and to my surprise he was quite gentle when using it. As well as a vehicle for play it gave me an opportunity to talk to him as he likes to spend about an hour each week with it. This has been the pattern for seven months, although Michael doesn't look for the dough straight away now. I introduce it when a tantrum seems imminent and it seems to have a calming effect when we sit down to play.

About two months later the volunteer visited to find Michael unwell. She was delighted to find that, for the first time, his mother had made him some play dough herself. In both examples the Home Start visitors are careful to leave control with the mother and to seek her agreement, while they demonstrate by example how play can be used to manage difficult behaviour and make both mother and child happier together. Understanding is 'caught not taught'.

PLAY IN WORK WITH THE WHOLE FAMILY

Play may be used in family work and family therapy to help in achieving a number of aims. It may be used in diagnosing the family's problem. It may be used to increase the ability of members of a family to communicate with one another, and to change their perceptions of one another and themselves. It may enable a family to change its perception of what it can do as a family – for example, that time together can be fun. It may be used to clarify and change alignments and boundaries, such as the boundary between generations, in a family. Where one person, usually the child, is scapegoated or used to carry the family's problem, therapy may be concerned with helping each family member to own their feelings and to stop projecting them on to the child. Where the child's emotional problems are judged to exist in their own right, play may be used in involving the family in the child's therapy. The following section will examine some examples.

Play in assessing the family's problem

The early practice of family therapy has been criticized for treating children as miniature adults. There has been a growing awareness of the value of play within the family therapy session. Dare and Lindsey (1979), followed by O'Brien and Loudon (1985), discuss the need for play materials. Penny Jaques, a psychiatric social worker, sees play as an invaluable means of communication for children during family therapy. She provides drawing and painting materials, a dolls' house with family, sets of domestic and wild animals, and Plasticine. She describes a six-year-old boy who was

> anxious and clinging and hated to leave his mother's side to go to school. While his parents talked he made a series of Plasticine babies, and then took great delight in cutting off their heads, a clear communication about his envy for the one-year-old who could stay with mum all day, and quite a revelation in a boy who had shown no overt signs of jealousy and was described as 'devoted to the baby'.

> (Jaques 1987: 9)

Play with wild animals may suggest a threat from outside to a child's sense of security, exemplified by the five-year-old who put domestic animals inside the fence with the wild ones outside. It may also express the child's own wild feelings.

Another five-year-old took six crocodiles and hippopotami and put them in the dolls' house where the daddy doll was positioned watching television. He put the wild animals in a circle surrounding the daddy doll and then stood back gleefully ... When his mother saw the set-up in the dolls' house, she commented ruefully that six crocs and three hippos wouldn't stop her husband working too hard.

(Jaques 1987: 10)

Jaques saw this as a crucial communication which transferred the definition of the problem away from the child to the father's unavailability, about which the boy was expressing his own and his mother's anger.

The child's communication in all these examples appears to be quite unconscious. Play is part of the process of diagnosis, clarifying the problem not only for the therapist but also for the members of the family, and providing the foundation for therapy.

Children may communicate through drawing and painting. The *content* may help the family as well as the worker to understand a child's inner feelings about important people and events. Jaques gives several examples. A child who was aggressive and demanding after her father's death drew a happy girl skipping among flowers, then blacked out the sun and covered the picture with grey raindrops, her unshed tears. The communication may illuminate family dynamics. A four-year-old showed how her separation anxiety was linked to her mother's unrecognized agoraphobia when she drew her house on wheels. A silent seven-year-old drew a ferocious shark, illuminating his family's need to be helped to permit the expression of strong feelings. The *process* or way a child paints or draws can also convey information, inhibition suggesting anxiety or low self-esteem, messiness suggesting lack of self-control or inner feelings of being 'a mess'. Jaques attends to the child's unconscious communication in play using a psychodynamic model to interpret it. Angry monsters, for example, are viewed not only in terms of the child's perception of threat from others but also as the projection of the child's own angry feelings.

O'Brien and Loudon (1985), using a more focused approach to drawing, often ask children to draw their family doing something, or at meal-times or bed-times. They might ask them to draw something that happened recently, a sad or happy time, school, or presents they would give each family member. They find drawing often illuminates the working of the family system, not only for therapists but also for parents.

Roz Huddleston, occupational therapist in a Lancaster psychiatric hospital, may ask children to draw their family as a way of assessing their view of a problem and comparing it with other workers' understanding of it. She finds focused drawing particularly useful if a child's free play seems geared to concrete activities such as a Lego construction, rather than communication. She writes:

Nine-year-old Simon was admitted to the children's residential unit because of enuresis, both night and day, sibling rivalry and temper outbursts. He was under-achieving at school and had poor peer relationships. Invited to paint his family he painted the title in a 'nice' colour, his word, perhaps representing his nice middle-class family. He painted dad first, with no arms, at a distance from the rest of the family (Figure 4.1). It suggested Simon's view of dad as emotionally distant, showing little affection (no arms) and spending little time with him. He painted mum next, also with no arms. His mother was reported to have felt unable to love Simon because of all the pain he caused the family. Then he painted his younger sister. She was the dominant child of the family and everything her parents could wish for, pretty, pleasant and intelligent. There was rivalry between her and Simon. He drew his youngest sister, still a toddler, again with no arms but smiling. He felt able to relate to this sister best. He drew himself last, standing on one leg between his sisters, again with no arms, representing his feeling about his value in the family. I asked Simon to tell me how the picture felt and he said he was squashed because there was no room for him. It suggested to me that he felt out-shadowed and pushed out by his sisters. I asked Simon to speak as his parents and gave him a choice of six different phrases. He chose 'Let Simon come forward'. He added that he was not sure that his sisters would allow this to happen. Following this, family work was done by my colleagues while I worked with him individually (working on his sham-confident false-self). I also had several sessions with him and his mother together.

Another child, John, was referred to the residential unit for running away from home and school; he had outbursts of temper which his father and step-mother could not control. I asked him to paint his family. He painted his dad first, in great detail and taking a long time. He sat back and surveyed it with satisfaction. His dad was very important to him, the only consistent figure in his life. The marriage was unstable and his step-mother had left the home for a while. John painted the mother figure without features, feet or hands, just fists, suggesting his perception of her as being unfeeling. He drew his step-brother and his natural sister, but 'forgot' to draw himself or his rival step-brother, who was the same age and then in foster care. Their absence could represent their physical absence from the family or John's feeling of not being part of it.

Some workers use play tasks in assessing a family's problem. Pauline Blunden, occupational therapist at the Drummond Clinic in Bury St Edmunds, might ask a family to build a tower with 12 large wooden blocks. This is a simple task in which even the youngest child can take part and it gives an idea of some of the family dynamics. She observes who directs the building, who builds the tower, and who is passive or takes no part. She notes if they enjoy the task or if they get easily discouraged if the tower falls. With a similar aim, she might ask a family to sort a pack of playing cards into groups, giving a time limit. Other tasks might involve a playful discussion of family likes and dislikes or planning a family day out (Blunden 1988).

Play as therapy

Family therapy does not often use play as therapy, although role play and sculpturing, even the drawing of a genogram, might be described as play techniques. These techniques help adults as well as children to perceive and work on their

Figure 4.1 My family, by Simon

relationships. They provide concrete symbols of these relationships (concrete operations in the Piagetian sense) which facilitate thought and foster playfulness, reducing feelings of threat and failure.

Alison O'Brien and Penny Loudon (1985) use a variety of concrete visual techniques in family therapy. Mobiles show how movement of one person affects everyone else. Balloons demonstrate the effects of cumulative stress. Balancing scales to which weights are added for each complaint about a 'bad' child, as opposed to the 'good' one, help some parents to realize suddenly the possible devastating effects of their complaints. A family, modelled from Fimo, is used to sculpture the family, to discuss family structure and to show how it changes with the family life-cycle. Used with wooden rods to represent the structure or boundaries around a child (or their absence or inconsistency), a family unable to agree on setting firm limits for their 'uncontrollable' four-year-old were helped to see how the lack of structure made their child insecure and to come to agree on a consistent routine. Other visual aids include a Fimo cake cut into segments, gears, wheels, magnets, rubber bands, plant symbolism, knots, a Newton's cradle and nesting dolls.

Bonnie Eaker (1986), in a wide-ranging article, explores many aspects of the use of play in family therapy, including such techniques as puppets, structured dramatic play and Gardner's (1981) mutual story-telling. She sees play as being valuable because it creates 'enough emotional distance between family members for the truth to be spoken' (p. 243) and 'serves as a cushion in sustaining resistant families in treatment' (p. 244). It can help parents who tend to intellectualize their difficulties as well as parents who have difficulties putting things into words. It can put parents in touch with the child within them and make them more able to reach their own children. Yet she warns against using family play therapy where abuse is suspected, if unlocking of family secrets might put a child at greater risk.

Play-based family therapy in Family Service Units is described in Martel (1981). With one family the aim was to relax the Victorian standards in the home, where there were no toys. Two workers introduced play with hand puppets, drawings, blocks and miniatures. Although the children, whose speech and other development had been delayed, blossomed, the mother felt threatened by their relationship to the workers (as Leverton warns) and stopped coming. Structured play and games were used with several large families with relationship problems where it was felt that normal family therapy would be too verbal and demanding. Games included drawing their ideal home, or their dream island: using cards, created by brainstorming 'feelings', in turn-taking games, 'I feel ... when ...', 'When I feel ... I ... and I would like people to ...'; telling stories with hand puppets: brainstorming memories, things that had frightened, angered or saddened them, or future wishes; making face masks and enacting a play; making a cut-out family tree; sculpturing the family. When one family's commitment waned the workers drew a picture of how they saw each family member. These hit the nail on the head and the family re-engaged in sessions. The workers felt that the families gained more from experiential learning, the freeing effect of play within safe limits, than from any interpretation or feedback they were given. Parents need to feel that they are partners in the process of change. Then they change in the ways in which they perceive and respond to their children, putting fewer projections and pressures on them and freeing them to develop normally (Cleveland *et al.*, in Martel 1981).

A carefully designed play programme was used to help the parents and seven children of the very deprived Watson family to listen to one another, to appreciate each other's contributions and to begin to cooperate, raising their self-esteem, instead of seeing themselves as 'useless' (Foster and Harwood, in Martel 1981). The first session used 'ice-breakers', with everyone decorating a name card, playing statues and saying one good thing that had happened that day. One room was quickly turned into a 'huff' room, with a notice on the door, as people stormed off so often. Later, family members were given roles in dramatic play, a plane crash. The family had to decide where and when the crash happened, who was injured, and how they were rescued or escaped, and enact this using props. Other games were a cooperative treasure hunt, a home-made jigsaw puzzle where each member had a piece but could not let go until all were in place, and musical 'chairs' on pieces of paper, in which no one was 'out' but the paper got less. To show that girls were as good as boys, each sex made a board game in separate rooms. To give the family some positive feelings the three workers wrote complimentary descriptions on cards for the others to guess who it was, the owner taking the card home. They made a Watson family advertisement, each member saying something positive about the others, and then each member making a separate advertisement using these. Mimes, charades and acting in pairs, photographs and videotapes gave everyone positive attention. As the group came to an end the workers made up a song about the family, asking everyone how they wanted to be said goodbye to – whispered, shouted or sung!

Susan Monson, an occupational therapist whose work with a bereaved mother and child has already been described, took her inspiration from work with the Watson family in planning, with co-worker staff nurse Martin Elliott, a final family session. The family consisted of a mother lacking in confidence, an unsupportive father, a handicapped child and a disturbed 'normal' child. Conventional family therapy elsewhere had not worked well. The aim was for a final session that would encourage family identity and self-esteem and help its members to enjoy doing things together. The workers explained to the family that they had planned some activities mainly for the children but they hoped they would all enjoy them. They introduced themselves with a jigsaw game they had made. Then everyone took turns in being the leader in Simon Says. Some of the leaders' instructions involved touching, such as 'hold hands' or 'hug each other'. Musical Islands followed where everyone ended up on one island.

Next was a fantasy journey. Together they did a large family collage on a box to make a rocket, the family beginning to work as a team but finding it hard and needing help and encouragement. Then the workers told a story about the rocket journeying to another planet, after which the family were given roles in dramatic play, with a few props and dressing-up clothes to help. Mother, in a hat, was thrilled to be captain but a little unsure of her role. Father was steward and only stopped joking and teasing people to serve tea. The handicapped child was the air hostess and sat on her father's lap shouting people's names. The other child was navigator: he was so carried away with the game that for a moment he thought it was real. The workers joined in. They created an asteroid storm by bombarding the rocket with rolled up socks, suggesting that the family needed to cling together in the turbulence, which they found hard to do. When the family landed safely, one worker took the role of a reporter and asked how the family had got on; the other worker took the role of a photographer and snapped pictures of the family. The captain said that all the members of her crew had done very well.

The session ended with a song about the family, with a verse about each of them. The mother kept the words and later sent a card saying how thrilled she was. The workers felt that the game had boosted her confidence considerably. The game was enjoyed by all, even the father. As a 'silly game' the workers knew it was a risk but felt that it achieved its aim in helping the family image. They had managed to do things together and to enjoy it, even though it was neither easy nor natural for them.

A song, accompanied by guitar, was similarly helpful to another family. The workers used a skeleton verse of the Beetles' song Get Back to Where You Belong, to which the family added. It gave a positive re-frame to a child returning home from care.

Minuchin's (1981) structural family therapy, concerned with spatial closeness and boundaries in families and re-dressing imbalances, is particularly appropriate for the application of play techniques. Where Minuchin would re-arrange the chairs of family members in a therapy session, Susan Monson and Martin Elliott might use play dough to bring all family members physically close to one another. For example, if a child takes itself away from the family then the therapist might ask the mother to bring the child back for play, giving her action a purpose. Parents are always told that they and not the therapists are in charge of their children during a session. The therapists feel that it is important for children to be active during family therapy because it is very difficult for them to sit for a whole session of talking with nothing to do, and also because it involves them in an age-appropriate way. They may use puppets or drawings, whatever children are comfortable with. When tracking the family story they may invite children to help draw a genogram, set out figures or model them in Plasticine. This may help in uncovering needs for future work – for example, a child's need to be told more about his absent father. They find some sort of warm-up game is useful and sometimes a play task is helpful in assessment. Three boys in a family were asked to build a bridge together with a large box of wooden bricks and pieces of wood. It soon became clear who was leader, who had ideas, who joined in most and who was least cooperative.

Involving parents in their child's therapy

The final example of play in family work is about involving family members in the

therapy of children who are deemed to have problems in their own right. Barry
Bowen, principal social worker in Kettering's child and family guidance service,
often starts therapy after a full assessment (including a genogram) by using
behavioural techniques such as 'effective praising' (Eimers and Aitchison 1978).
Part of this includes teaching parents how to praise and cuddle their children, and
if marital problems are suspected he may use role play in which parents start by
practising on one another. This indirect marital therapy 'moves things along a bit.'
A family that comes in 'with their faces on the floor' ends up laughing. 'It helps
the child to see mum and dad laughing'. Bowen draws on White and Epston's
(1989) notion of 'externalizing the problem'. He finds that the use of metaphor and
analogy can be very powerful, especially when the family's own metaphors are
used (Bowen and Nimmo 1986). People change more easily because it feels less
dangerous. This is illustrated in his work with Kevin, an eight-year-old living at
home with his quarrelling parents and described as 'impossible' at school.

The part-time hulk

When a child is written off by everybody including itself, the 'monster'
technique is wonderful. It is a global concept which does not focus on individual
bits of behaviour. I drew a little stick picture of a happy child and then, with the
parents contributing, I found out what Kevin was good at – swimming, helping
out, football. This, I said, is the real Kevin. From this different perception I went
on to find out when he got sad or upset. I explained that the 'Incredible Hulk'
on television grows big and turns into a monster when he gets angry. He looks
very big and powerful and frightens everyone. No one likes him and he is
unhappy. I helped Kevin to draw him using a whole page (Figure 4.2). I asked
him and his parents what the monster does and wrote down 'shouting, spitting,
swearing, messing about at school, breaking windows, shop-lifting'. Asked to
name the monster, Kevin called it the 'Part-time Hulk', because he is not there
all the time. I then compared him with the little stick drawing and asked how
old the monster was; Kevin said three. Then I said, 'The monster is only three
but he frightens everyone, especially Kevin. You've got to beat the monster.
Every time you beat him he shrinks a bit and you grow a bit. How long do you
think it will take to get the monster down a bit? Two weeks?' I told him that
before he came back in two weeks he was to draw a picture of the monster and
himself the right sizes for then, checking with mum and dad and his teacher. He
did this but the monster was still bigger than the stick figure, although it had
shrunk a little. I sent Kevin a letter of congratulations but said that he still needed
to work on reducing the monster. 'The trick is that if the monster gets smaller
than you he will never beat you again. If you can get him down to pet-size you
will get a certificate to say that you can teach people how to do hulk reduction.'
When he succeeded I sent him another letter and a posh certificate for his wall,
suggesting it needed a proper frame. Some time later there was a major upset in
the family and Kevin regressed. We looked at his 'Part-time Hulk' again and

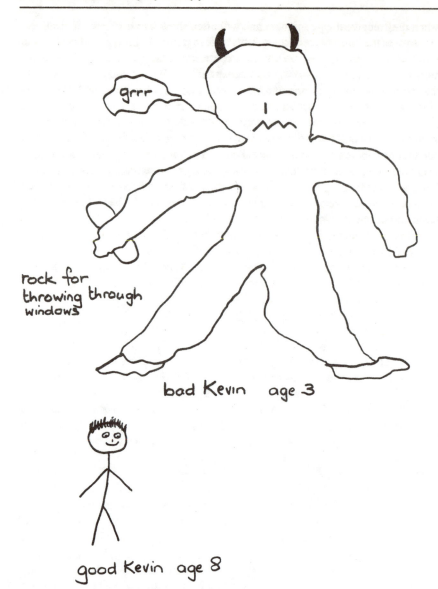

Figure 4.2   The part-time hulk, by Kevin

agreed that he got bigger when people were not looking at him, so we needed to look at him again together.

The use of letters to the child after each session of 'hulk therapy' is crucial to Bowen's approach, as it is in Wood's (1988). He finds that children are very excited when they receive their own letter and will often show it to teachers and relatives. He stresses the importance of the parents' role in joining in the game of beating the monster. Parents must be present and contribute positive aspects of the monster/child. Each time they come they are asked how big the monster is. He finds that parents like the game and find their own 'child' in the course of it. The method works in changing parents' and teachers' perceptions of the child and the child's perceptions of itself. The fantasy is tuned in to the child's wave-length, based on what interests a child of this age. Bowen uses this technique for children who have conduct problems which may conceal emotional problems, and also for children who are scapegoated or in danger of being scapegoated. However, it is unlikely to be effective in families where the scapegoating has a function for the family so that parents, however unconsciously, may not want their child 'cured'. It requires a basic commitment from the family to the child.

In this example the focus was on therapy for the child but involving the parents. In many instances, therapy through play is offered to a child without the direct involvement of parents, although work with parents may be going on in parallel to work with the child. Play therapy in direct work with unhappy children living with their families is the subject of the next chapter.

Chapter 5

Play therapy for children living in unhappy families

In this chapter we look at ways in which play can help children whose emotional difficulties arise out of an unhappy family situation. These children are still living with their families, although for some the family structure may have changed. Separation and divorce, remarriage and cohabitation, childbirth and step-parenting can mean that adults or children have left or been added to some families. The children may be the victims of cycles of damage and deprivation going back over the generations. Some of these children have lacked 'good enough' parenting for part or all of their lives. Some have experienced neglect, attachment failure, emotional or physical abuse. Some have observed severe conflicts, verbal and sometimes physical violence, between adults in the family.

Children whose emotional difficulties stem from their experience in the first two years of life are likely to have more deep-seated problems than those who have suffered later. Many of these children will have experienced adults who are indifferent, resentful, jealous, angry and violent, intermittently throughout their lives. They often identify with these adults and in turn display these attitudes in their relationships with others, covering up their pain by projecting their feelings. Therefore the best clue to how these children are really feeling often lies in how they make the worker feel, whether it is useless, no good, wiped out or annihilated, helpless or 'bad'. Play may contain this indirect communication even when it offers little that can be interpreted as a direct communication. These ideas are further explored in Boston and Szur (1983), and Copley and Forryan (1987). Children with long experience of deprivation may need therapy which involves some form of regression. For example, eight-year-old Mick, described by teachers as a bruiser and street-wise, curled up with a cushion in the sand tray for the start of each session throughout his first eight weeks in a school unit for maladjusted children. Children whose experience of family disruption has been later and more limited often have a greater capacity for recovery through understanding what has happened and making sense of it through symbolic play.

This chapter looks at non-directive play therapy in a Family Service Unit and in the Children's Hours Trust. It explores the painful process of containment and regression in an occupational therapist's work in a child psychiatric unit, and in a social worker's therapy in a similar unit. It explores a variety of focused play techniques used by social workers in two Family Centres run by the National Children's Homes. Finally it examines some examples of group work with children.

NON-DIRECTIVE PLAY FOR ABUSED CHILDREN IN A FAMILY SERVICE UNIT

In a Family Service Unit (FSU), play therapy was seen as a much larger package of intervention with the whole family. It was used where it was felt that a special piece of work directly with a child might help to change the situation in the family; opportunity for change might be faster in the child who is still developing. Barbara Kezur, (in Martel 1981) describes her use of Axline's non-directive play therapy. She considers that abused children have rarely had an opportunity to learn to live with and deal with their feelings, or to challenge the negative view of themselves that they have come to accept. Her playroom provides a safe space, with no interruptions, where the child can feel free to play, to make a mess, to lie on the floor, to throw things, or to cuddle on a pillow or in an armchair. Play materials to encourage the expression of feelings include sand and water, painting and drawing materials, Plasticine, a dolls' house, soldiers, plastic weapons, a puncho, cars, blocks, puzzles and games, telephones, money, books, doctor kits, as well as a nearby loo. She aims to offer children an empathetic relationship of unqualified acceptance and belief in their potential. She provides both freedom and boundaries. The child chooses what to do, within the 45-minute session, but is told that people may not be hurt nor excessive damage done. Children are told that she may discuss the session with their social worker but not with their family. Kezur emphasizes that 'Each child's willingness to reveal feelings and his inner self to the therapist must emerge when the child is ready, not at the insistence of the therapist' (Martel 1981: 9). Like Axline, she uses the technique of reflective listening as children's feelings are expressed in words or play.

Kezur finds that many children come to therapy feeling that they are not very likeable and that their feelings are wrong and must be hidden. Play therapy helps children to express and own their feelings at a conscious level. This gives relief and the opportunity either to integrate conflicts and feelings within the self or to work through and resolve them. Children may find different ways of expressing their feelings and may come to feel more able to make decisions where they have some choice, as well as accepting what is beyond their control. For example, Deborah, an eight-year-old, the eldest child in a depriving and non-nurturing family, was depressed and not attending school. Play therapy over five months brought out her angry and fearful feelings, and a transference wish that the therapist was her mother. Her attitude to school improved. She became assertive, lively and angry. Davey, a six-year-old, was the oldest of three boys living with their mother, with their abusing father coming and going. For a long time distrustful and needing clear limits, after a year's play therapy he had gained in self-esteem and self-control.

Joan Neusner, also a FSU worker, similarly used Axline's model of play therapy in a year's work with seven-year-old Peter (in Martel 1981). She describes him as the baby of a disturbed family of five children, living in a fantasy world of spirits and wild animals and making no progress at school. She saw him weekly in the playroom. Peter chose activities for each session, and she usually 'rather passively reflected back' his own play and verbal material. If she made interpretations he resisted by refusing to hear. She decided to limit the amount of play material as Peter was distressed by things, such as beads and paint, which he could not manage. There was an initial honeymoon phase of good behaviour. This was followed by a period of resentment and testing out, of 'hostile ambivalence'. He played obsessively with model animals in bloodthirsty enactments, progressing later to play with people and family figures. Often he was immobilized by anger. At a later stage he wanted to regress and was given water play and brown dough. His play became very destructive; he messed up the room and urinated on the floor, and this was accepted. He reverted to baby talk. He went on to show an interest in the therapist's family and began to make progress. Neusner respected Peter's fantasy life and his need to regress in the playroom where he could work on internal problems. Outside the playroom, when travelling to and from the centre or on visits to the park, she expected normal sociable behaviour. In public situations his fantasy life was not permitted. She feels that this was important in helping him to distinguish between his inner and his outer worlds, important for a child who tended to get lost in his fantasies.

The demands on the worker of this style and length of play therapy are very great. The worker's trust in the child's ability to sort out his inner problems himself, given a containing relationship, is fundamental. As Peter was not aware of working through his feelings, an active interpretive style would probably not have been appropriate. Although Kezur claimed to be working only with children's conscious feelings, both FSU workers appear to have let the working through of *unconscious* feelings form an important part of the therapy. The process of therapy in Neusner's account moves from a honeymoon phase, through hostile ambivalence, in which anger, sometimes immobilizing, was expressed at first generally and later more specifically, to a stage of regressive play, before a final stage of progress in coping with the real world. It has strong echoes in Lyn Bennett's work, which will be discussed shortly. First, we turn to an account of work in the Children's Hours Trust in which the approach to play, like that in the FSU, is non-directive, and uses reflective listening.

CHILDREN'S HOURS – GIVING TOTAL ATTENTION

Jenny Senior, speech therapist and taker of Children's Hours using Rachel Pinney's creative listening approach (see Chapter 2), believes that these special playtimes are a source of happiness to many children. 'Children can gradually discover in this setting that their play is respected, their thoughts and feelings valued and that they are taken seriously. Tensions are released and self-worth and self-respect begin to develop.' Jenny Senior's account of her work with Keith illustrates the

Children's Hours approach. It also raises some interesting questions about the continuation of a therapeutic approach in public situations.

Keith, six years old, was referred because of severe disturbances at home which had resulted in family break-up. He was described as violent and hyperactive. To make contact with such a child requires that your limits during the sessions are as broad as possible but set decisively and without emotion. I approached his first session with some trepidation and went round the playroom removing anything sharp or breakable. In rushed Keith. There was just time to take in that he was small and darkly handsome with an engaging shy grin and more than his fair share of charm. There was barely a moment to greet him and state the terms of his first 'Hour'. He could do anything he liked except dangerous things – but I would look after that – he could ask me to do anything he wanted, and when the big hand said three o'clock time would be up; I would be with him, as would the two observers present.

Keith made for a cardboard box on a shelf and knocked it to the floor. Soon he had all the boxes and their contents strewn around. He found a felt-tip pen and ran round the room with it, drawing on walls, boxes and bricks. I re-capped him as he did so, so that he would know this was all right with me, 'Up you go, across the top, down the wall, over the house and into that box ...'. He ran outside and we all followed. (One of the joys of Children's Hours is that the world is your playground, the taker of the session looking after the needs of others.) Keith headed for an open space. I was put into a prison, fenced in on two sides, and put to work to make prison supper in the open stove (a rubbish bin). The others were given roles as prison warder and a stranger who came in to rescue the prisoner. The warder was told to be asleep, to wake up too late and to give chase. A child like this who is angry with his closest grown-ups loves the chance to dispense with the taker (on this occasion, into prison) and this is only possible if you can quickly delegate an observer to be in charge of the limits of behaviour. Keith resisted every form of prison, whether it was being stuck in his tower-block flat, tied to a classroom or made to obey apparently pointless rules; he would agree to sensible requests. When he felt humiliated we were on a knife-edge, needing careful and timely handling.

We were at a bus stop and Keith was astride the rails, riding his horse. A man came along and angrily told Keith to get down. He did, but when the man got on the bus Keith was swearing and shaking his fist at the departing bus and he began to elbow and push me. I had made the mistake of responding directly to the man's anger. I was supposed to be in charge of limits and Keith was being humiliated. Had I continued to tune in to Keith, acknowledging his play and his feelings, I think the outcome would have been more akin to what happened in the following session. We were in a used car lot near some flats. Keith tried lots of door handles until he found one that opened. I said, sorry, I couldn't let him get in. He tried to get in and I picked him out. He then wanted to be the one to shut the door. This happened twice; he seemed better able to accept my limits today. An angry man appeared and started threatening Keith with the police. I spoke to Keith, not the man, saying this person didn't quite understand, did he. Keith was happy with this and we went off leaving the man somewhat bewildered. This time, when an inflammatory situation arose, I spoke solely to Keith, so that my attention, which was his due in his 'Hour', was not diverted. His security and self-esteem were therefore not undermined.

The time limit was my chief difficulty. With any other child you could say 'You don't want to go now ... You wish you could have another ... a trillion ... more hours, but in fact time's up' and off they would go, their feelings and wishes having been affirmed. Not so with Keith. He had a delightful hour getting to know a series of dogs and their owners in a park. It was time to go. 'I'll throw the stick for him once more', he said. I repeated, sorry, time was up. Then I made the mistake of chasing him. This was fatal as he ran faster. Down by the lake I lunged forward, and got stuck in black mud to the knee, while he ran laughing into the water. Ten minutes later I had taken the only possible course and said 'I'm going back now, see you at the road'. Suddenly a voice beside me said 'You know, you shouldn't have done that'. I grinned sheepishly and agreed.

An unusual birthday party shows how Keith chose to make reparation through play. Keith assembled Rachel, me and two other observers in a small hut in the adventure playground, where birthday ingredients had been put on a tablecloth on the floor. He cut the cake and put a piece on a plate which had to be passed round the circle until he said stop. Some unlucky people didn't get any. Rachel (Pinney) was told she could come in if she behaved, but she was soon banished. Every so often Keith would go outside to check that she was where he'd left her, giving her a push for good measure. Once she nearly lost balance when her crutches fell to the ground. Keith was unnerved by this. So often he had played at robbing and fighting, but he always stopped short of hurting anyone. He left the party and picked up Rachel's crutches and then fell down. I tested all his limbs – no life at all. 'Fetch a doctor', he said. I fetched Dr Rachel, who ministered to him carefully, then pronounced the patient fit to walk. In this case of role reversal, Keith's genuine feelings of concern were acted out by taking Rachel's part, putting himself at her mercy and being restored by her.

During one 'Hour', Keith played with a Newton's toy and got all the balls and strings tangled into a huge knot, which he wanted to untangle. For 25 minutes this 'clumsy, hyperactive' child sorted out one thread after the other with total concentration, then raised his arms in triumph. After two years, Keith's outward difficulties were far from resolved but his inner resources were growing and his self-esteem more evident. Against a backdrop of violent changes in his life, his 'Hours' provided him with a thread of continuity and consistent handling, with a release of tension and the experience of happiness.

There are very few workers, except perhaps those in residential settings or foster parents, who can offer such an intensive play experience, involving many people over a long period. Many would admire Jenny Senior's courage in taking play into unpredictable settings where her potential control of the situation is less, as well as her honest account of successes and failures. Unlike Peter, in Neusner's work, Keith was not liable to confuse fantasy and reality and so there was not the same need to keep the real world and the world of therapy separated. Keith's feelings were acknowledged in the midst of coping with real situations. Control over limits, however, rested solely with the worker, rather than in any support from the setting, which makes her work more arduous and risky as well as, as was clear from her account, exciting and rewarding.

THE PROCESS OF THERAPY – THE WORK OF AN OCCUPATIONAL THERAPIST IN A CHILD PSYCHIATRIC UNIT

A great deal of the intensive play therapy for children living in unhappy families is carried out by specialist occupational therapists working in child psychiatric units and hospitals. At Park Hospital for children in Oxford, occupational therapists work in a well-equipped playroom containing nursery toys, miniature people, animals and cars, puppets and a home corner for domestic play. Three other rooms open into the central playroom. A wet room contains wet and dry sand, clay, paints and water. There is a quiet room full of big cushions. There is also a kitchen. In an enclosed inner courtyard there are rabbits. Children of any age up to fourteen may be referred for help with any kind of emotional problem. Out-patients are likely to have one hour a week play therapy: in-patients may come more frequently. Approaches to therapy are eclectic, based on the assessed needs of the child.

In this setting, Fiona Hawkridge used Axline's method of reflective listening in play therapy with an anally retentive child. His fascination with a toy castle was followed by modelling in brown clay of a circular wall totally enclosing the area within. She understood this to reflect his need to keep his emotions and anxieties protected inside him and interpreted this to him. Lyn Bennett used puppets to help an eight-year-old boy who had never spoken in school or outside the home. In his first session he whispered a few words and she just responded as if it were perfectly normal. After a few sessions he became silent again, and he was helped to talk through puppets. The therapist held a puppet 'who finds it hard to say things' and the boy told her what to say. In the following absorbing account, Lyn Bennett describes the course of play therapy with a very disturbed child. It illustrates the process of therapy and shows clearly the difficulties which beset the worker.

Andrew was admitted to hospital because of severe behaviour problems. He was very aggressive, both verbally and physically, in school and at home, and he had been excluded from school. He was ten years old, the middle of three children. He lived with his mother who had divorced his father two years previously. Contact with his father was very rare. I think he had already been quite a handful but he had got considerably worse since the breakdown. We discussed him as a team and anticipated that there would be lots of problems. Out-patient work had been tried unsuccessfully; he was uncooperative and aggressive. The prospect of working with him was quite alarming. Soon after he came into hospital I went along to the hospital school to introduce myself. He had got away from everyone else and was up a tree, pulling bits off and throwing them. I decided that it was a bit too stressful at that point and I waited until later in the day. I found him sitting on top of the wardrobe in his bedroom, hurling objects and abuse at whoever appeared at the door. I told him who I was and that I would see him three times a week while he was in hospital. He shouted abuse at everything I said. Right from the start I became aware of his sense of humour and I felt some warming towards him in spite of everything. There was a little twinkle in his eye when he was being abusive, so that although I felt apprehensive I felt positive as well. I told him what time I would see him the next day.

The following day he managed to get into the school and when the time came I went to collect him. He fled to the other side of the room like a frightened animal and said he wasn't coming. I thought he was probably very confused about all the different things in the hospital. Although I'd used the word occupational therapy as well as OT, I think he had OT, EEG and other things muddled up in his mind. He didn't know if I was going to put electrodes on his head or what and was terrified of the unknown. I asked the teacher if I could stay for a while. I noticed that Andrew never went very far away but circled round me, giving me his attention and always talking to me. The teacher also picked up that Andrew was frightened, and he said 'How about if we all go over to the department and then you can at least see what it is like?' Andrew agreed and we all went. Once there he was like a terrified caged animal. He took a quick look round and it was as if he couldn't quite take it in. He panicked and fled to the windows. They are child-proof and only open slightly so the teacher and I were both very calm, knowing that he couldn't get out. But somehow he did! He was out and across the field leaving us both standing there with our mouths open. There was a great look of triumph on his face. He didn't run right away, only to the limits of the grounds. We thought he would go back to his class eventually and the teacher agreed to tell him I would wait for him in OT for the rest of his time. I didn't expect to hear anything but about ten minutes before the end the telephone rang. It was Andrew saying 'I'll come'. He appeared at the door with a look of bravado. All he could do was look around before the time was up. The limit was there and he accepted that. I was very pleased that he had managed to come.

After that, when he saw me arriving in the morning he would say he wasn't coming, but he always did. I never had to fetch him; he always turned up on time. I tried to keep his three sessions to a regular time. On a Monday he took the responsibility of looking at his timetable for the week to see when to come. I found the first block of sessions difficult but I warmed to him in spite of that. After that first meeting I felt very strongly that he'd always been a child who had been challenged, and I felt he wanted a lot of space. With some children you feel you want fairly structured limits so that they know where they are; here I felt I wanted him to have a great deal of space and not put too many limits on him. I wanted to see him when there was no one else in the department, since I did not want to say that he could not go into a room because someone else was working there. So I had a lot of discussion with other people because he was so violent. I felt confident that he would not hurt me, and he never did. I don't think he even threatened to attack me. He broke things, usually things that he was making, to do with him.

That first block of sessions was very hard going. He could not tolerate being in the same room with me for more than a couple of minutes, but he still wanted my attention. I decided right from the start that I was not going to go after him and debated whether to end the session if he left the department. In the end I let him go as far as the end of the corridor and when he came back told him I needed to be able to see where he was. After that he never went far and always came back quickly. I was not sure about that decision but it seemed to be the right one. During that time he did very little. He fiddled with things, picked them up and put them down. He might occasionally attempt something, construction or pottery, but he would quickly become frustrated and break it. He showed no inclination to play imaginatively. Then he started going to the cupboard with the nursery toys and would settle to play. He would get a bike that he could hardly fit on. His knees would be right up in the air and he would pedal like crazy, round and round the room. He was beside himself with fury if anyone other than me saw him like that. One day he picked up a feeding bottle and was drinking from it when his doctor unfortunately walked in. Andrew was distraught and screamed abuse at him. A great deal of regressive play followed, including drinking from the baby bottle. I was just there, not saying a great deal, occasionally commenting or answering his day-to-day living sort of questions. I would position myself somewhere central and I found that he stayed around where I was. I was beginning to feel he was settled.

I thought I had experienced the testing-out bit, because it had been pretty hard going. But it was really the honeymoon period! I then had a week when it was almost unbearable. I think children are very good at picking a time when you are feeling vulnerable and I was feeling I was the worst therapist in the world. He did not physically attack me, but I began to think that that was all that there was left. He became totally abusive, not just in the sessions but wherever I was in the hospital. On a ward-round his face would appear at the window and a torrent of abuse would come out; or if I was talking in the corridor he would get right in my face and be really abusive. He would constantly threaten me and there was nowhere I could go to get away from it. He came to sessions, although he threatened not to. He could not settle to anything but constantly broke things. Again it was only his things he wanted to break. Away from the situation I was thinking that he was pushing me to reject him, and I felt he was pushing me pretty far.

On a Friday, at the end of a week of this, he burst into the department. He was still being very stroppy but I just sensed there was something different in his manner. He looked at me and said, 'Do you know Lyn, I like you. Not all the time. But I do like you.' I gave a sigh of relief and we went on to cook. His other comment that session was 'When I'm in here I can be free'. It was not plain sailing after that but it was obviously the turning point. He had a period of a lot more constructive activity. (He did not do any imaginative play.) He was really experiencing the relationship and surviving it. There was a noticeable difference in him everywhere after that particular week. He was a lot calmer and he became quite liked. Family sessions improved as well. It would be naïve to say that everything was all right in the end. He was still difficult, but nothing like he had been. We started some group work. I felt very strongly that I did not want to be involved in the group at this point because I did not think he could cope with sharing me. Also I would have had to set limits in the group that I did not have in sessions. Others took the group and it worked quite well.

He went on to a boarding school for difficult children where he has done very well. I saw him at half-terms and once during each holiday, when we did craft and constructive activities. At the end he was a very pleasant child.

Lyn Bennett's account of the process of therapy closely matches the stages of therapy outlined by Moustakas (in Haworth 1964, see also Chapter 3). At first Andrew experienced diffuse, generalized and pervasive feelings of anger, hostility and fear. His only means of coping was fight and flight. Moustakas describes the child's anxiety at this stage as often 'so pervasive that the child is immobilized and unable to start anything, or complete anything, or even to think clearly and attack problems logically' (in Haworth 1964: 148). Even when Andrew felt safe enough to stay in the playroom he could not play constructively. The therapist's acceptance enabled him to move on to the second stage in which fear and hostility become more focused, in this case on his therapist. Her continued acceptance allowed him to regress and then to move towards the stage of experiencing confused and ambivalent reactions towards her. His feelings then became more positive and he reached the final stage in which his positive and negative attitudes became separated and more consistent with reality.

Moustakas points out that the therapeutic process does not automatically occur in a play situation. 'It becomes possible in a therapeutic relationship where the therapist responds in constant sensitivity to the child's feelings, accepts the child's attitudes, and conveys a consistent and sincere belief in the child and respect for him' (in Haworth 1964: 419). Lyn Bennett shows how hard this can be. In order to help Andrew she had to survive his hostility, his attempt to annihilate her. Only when she had withstood this, retaining her identity and still 'holding' him, could Andrew start to find and integrate his good and bad feelings and hold himself together. It is significant that at the turning point they chose to cook together, an oral, mothering activity. Apart from Andrew's profound expression in this session, feelings were not talked about. The here and now of the relationship was what mattered. A therapist's survival is not automatic. What kept her going was her faith that there was a relationship there and the fact that she genuinely liked him. Support for the therapist is essential. In this case it came from the weekly team meeting as well as informally from colleagues.

AXLINE PLAY THERAPY BY A SOCIAL WORKER IN A CHILD PSYCHIATRIC UNIT

Jo Carroll, now a freelance play therapist, carried out direct work with children while a social worker in a child psychiatric unit in Wiltshire. Her approach varied according to children's need, ranging from psychodynamic play therapy to life-story work and directive work. Work might be short or long term, but was often over more than six weeks. She would see a child once a week, for up to an hour, finding that an hour is too long for many children. In her play therapy with Sally, which is described below, she uses Axline's non-directive approach. As with Lyn Bennett her acceptance of the child is crucial. 'There is no question of pleasing or displeasing the therapist because everything is acceptable. As a result, the child no longer has to worry about being right or wrong, she just *is*. Her anxiety level falls, and with it the defences she uses to protect herself. Within this space she can now use her energy just to help herself' (Carroll 1990: 7). The process of therapy follows the now familiar pattern. There is initial confusion, followed by anger and testing-out. Only then, when acceptance is assured, does the child dare to regress and eventually come able to grow up again. Jo Carroll writes:

Sally was just four-and-a-half when she was referred by her playgroup leader, who was concerned by her daytime wetting and some sexually explicit play. She had a deprived and distressing history, but was still living with her parents at the time. I saw her weekly for nine months. Initially, she was confused by the unusual 'rules' of her play. She repeatedly overfilled her teacup with water, watching me constantly and waiting for the reprimand which never came. Slowly she learned that she alone was responsible for the amount of water in the teacup. With this understanding came some extremely explicit sexual play. I felt that I was being tested out to see if I could survive both the content of the play and the feelings that so clearly went with it.

This was followed by two sessions when Sally was reluctant to see me. I continued to accept her just as she was, and as she obviously didn't like herself at the time this was painful for us both. When Sally was very angry with me I repeated over and over again that it was OK to be angry with me but I would not let her hurt me. She eventually retreated into infancy, climbing into the dolls' pram, crying like a baby (with a tiny cry, not the wail of an older child pretending to be a baby) and demanding constant comfort and attention, which she received. During the ensuing months she slowly 'grew up'. We had weeks of messy toddlerhood, with water and paint everywhere. This re-experiencing was clearly reparative for her, and she enjoyed every minute of it. Looking back, I can also see that she was postponing 'being four'.

One day, her play suddenly changed. She took the doll which she used to represent herself and painted it; the legs and genitals were red, the hands orange and the breasts were black. I abandoned Axline briefly and asked her gentle questions, but she offered no explanation. She simply asked me to look after the doll for her. Two weeks later she wanted the doll washed clean again, and asked me to paint 'I am five' for her. Following this she asked me to draw round her on a large piece of paper on the floor, and was very proud of how big she looked.

Sally used the opportunity of play therapy to regress completely, to re-experience her unhappy infancy and toddlerhood in a more satisfying way, to externalize her feelings about herself at four, and to grow into a normal, happy five-year-old.

(Carroll 1990: 7–10)

The therapist's acceptance and containment of Sally, which is apparent throughout, is symbolized in Sally giving her the doll, her unclean self, to be 'held' and looked after.

FOCUSED PLAY IN ASSESSMENT

In all the therapeutic play situations described so far the approach to play has been non-directive. Within the limits set and the provision available the child has chosen how to use the time. We turn now to consider some examples of focused play. Some workers use these techniques alone but often they are used in conjunction with some free play. They are more likely to be used when an assessment of a child is needed and time is short.

Sandra Foster is a social worker in a NCH Family Centre in Hull. She uses play in assessments of abused children, finding out their feelings and attachments so that plans for the future can be made. She finds that children usually want to go back to their parents but often cannot because their parents do not want them. This entails further therapeutic work to help children deal with their feelings at this point. Although she uses focused techniques she aims to give power to the child in the sessions. She ensures that the children understand why they are there and for how long, usually for at least six weekly sessions. She plans each session carefully, taking into account what happened in the previous session. This planning is illustrated in her account of her work with Stephen. This account also shows her use of sand play as a play therapy technique.

Stephen was 15 years old when I met him. His parents had separated when he was two years old and he had stayed at home with his father, who was subsequently awarded custody of him. When Stephen was four his father became ill and Stephen was received into care. From then until he was twelve, Stephen had periods with foster parents, relatives and his father. When he was twelve he was placed at a residential school for emotionally disturbed children, spending school holidays with his father or with relatives. During one holiday his three-year-old cousin alleged Stephen had asked him to touch his willy. When interviewed by the police Stephen disclosed that he had been sexually abused at school by another boy over a period of three years. The school's response to this was that they suspected Stephen was being sexually abused by his homosexual father during the school holidays.

I was approached to offer individual work with Stephen to explore attachments, sexual abuse, hopes and wishes. Despite his age and his high level of academic achievement, Stephen was emotionally and socially immature and was extremely enthusiastic about engaging in play sessions.

First session. The aim was to put Stephen at his ease so that we could start to get to know one another. We were not in the playroom as I was not sure where he was in terms of maturity and I did not want to lose him at the first session by offending him. I was not sure at this point whether sessions would take on a verbal counselling format. While Stephen had communicated easily he also enjoyed using the felt pens I had taken into the room. We started a 'life snake' of his early life experiences and his feelings around them.

Second session. We continued his life snake. Stephen was still talking but blocking certain events. I introduced the playroom at the end of this session and he was keen to use it.

Third session. In this first session in the playroom I planned to use *Talking Pictures* (P.King 1988) as a tool to free him to talk about areas he was blocking last week. We used All My Faces, My Secret Cupboard, Who I Would Like to Visit Me in Hospital. He was able to talk more about abuse at school. Then he asked if he could play in the dolls' house, furnishing a bedroom for himself and one for dad. Free play in the sand tray followed. He also wanted to paint but there was not enough time.

Fourth session. I wanted to give Stephen the chance to be angry as last week he had spoken about abuse. I did this by play with wet clay and how it made him feel. He was not responsive. The timing was wrong on my part; he had not had time to paint last week and this was now top of his agenda. His picture of a hot air balloon gave me the lead to say 'You could go on a journey in a balloon'. He decided he would go to Mount Everest, K2 and Mount Vesuvius and added these to his painting. I asked who he would take with him on his journey. 'Dad', he said.

At my suggestion he painted two apple trees, the apples standing for people. He put himself and dad together. On his second tree I asked him to place apples (people) showing how close he wanted them to him. He put dad and mum closest to him. He was sad about mum's absence and seemed to know little about this; his only knowledge comes from an aunt. The session again ended with sand play. Throughout the session it was clear that dad was significant.

Fifth session. I used the sand tray and story-telling as a method of enabling Stephen to express his feelings. I had on display several small items, including male and female figures, cars, animals and miniature toys. I asked him to choose five items and then invited him to place one item in the sand. I then asked him to close his eyes to and start thinking of a story whereby he could introduce his second item, moulding the sand to create the scene and eventually using all five items.

Stephen selected two cars, two male dolls and a motorbike with rider. His story was of a horrific road accident with the cars and the motorbike in a pile, and ended with the two male figures coming along and rescuing the motorbike rider. Reflecting back on his story, I offered Stephen an interpretation, adding names to his characters. I said, 'I feel this (the motorbike rider) could be Stephen'. He agreed. He saw the two male rescuers as his dad and dad's friend. The mangled wreckage of cars and motorbike were how he felt about his present circumstances. He was afraid to return to school after the holidays and wanted dad to support him in his refusal to return. Dad's need for a friend not only showed insight into his dad's sexuality (which dad had previously explained to him) but of dad's weaknesses and need for support from his friend. Following this Stephen created another scene in the sand.

Sixth session. This last session was for reflection and free play. Stephen showed surprise at how much work in painting and drawing he had done.

Work with Stephen led to the conclusion that the incident with his cousin was Stephen's way of attracting attention so that he could disclose his own abuse at school. Despite the school's concerns, there was no evidence of sexual abuse by dad. A spin-off from my work was individual work with dad by another family centre worker, focusing on Stephen's need to know more about his mother and enabling dad to talk more freely about her without feeling threatened. He also needed to talk about how to cope with being a full-time parent. Stephen's wishes were followed and he was allowed to remain in his father's care. He was eventually transferred to a local school for children with emotional difficulties which he attends as a day pupil.

This case study illustrates both the strengths and the weaknesses of focused play techniques. The worker's timing in choice of a technique must be matched to the child's readiness to make use of it. Stephen was not interested in using clay to express anger because he had planned to paint. The worker had to drop her plan and quickly follow the child. She did so successfully and in the process learned more about how important dad was to him. Her ability to be flexible and responsive was important to her success.

In contrast, story-telling through sand play appealed to Stephen from the start. This was not an accidental choice of technique. The worker had noted that he often spontaneously wanted to play in the sand. It seemed, therefore, a natural and comfortable medium to use when she was at the stage of wanting to test out her hypothesis of Stephen's perceptions of his father and their relationship. Once given the technique he made good use of it as a tool to express how he viewed his present situation. Sandra Foster points out that when using this technique she does not tell children that they are going to make up a story until *after* they have selected their five items. Once Stephen's story was enacted, she offered a tentative interpretation. In this instance he accepted the interpretation enthusiastically and elaborated on it.

She emphasizes that if he had not accepted her suggestion of his presence in the story she would have accepted his characters as fictional and the story at face value. She finds that children tend either to make up a story using all the items and become involved in its interpretation or to get stuck after placing the first item in the sand and unable to create a story.

This approach is closer to psychotherapy than to Axline's non-directive, reflective listening approach. In skilled hands it reaches strong feelings in a short time and is a powerful tool for assessment. The risk lies in the child being surprised and overcome by feelings, and retreating to avoid pain. A rejected interpretation may not be wrong. The worker must always be alert to the child's response, and be able to show acceptance of painful feelings, however briefly, rather than avoid them. A lesser risk is a wrong interpretation which the child can just dismiss, possibly along with the worker. In Stephen's case, of course, the interpretation was helpful. It made clear his feelings about his father, contributing to sound planning for his future.

Sandra Foster learned this sand play technique from Jenny Biancardi of the Morpeth Centre for Psychotherapy. It also has echoes of Erikson (1965) who would invite children to make a construction from blocks and tell a story around it. Jo Carroll makes up stories about another child in a comparable situation, perhaps using a puppet to tell the story. Another story-telling technique is Gardner's (1981) mutual story-telling. In this the therapist asks the child to tell a story (the diagnosis). Then she re-tells the story, using the child's language, characters and initial setting, but with a more appropriate resolution. The new story must avoid unconscious meanings which might cause anxiety.

Sandra Foster also uses sand play in which children build sand-castles, which is often their first reaction to sand. Using play people, she invites the child to place itself in the castle, together with other people the child would want with it. She would ask which people were not allowed across the moat. Or she might ask who would want to live in the castle, or who would protect the child from the snakes in the sand. She notes that children instinctively bury things in the sand; she has monster toys available so that children can bury the monster in their lives and express their anger towards it.

Jo Carroll, whose play therapy with Sally has been described, first became convinced of the value of play therapy as a means of helping distressed children to understand themselves and be understood through an eight-year-old's communication through sand play. The boy had been received into care because his mother was homeless. He stayed in a special school, going to foster parents at weekends, with his mother visiting when she could. He was described as aggressive and defiant, with frequent wetting and soiling. Jo Carroll continues:

> I tried to talk to him about the situation and how we planned to change it but I was not sure how much he understood. I used my little people and houses to show him that his mother still existed even when he could not see her. Finally I just watched as he showed me how he saw his situation. He went straight to the sand and built three castles, filling the spaces between them with water. He

built bridges between one castle and another, then crashed them into the water. He clearly understood that he had three 'homes' but he could not bear the space between them. I had tried to help him using my words and toys, but until I had enabled him to explain his distress to me through his play I made no progress. I feel that the most valuable aspect of our time together was the opportunity for him to share his view of the world and to have that validated.

This example of sand play shows how a sensitive worker can judge when focused methods are inappropriate and switch to a non-directive approach where the child determines the pace of work. Most workers in practice seem to use a mixture of non-directive and focused methods. Moreover, where focused methods are used, workers often use Axline's reflective listening in their response to the child's play. Yet there can be difficulties in striking a balance and using both appropriately.

A social worker who recognizes these difficulties is John Diaper, project worker in a NCH Family Centre in Bodmin. He considers it important that both the child and the worker should feel comfortable with the technique they are using. Play must be fun and without pressure, since a child under pressure will say anything just to stop it. He uses play to help children communicate their more or less conscious feelings. Although he recognizes that free play may reveal a good deal about a child, (for example, a five-year-old girl who was presenting serious problems in a foster home disclosed sexual abuse during a 'free fun' period), he makes more use of structured techniques, particularly in assessment. He describes these as follows.

Structured techniques in play-based assessments

Construction toys

Duplo (large Lego) is used to make buildings and people. The child often talks while building and then acts out situations. For example, one five-year-old who was a ward of court built himself and all three adults who were arguing over him, and then used the model of himself to smash all the others. Another seven-year-old boy who was having school attendance problems built the school and insisted on having an area 'where we hang our bags up'. He then labelled all the parts of the building as 'happy' or 'OK' except for this area which was 'unhappy'. In pushing this further it became obvious that he was being bullied in the cloakroom area. This had not previously been known.

Large bricks (Lincabrix) can be used to build houses. The child is told this is its house and it has control over who lives there and who does not. (This is like Sandra Foster's use of sand castles.) One five-year-old would have his mother and either 'father' or grandmother in the house but not all three at once. It came out that 'Nanny hates Dave'.

Dolls' house and dolls

A large dolls' house with furniture and a selection of dolls to scale are used. I usually start by asking the child to put the furniture in the dolls' house as near as possible to how it is in its home. This gives some idea of the sense of order or confusion in the home. I then ask the child to select dolls to represent family members, to put everybody to bed and then take me through a normal school or weekend day, or sometimes a particular day I want to focus on. I also use this technique to look at alternative strategies, 'So that's what happened when you ... What do you think would have happened if you had ...?'

Telephone role play

Working telephones in different rooms are used for role play. This has the advantage of avoiding eye contact and helping to re-dress the power imbalance between worker and child. The child easily controls the end of the conversation by hanging up. The child can decide who it and the worker are going to be. (Sandra Foster similarly uses a small tent in the playroom in which the child can sit unseen while telling 'secrets'.)

Drawing and flip charts

As well as free drawing, the part-completed drawings by Philip King (1988) are very useful, especially in assessment work. Flip charts are useful for large drawings or with older children to help them work through something. For example, a ten-year-old boy felt he was to blame for the break-up of his parents' marriage. After several sessions we listed his reasons on a flip chart. We then went through the reasons one by one, over several sessions, and as we eliminated each one he put a line through it. When none of the reasons was left he asked if he could paint them out. He painted the whole chart completely black.

Water play

A bowl full of water is changed into 'good stuff', using food colouring, by the child suggesting things which it feels are good, like cuddling, attention and love. Different members of the family are represented by labelled glasses. The only rules are that the more 'good stuff' someone has the happier that person is, and whenever a person gives out 'good stuff' to someone else the person gets the same amount back from the jug. It is then possible to act out situations. A seven-year-old boy whose father lived away except for alternate weekends said he felt unhappy because mum and dad spent most of the time at home arguing. We set this up with 'good stuff' and he promptly poured half of his out. When I asked how mum and dad felt he paused for a long time and then silently poured out some of both mum and dad's 'good stuff'. It is also useful for looking at children who block love. One five-year-old girl was fairly empty of 'good stuff' and I put a lid on her beaker and then tried to fill her up from her mother's beaker. Of course, the 'good stuff' went into the bowl and not into her. We were then able to explore what 'lids' she used.

The last three of these play techniques are illustrated in John Diaper's assessment of Sean.

> Six-year-old Sean was referred to the family centre for assessment because of disruptive and aggressive behaviour at school, and bed-wetting and jealousy of his 15-month-old brother at home with his parents. A sister had been a victim of cot death when Sean was three years old. Sean was seen frequently over four weeks. He was energetic, with little concentration, and seemed to push and shove his way through life. He was very talkative, especially about what he had done or been in a fantasy life, which he described as if it were true. He never mentioned his sister's death, but I was told he had worked through this.
>
> I would spend time playing with Sean and then offering him paper to draw anything he wanted. I then gave him some partially completed drawings (P.King 1988) and asked Sean to imagine himself into the situations and finish the drawing. I watched carefully, labelling people and objects as he drew and writing on what he said. I let him stop when he had had enough. One session was at home so that Sean's parents could see what I did and that I took an impartial stance. Another time I asked the parents to help Sean complete some pictures. In his drawing of faces, sad ('when my mum tells me off') and happy ('when my mum don't tell me off'), Sean showed he wanted his mother's approval. He drew My Favourite Food, sausages and three baked beans, 'because my mum only give me three'. He drew a shark, 'because it eats everything up'. My Secret Island had 'no more people, just me'. He drew My House which included an enormous toilet and, deliberately, no television. For Who I Would Like to Visit Me in Hospital, he liked the idea of being 'poorly' and drew himself with a sad face. The only person he wanted to visit him was his grandad, with whom he was due to spend the weekend. He was quite firm that his mum and dad would not come. Similarly, in his drawing of The People I Would Get to Hold the Rope for Me, to stop him falling down a cliff, he drew only myself. When prompted he said 'Mum and dad would let me fall', and added 'They like me but they don't want me'. I asked if he liked mum and dad and wanted them, and Sean replied, 'I like mum and dad and want them but they don't want me'. He was noticeably upset so I ended the session and went on to playing with the toys.
>
> We had several conversations on connected telephones in which I became Sean and he became someone else. This was not so successful because as soon as I steered talk round to awkward or possible painful issues he would just say 'Bye' and hang up. However, it became clearer that Sean desperately wanted more attention and affection from both his parents.
>
> Sean took exceptionally well to water play with 'good stuff', coloured water representing nice warm things like attention and sticks of rock (Sean's idea).

Only twice did Sean fill up his glass with 'good stuff' from his mother. He usually poured most of his mother's water into either his brother's or his father's glass. He frequently filled up his mother's glass from his own, showing that he kept on giving her love and affection but felt he got little back. It was interesting to note that he felt he got a fairer share of his mother's attention when his father was there too. He showed that he got love and attention from his father, although not enough, but had more when his mother was not included. His brother received 'good stuff' from everyone but gave none out, perhaps typical of a 15-month-old who naturally soaks up attention. His teacher, myself, and one or two others were seen as giving 'good stuff'.

From this assessment, John Diaper concluded that much more work needed to be done to help his parents give Sean the love and attention he craved. He warned that unless preventive action was taken, Sean would eventually become enmeshed in either the care system or the delinquency system or both. His prediction proved to be only too accurate.

PLAY IN GROUP WORK WITH CHILDREN OF SCHOOL AGE

Group work is sometimes offered to children with emotional and behavioural difficulties. It may run in parallel with individual work or, as with Andrew, form part of the final phase of therapy. Individual or group work with parents, or some form of family case-work or family therapy, provided alongside work with children, is often seen as a necessary pre-condition for its success, especially when the aim is to prevent reception into care. Otherwise it may only increase negative 'labelling' of the child.

Games in group work

John Diaper, with another social worker as co-leader, ran a group for boys and girls with ages ranging from six to nine years, where the primary aim was to prevent reception into care. Secondary aims were to help children come to terms and cope with existing home situations, to improve basic communication, to convey the idea that everyone has the opportunity to change and grow through making choices, and to improve self-image. The group time was spent in carefully planned games, moving quickly from one to another as the children could not cope with unstructured time. Alternating between a constructive game and a so-called silly game worked well. A common theme for games over several sessions was helpful.

One of the themes was 'choice'. Despite adults making many choices for children there are still choices which children make every day which can affect their happiness. The workers invented a massive board game, using the whole room, with huge dice and the children as players. A turn would involve a choice such as 'Do I get up when mum calls me or do I miss school?' Similarly in a game of traffic lights, red was 'stop', amber was 'think' and green was 'choose'. (Choice is also one of the themes of group work with children in divorce, carried out by Leicestershire Court Welfare Service, see Chapter 7.)

Although these games were invented there is also a considerable literature available, including Dearling and Armstrong (1989), Panmure House (undated), Masheder (1989), Silveira *et al.* (1988) and Orlick (1972 and 1982).

Activity groups

Occupational therapist Susan Monson describes a different style of group work in a child psychiatric unit in a children's hospital. She runs group sessions in partnership with each of the in-patient group nurses. Small groups of about four children meet weekly for an hour after school. The aim is to help the children with their different problems which invariably include a low self-image and difficulties in making relationships. She writes:

> The following examples give some idea of what we try to achieve in group sessions. What is done is less important than how it is done. The same activity can often be used in different ways to help different children. The children are given some choice of activity when appropriate.
>
> Cooking can give a real sense of achievement to children who have low self-esteem. It can help them to work constructively in a group. A recipe might be chosen that involves everyone helping to make the same thing such as a marble cake. Or it could be one that needs careful step-by-step concentration or helps fine motor control. Some recipes need a lot of beating and give an outlet for aggression, such as Crash-Bash biscuits. Other recipes can give opportunities for individual choice and creativity, for example, decorated biscuit shapes. Sharing the cooked things with other people is a chance for the children to give something they have made themselves and to receive praise. Most children enjoy making and eating food so it is usually a very positive activity with a real sense of achievement. Cooking is particularly valuable in the way in which it links with home and family.
>
> Painting can be enjoyed in different ways by different children, useful when children in a group vary in age, stage, ability and therapeutic needs. Art can be used as an outlet for feelings and as a way of expressing problems for which a child lacks words. Children can work individually, in pairs or in a group. Depending on the presentation, art can be stimulating, relaxing, challenging, an opportunity to explore or a chance to regress. When the emphasis is on the doing, rather than on the end result (which can so easily be judged a failure), and when children are encouraged to use their own ideas and imagination, then art can be a very therapeutic activity.
>
> Through playing with sand and water children can catch up on experiences they may have missed out on or regress to early play if present problems are overwhelming. Within a framework of simple rules, made so that nobody is hurt and nothing is broken, the children can be given freedom to enjoy messy play

and to be destructive without really doing any damage, as when building and knocking down sand castles. Wet or dry sand is ideal for imaginative play, either on its own or with miniature people, houses, and animals. Older children rarely get the chance to play in this way but respond well to these natural materials.

We try to make these groups a positive time since disturbed children often get into a negative pattern that is hard to change. Positive experiences can help both their own self-image and their relationship with staff and peers.

Occasionally a parent has been involved in these sessions, in a similar way to parent helpers in playgroups, after careful consideration of the needs of all the children in the group. The parent was treated as an adult member of the group and enabled to join in and help without taking over. It was possible for the parent to copy play ideas and ways of handling the child, to share in the enjoyment of the session and to be given status which also reflected on the child. Joining the group was helpful for some parents, as Susan Monson describes.

A father, who had a poor relationship with his son, joined a woodwork group and his help was much appreciated. Afterwards his son told everyone how his dad had been in to help, that he was teaching the children, that he was clever and knew all about tools. This was a real contrast to his usual negative feelings. He felt that his dad must care about him if he took the trouble to come, and the father was able to see himself in a more positive role.

Other activities offered in these and other workers' activity groups include finger painting, clay, collage, woodwork, cooperative games, including hiding games, and outdoor activities such as gardening, tracking, nature walks and making dens, and also music, dancing, puppets, dressing-up, play acting, miming games and psychodrama.

Play therapy in a school group

Another group which offers a wide choice of activities is run by Rose Larter, a teacher in a primary school unit in Reading for children with emotional problems. The children continue to attend their normal classes, in which they have exhibited difficulties in behaviour or are described as 'odd', and have an hour a week play therapy session in the unit. Two children come at a time, making for a less intense and more natural atmosphere than if there was only one. For example, one child was saying that he had seen his dad, so the other child was asked if he had seen *his* dad, a natural way of introducing a subject that he had avoided.

The aim of the group is to allow children to express their feelings, to be listened to and to be more themselves. Rose Larter refers to Winnicott in emphasizing the value of play. Sessions usually start with a nurturing time on big cushions, perhaps singing, looking at books or reading stories. She tells parents 'We always read and have a story; the rest of the time is theirs'. Books are everywhere. Painting and drawing are encouraged. Water play and other messy play, cooking and play with dolls are all available.

A child who has benefited is Emma, whose mother was divorced some time ago but remains angry. Emma is the oldest child in her class but a reluctant reader, with pressure from home and school to achieve more. Unable to make friends at school, she acquired a reputation for scratching other children. In play therapy she made up a story about a ladybird and other creatures, with her teacher as 'secretary', and drew beautiful tiny pictures with opening windows to stick on to the names in the story. The last line of her story was 'We started being friends'. 'That's my favourite bit', she said. Her school is delighted with her progress and says 'she's no bother at all'. Emma recently told Rose how two girls were playing with some pearls in the playground, 'I wanted them and could have scratched those girls but I decided not to, so I walked away'.

Chapter 6

Play for children with illness, disabilities and learning difficulties

This chapter explores the use of play in two distinct but overlapping areas of work, children with disabilities and children in hospital. Play therapists and play workers, teachers and nursery nurses, speech therapists, occupational therapists, physiotherapists and sometimes social workers and psychologists, all these may use play in work with children with developmental delay or learning difficulties, or other disabilities, short or long term, which may be physical, mental or both. Play provision for young children may be in ordinary pre-school playgroups or nursery schools into which these children are integrated, in special playgroups and opportunity groups, in educational home-teaching services, in a hospital setting or a child development centre. Play work for older children may take place in schools, including residential schools, and in holiday play schemes and 'handicapped' adventure playgrounds. Hospital play specialists, teachers, nurses and nursery nurses, and occupational therapists use play in work with children with illnesses and disabilities who are in hospital for long or short stays.

PLAY FOR YOUNG CHILDREN WITH DISABILITIES AND DEVELOPMENTAL DELAY

Concern for the development of children with disabilities and developmental delay, particularly in the years following the 1981 Education Act, resulted in the burgeoning of structured developmental programmes for children, such as the Portage scheme. While play is one of the methods used in these largely behaviourally oriented programmes it is often both adult initiated and adult controlled. Assessments of children are frequently based on adult-imposed tasks and instructions. The Newsons (1979) stressed the need to observe children in a more playful situation where their initiative is welcomed and the role of the adult is to help children to perform at their highest level of ability.

Many workers in this field are teachers and nursery nurses whose training, drawing on the theories of Piaget and Bruner, leads them to see play as valuable in promoting intellectual and language development. Emotional development is rarely accorded the same significance and there is often little attention to the relationship between emotional and intellectual development. Another difficulty appears to be in striking the right balance between the extreme views that, on the one hand, only adult-imposed graded tasks using toys, such as posting boxes and jigsaw puzzles, will help the child to progress, and, on the other hand, the view that adults should not interfere in children's play. Yet children's needs for structured help can still be met in a playful situation which, wherever possible, meets their emotional need for autonomy and creativity in building a sense of identity.

McConkey (1986a and 1986b) offers a guide through the confusion, noting evidence that play, in particular pretend play, helps to develop children's ability to think and to learn language. There is a widely held belief that developmentally delayed children do not play. McConkey (1986a) quotes a range of evidence refuting this view. He observes, however, that a great many disabled children lose out on opportunities for pretend or creative activities. If children normally use play to help them make sense of their world then a child with disabilities may be doubly handicapped if this need is not met. McConkey goes on to emphasize the important relationship between intellectual and emotional development. He writes, 'I doubt if teaching and therapy can ever inculcate a sense of autonomy, self-sufficiency and cooperativeness to anything like the same extent as play can do' (McConkey 1986b: 31).

In recent years many children with disabilities have been integrated into the normal play activities of playgroups and nursery schools. Yet despite wider recognition of the value of play to children with disabilities there remains an underlying doubt that playing *really* aids learning, due, McConkey feels, to

> the well-established tradition of the able-bodied doing things for handicapped people. The notion of letting handicapped children do things for themselves and in the way they want to do it is therefore fairly radical. Nevertheless, I believe we have much to learn by adopting this approach, particularly in the realm of play.
>
> (McConkey 1986a: 86)

Play is far more than a technique to foster intellectual development. It is central to the development of autonomy and mastery, and so, as Erikson and Winnicott have shown, to the development of a sense of self and self-esteem. A child with disabilities who is unable to achieve this through unaided spontaneous play needs help from an adult which fosters all the attributes of spontaneous play rather than taking them away even further. As Newson and Hipgrave remind us, although an adult provider and playmate may be needed,

> In our enthusiasm to help the child to learn we must not forget the voluntary and exploratory nature of play ... Our aim when we play with him is not only to help the child to want to learn new skills, but also to give him the feeling that he has some mastery and control over the things around him.
>
> (Newson and Hipgrave 1982: 67)

Adults joining in play can enhance rather than hinder it provided that a number of conditions are met. McConkey lists these. Child and adult should take turns in leading the play – for example, in Peep-bo or undressing teddy. Adults should join in playing at the child's developmental level, rather than pushing the child too hastily to play at a more advanced level which it cannot manage or sustain. This requires a fine assessment of the child's developmental level in play (see Chapter 1). Adults should join in as active playmates rather than encouragers from the sidelines, since children need to see adults modelling play. More than this, adult sharing of play helps to equalize the relationship. If these conditions are met then 'there is no better way of developing children's imaginative play and encouraging their language development' (McConkey 1986b: 30). This matches the way in which mothers play with their babies, pacing the interaction and helping their infants to take turns by leaving spaces in the interaction for them to fill.

Pretend play

McConkey suggests that the best educational toy for a developmentally delayed child may well be a not too life-like rag doll, rather than the usual sorting box, since it enables young children to re-create the events of their daily life, such as washing, dressing and eating. He sees pretend games as vital, especially for children who have not begun to talk. Make-believe actions, such as pretend hairbrushing or telephoning, can be used as well as toys, as can pictures and drawing.

Gill Howgego, leader of the family play therapy group in Dingley Child Development Centre, keeps at hand a basket of real baby equipment, a plastic bowl, flannel and soap, towel, potty, hairbrush, feeding bottle and doll. In one-to-one play with a child she shows the child the things in her basket, and observes what the child uses and how much of a sequence of events the child can play out. This helps her to decide at what point and at what level to join in with play in order to help the child to develop more complex pretend play.

Interactive play

Some kinds of play lend themselves more readily to interactive play than others. Rough-and-tumble play can be a way of reaching, for example, a child with communication difficulties. The use of music sessions to initiate non-verbal 'conversations', drawing on knowledge of early mother–infant interaction, is described by music therapist Wendy Prevezer (1990):

> We use three main strategies for this tuning in process, which in practice often overlap within one activity. These strategies permeate the way we use children's songs and rhymes, their active and lap play, and many structured and improvised games. In a child's first few sessions we experiment with a wide range of these activities, looking for a positive response, however small.
>
> The least structured way of tuning in to the child involves joining in with, imitating and later extending, his own spontaneous sounds and movements, and treating them as if they were intentional attempts at communication, even when

they are clearly not. This child-centred approach provides the most straightforward way of drawing the child into a turn-taking situation. Most children respond by giving more eye contact, and eventually by using a wider range of sounds in a much more positive and intentional way ... The moment a child first realizes that he is leading or 'in control' is often visible on his face, and then his confidence grows ...

The 'running commentary' involves using words in a simple extemporized song to fit in with whatever the child is doing at the time, whether it is jumping, rocking, or looking out of the window. The third strategy provides a more structured framework using a song with short verses, which are flexible enough to accommodate anything the child might do or suggest. For example, we might sing 'Pat, pat, pat your leg' or 'Crawl, crawl, crawl around', to the tune of 'Skip to My Lou'.

One other important technique, used throughout many kinds of activity, is the leaving of 'dramatic pauses' before key words in familiar songs ... (which) seems to compel a child to 'slot in'.

(Prevezer 1990: 4)

Work involves two adults for each child. Wendy Prevezer uses an electronic keyboard so that she can see and follow the child. A nursery nurse sits facing the child with the child's knees between hers. While this work is with autistic children in a special school the basic strategies are widely applicable to children with communication and learning difficulties, and can be used on a one-to-one basis with the adult singing, rather than playing a keyboard.

Susan Monson and Margaret Petchley's interactive games for autistic children are described later in this chapter.

Sensory play

Sensory play environments may be developmentally appropriate to some children and may also offer opportunities for playing and 'being' which do not occur naturally. Soft play areas filled with a variety of vinyl-covered foam shapes or air-filled mattresses provide a response to any movement a child makes. They are also a good place for interactive rough-and-tumble play between adult and child, or between children. Darkened rooms with coloured lights and soothing music offer womb-like comfort, valuable for anxious children in hospital or in an unfamiliar setting. With different music (or birdsong), and visual effects such as a rotating mirror ball with pinspot light, and perhaps a humming, vibrating tube of moving bubbles, the same room can be stimulating (see Jean Gregg's use of a sensory cubicle, described later in this chapter). Ultra-violet light and a resonance board intensify light and sound so that they can be picked up by sight- and hearing-impaired children. In her school for children with learning difficulties Longhorn (1988) provides a sensory curriculum including touch, taste and smell, and a sensory perception room providing a resource bank of equipment. Swimming offers freedom to play for many children with disabilities. Newson and Hipgrave (1982) offer many ideas to help children to get meaning from the use of each of their senses, from sand and water play to 'feely bags' and rolling in leaves. (See also Chapters 2 and 9.)

Play to meet the needs for autonomy of children and their parents

Dingley Family Play Therapy Group is a voluntary organization, originally funded through the Pre-school Playgroups Association and now by social services. It forms one element of the multi-disciplinary team at Dingley Child Development Centre in Reading. Parents come with their young children who have disabilities or are developmentally delayed, together with any young brothers or sisters. These parents often find the task of mothering particularly stressful. It can be both physically and emotionally draining, with limited rewards when their children progress only slowly. They have a particularly strong need to be 'held' so that they can in turn 'hold' their children. As parents join in play with their own and other people's children, and see playleaders and other parents appreciating their company and enjoying play with their own child they may find it a little easier to accept their child's disabilities. Playleaders work in partnership with parents, recognizing parents' knowledge of their children and their play. Anxious parents often start to relax as they join in play in which other parents and children are involved too. This might be anything from rough-and-tumble play in a 'soft' play area to a group collage or music session. Children with communication difficulties are often particularly unrewarding to 'mother' and this can lead to difficulties in attachment. Rough-and-tumble play encourages physical contact and communication. So does music and singing, as Margaret Shephard (1989) has shown, where parents hold their children and their bodies start to move in synchrony. A parent can physically feel the tense child relax and become peaceful.

The group provides all the play activities normally found in under-fives settings: sand and water, dough, painting, cutting and sticking, jigsaw puzzles, home corner and pretend play. Play is seen as essential, not only to cognitive growth and the next developmental stage, but also to children's need to 'be' and to enjoy themselves at whatever stage they have reached. Children are encouraged to take the initiative and, whenever possible, to develop their own themes in play. By being in control of their play, children's mastery, however limited, of their environment increases, and with it growth in the sense of self. The role of the adult (worker or parent) is to provide tempting and developmentally appropriate play materials and activities and to entice the child into playing.

Different approaches work, depending on the child. With one relatively able but non-communicating boy, problem-solving toys were placed in his path so that he almost literally fell over them; he was attracted by the practical mechanical problem the toy presented and the reinforcement for success, such as a funny noise (a moo or a squeak) or a flashing light. An effective way to interest many children in something is for the adult to start playing with it. A musical marble run is particularly appealing. Once the child is playing the adult can gradually join in as the child begins to tolerate the adult's presence. The adult may tempt the child to extend the play into something more complex, or into a turn-taking game. In Bruner's term the adult provides the 'scaffolding' for the child's play. The adult can provide a slow running commentary on the child's actions ('Teddy's having a drink') and use questions sparingly. Instead of condescending praise ('Good boy') mutual enjoyment and appreciation of what the child is doing is preferable ('Lovely!' 'That worked well!' 'I like that!'). From a worker's modelling of play and the essential subsequent discussion, parents may learn new ways of helping their children. Equally parents may demonstrate effective ways of communicating and playing with their children to the benefit of workers and other parents.

The Dingley playgroup, which I led in its first years, has also offered play therapy, based on Axline's non-directive model, to those children whose developmental delay, communication disorder or physical disability is suspected of involving an emotional element or consequence. An example is my account of play therapy with four-year-old Mark (see later in this chapter). Gill Howgego, the present leader, has used therapeutic play to help a young child who developed epilepsy following a viral infection. The parents had a new baby while the child was in hospital. Described as having been 'a dear little girl' her violent and angry behaviour and temper tantrums alarmed her family and carers, and frightened the child herself. Holding sent her into a frenzy, tearing out her hair, banging her head and poking her genitals. She delighted in messy play which Gill saw as healing after her illness. She began to want a baby bottle and got into bed in the home corner. At lunch-time she wanted a baby cup to drink from. That happened for quite a little while until she began not to need to do it. At the same time her tantrums were becoming less frequent and less intense, and she seemed more in control.

Another voluntary organization in which play forms an important part of work with children with special needs is the London-based KIDS. It provides a wide variety of services to children and their families. Its family centres offer integrated playgroups and developmental play programmes, home visiting, toy libraries and holiday play schemes. KIDS offers close partnership with parents, and whole families may attend its playgroups.

Interaction play for autistic children and their parents

Play and games which require interaction can help parents to find ways in which they can begin to get through to their children and have some success in fostering their development. It is also a good way of strengthening the attachment between parent and child. Susan Monson, occupational therapist at Marlborough Children's Hospital, some of whose work was described in earlier chapters, also works with autistic children and their parents. She writes

My approach is based on the current majority view that autism is a biological disorder caused by organic dysfunction (Gillberg 1990). Sensory integration theory (Ayres 1985) also stresses the neurological basis of the condition, particularly problems like oversensitivity to touch or other stimuli. Rudolph Schaffer's studies of mother–infant interactions show how the mother's task is 'to dovetail her behaviour to that of the infant's' and he recognizes that amongst babies 'there are some (found principally among the brain-impaired, the autistic and the mentally handicapped) who may be almost impossible to mother in the usual sense, for their capacity to enter a reciprocal relationship may be so impaired that normal mutuality just cannot develop' (Schaffer 1977: 31 and 99).

In the hope that these early interaction patterns, normal for most mothers and children, could be taught to some extent to autistic children I worked on a one-to-one basis using musical conversations, give and take games, turn-taking and interaction activities. I was encouraged by the children's response but quickly realized that it would be far more valuable for the mothers to be doing this with their children so that they could break through the barriers of autism and enjoy a closer relationship. I use normal and enjoyable activities whenever possible, in a structured step-by-step approach, but it is sometimes necessary to be very firm and intrusive for a few minutes. I work increasingly with mothers and children at home and marked improvement has been made by all the mothers and children I have worked with. (Naturally this is only one aspect of the help offered at the clinic.)

Autistic children need to be taught to play as they understand little speech and they find it difficult to copy. The use of physical prompts and guidance has proved a most helpful technique and one that parents pick up easily. Since I started work in this field, close liaison with speech therapists has been particularly helpful and rewarding.

Susan and her present speech therapy colleague, Margaret Petchley, have made a videotape of their work with four-year-old Jamie and his family, described here.

Jamie is being helped to thread a wooden peg attached to a cord through the holes in a large flat wooden 'pear'. His mother holds him round the waist, facing his father. She takes Jamie's hand, helping him push the peg through the pear to his father, who posts it back through the hole, wiggling it and calling to Jamie to take it. Jamie takes the peg and is encouraged to put it through another hole. His mother helps by holding his hand but lets him do it independently whenever he tries. They play similar games with a musical marble run, Jamie being helped to take turns with his father as his mother holds and encourages him. He pushes large beads along a curly wire loop, his parents at each end urging him on. Rocked in a see-saw by his father facing him, he several times looks at his father, as he does while being bounced astride his father's leg, as his father talks and his mother sings See-saw Margery Daw. Jamie bangs a triangle held close to his mother's face and chases bubbles which she blows. When she stops he sits and looks at her. Another time, father holds Jamie's hand, helping him to pretend feed a puppet from a spoon, while his mother uses the puppet to attract his attention. Jamie's parents were delighted with his responsive play and over the following months his play and communication continued to improve.

Recently both therapists have been running a weekly joint session with Jamie and another autistic boy, which they have also videotaped. The aim is to help the two boys to respond to each other using interaction, turn-taking and to-and-fro activities. By trying out different ideas they find which ones the boys respond to best. A sand wheel, with a small pot each, a bell to post down a cardboard tube, a ball or toy bus to push to each other, musical conversations where they play a few notes in turn on a glockenspiel, and a see-saw boat for them both to rock in, these are some of the things that are helping them to play together.

Contact with home continues and nursing staff run a fortnightly support meeting. A workshop for three mothers and their children, involving the nursing staff, gave much needed encouragement and the chance to work in a group. Support and encouragement are really important as working with autistic children demands great patience and perseverance, especially from the parents.

PLAY FOR CHILDREN WITH LEARNING DIFFICULTIES AND EMOTIONAL PROBLEMS

Learning difficulty, developmental delay, communication and language disorder, and physical disability may be linked with emotional problems in varying ways. It may be that their physical or mental limitations have deprived children of the opportunity to experience the world and to develop their creativity and sense of self through play. It may be that early experiences of neglect or deprivation have led to potentially normal children being denied opportunities for development, resulting in learning difficulties. It may be that early experiences of separation and loss, of unresolved pain, anger and fear, may leave children unable to take advantage of present opportunities. Sometimes there are complex combinations of these factors.

A number of workers use therapeutic play approaches to help children and young people, even young adults, who have learning difficulties, and also who need help in making sense of what is happening in their lives. Play may help them to communicate some of their feelings.

Social worker Sandra Foster used play methods in a long piece of work with a 14-year-old with learning difficulties. For example, using her technique of getting the child to tell a story linking various objects in sand play (see Chapter 5), she would point out an unnamed object and suggest 'Perhaps that is Suzie', making tentative interpretations into her life but ready to be corrected. Family placement worker Kate Burke used sensory work and music therapy to help a young adult, who had been in mental handicap institutions from the age of seven, to become more able and confident, and ready to cope with a move to a new setting. Christine Bradley has set up a therapeutic playgroup, using psychodynamic principles and non-directive play, in a residential school for children with physical disabilities (see Chapter 2). Children with communication disorders often experience acute and disabling frustration. Roger Arguile gives an absorbing account of his use of art therapy to help a child with severe aphasia in a residential special school (in Case and Dalley 1990).

Non-directive play therapy can offer much help to some children who initially present with learning difficulties. This section includes two accounts of work of this sort. The first is about my work in a child development centre with a four-year-old who had spent much time in hospital. The other is about the provision of play therapy in a residential school for children with learning difficulties.

'Mark is very frail. He's recently had a major operation and he's been in hospital for a large part of his life. His speech is very unclear and he has had almost no experience of other children and couldn't cope with nursery school'. The teacher-counsellor's description of Mark did not prepare me for the ball of energy that flew in the playroom door one January morning. His eyes were alert and observant, his speech so rapid and soft that it was almost impossible to follow. He was slightly built but threw himself energetically into play with the sand, dough, in the home corner and under the climbing frame. He played happily alongside Angela, who was new too. Mark's mother sat watching him anxiously.

The next week Mark was playing under the climbing frame when a solidly built but developmentally very delayed three-year-old clutched fiercely at his face and hair. Mark hit him hard, with an anger I had not anticipated. Later I watched Mark and Kevin, another very large and solid three-year-old, wearing hats and rushing round giggling together. Over the next month I saw very little of Mark because he changed his day to one when I was not there. My co-worker Gill Howgego said he often played with Angela or Kevin. She was pleased with his progress but anxious about his tendency to attack other children. We decided to invite Mark and Kevin to an afternoon play therapy session. With no other children or adults we could give each child our fullest attention. The first session went smoothly, both children playing independently although aware of and enjoying one another's presence.

We began the following week with trampolining in the soft play area as a way of focusing both children's need for physical activity and expression of aggression. If anything it had the opposite effect to that intended. Mark was diving straight on to the play mat and wriggling on his back. Kevin was literally throwing his weight about, giggling, making loud shouts, then wandering aimlessly, mouthing pieces from a posting box. Mark had joined in the horse-play at first, smiling and laughing. Once back in the playroom he started to hit Kevin really hard in the face with a handbag. I took him firmly on my lap, saying 'I will not let you hit Kevin. You need to sit down until you are ready to play again.' He quietened down and let me read him a story. He and Kevin then found newspapers and each settled down peacefully 'reading'. After a while play deteriorated to hitting again. Later in the session both were painting, on opposite sides of the easel. Each painted big patches of colour, Kevin's yellow and Mark's orange. Now and then Mark reached over the top of the easel to dab his brush at Kevin's painting. He brushed his own paper hard. I told him it was all right to brush as hard as he liked.

Mark continued his sudden attacks on Kevin, hitting or scratching his face for no apparent reason. I stuck to the strategy of picking up Mark at the start of an attack, holding him firmly on my lap, saying calmly that I knew he was angry, that it was all right to be angry but I would not let him hurt Kevin. One afternoon I had held him on my lap several times to calm him when he picked up a very large teddy bear. He started to undress him, asking for help. He then said, 'You be the nurse', and he put the bear on the bed in the home corner and began 'examining' him. I promptly fetched the hospital play kit which he used at once to give teddy injections and listen to his chest. I was saying things like 'It must hurt ... I expect teddy feels like crying', watching Mark carefully, who was nodding at my comments. He fetched two long pencils and carefully stuck them into the bear's crotch. I continued reflective comments until he had finished playing. Later talking to his mother, she told me that the last of the series of plastic surgery operations Mark had needed to rebuild his penis had been extremely painful.

After that cathartic day Mark coped much better with other children. In playgroup the next morning I watched him play a complicated game involving cardboard tubes with Daniel, both totally absorbed. In play therapy Mark invariably sought the hospital box and he always chose the same teddy, undressing it on the bed and 'treating' it. Once he lay down himself and asked me to be the doctor, which I did. Another time he told a passing child to be a nurse to teddy while he was doctor. He then told me to lie down and he examined and 'treated' me.

In this way Mark began to come to terms with his painful experience. He started nursery school after Easter where he became a friendly and acceptable child, to his mother's delight. His mother was also relieved that they could go to the park without her watching like a hawk in case he pushed anyone off the slide. The family went on holiday by the sea and Mark loved every moment of it. His mother said that now whenever they went past the Centre he would always say, 'There's my other school'.

I am grateful for the chance to meet such a courageous child who faces life with zest and enthusiasm despite the pain that he knows it can hold. Mark's anger was at first unfocused but its recognition and containment in play therapy enabled him to focus it appropriately. His constant re-enactment of his operation and my recognition of his hurt and angry feelings, working within the symbolism of his hurt teddy, helped him express and work through his pain.

Bourne Place is a residential special school, run by the National Children's Homes, for children with learning difficulties and emotional problems. The aim is to provide an overall therapeutic environment, with play therapy being a major component of the school's work. The play therapists stress the need to work as part of the school team – for example, telling other staff how a child is feeling in general, without breaking the child's confidentiality (except in the frequent disclosures of sexual abuse), and warning them if a child has had a difficult session which might carry over into classroom behaviour. This helps cope with natural envy of the luxury of one-to-one work.

The two play therapists use non-directive play therapy, but with different styles. Margaret Coles has training in psychotherapy and uses a great deal of interpretation to the child of the feelings which she understands its play to represent. Christine Froude is a teacher in the school and has trained in art therapy. She tends to work within the symbolism of the child's play. This approach is more appropriate for adoption by workers who do not have supervision from a psychotherapist, and the following is her account.

Play therapy began 'officially' in this residential special school five years ago. When my colleague and I started we were working in an old pottery room, which, although wonderful for making a mess, was cold and draughty with no hot water and little privacy. At that time we were seeing two or three children whom we selected for individual therapy sessions. Since then we have come a long way. The old pottery room has been converted into two purpose-built rooms. One is large and contains sand, water, a dolls' house, paint, glue and many other art and play materials. It has a sink with hot and cold water, and one-way windows. It is ideal for children who need a larger experiential space. The other room is smaller and carpeted, with some less messy art and play materials, but it is generally a much 'quieter' and more contained space.

We now see 12 children for 50-minute therapy sessions on a weekly basis. This time is part of the school curriculum. A consultant psychotherapist visits once a month to supervise our work and to assess children who may benefit from the therapy that we have to offer.

I began seeing Phillip about two years ago when he was nine years old. He was referred because of his very aggressive behaviour towards other children and his inability to express his feelings through the normal channels of communication. His life had been one of confusion. He was one of five children. There was a question of sexual abuse towards his younger sister by his grandfather, and Phillip's natural father had left the family home a year or so before I began seeing him. Mother had a new common law husband and Phillip was beginning to show a lot of resentment towards this new father figure. On top of this he had been sent to our school because of his educational needs, so I suspected that he must have feelings of being sent away (punished?) and perhaps even responsible for events at home.

My initial aim was to help Phillip, through art and play, to express his feelings and, I hoped, come to terms with the new father figure and say goodbye to his natural father. I felt this was achieved quite successfully in the first few months of therapy. Phillip used clay models of dad and himself to express deep anger and resentment at dad's departure. Just before our long summer break he seemed calmer and happier than he had for some time. He put the clay dad away in the cupboard and said goodbye to him. It appeared that he was now ready to begin a new relationship with a new dad.

But the holiday brought about disastrous events for Phillip. His younger sister was taken into care and his grandfather was imprisoned. His new dad had sexually abused Phillip's 14-year-old aunt and had been banished from home awaiting prosecution. Phillip, quite naturally, returned to school in a totally chaotic state and our sessions reflected this. For several weeks he was unable to 'use' anything and could only dash around the room shouting and screaming, hide under tables and chairs, and attempt to destroy materials. This left me feeling exhausted and useless, and I felt all our good work had been undone by events outside our control. It was after this period of chaos, however, that the most important and revealing sessions began. It is those two or three sessions which I wish to report here, since they show how powerful is the art of play. For a child who could not say how he felt play revealed all and went some way towards the healing process.

It felt as if Phillip was very uncomfortable in the room. He was flitting anxiously from one activity to another, unable to sustain anything. I said to him 'I know you had a terrible holiday and you must be feeling very hurt and upset'. He nodded agreement. I suggested that at the moment it must be very hard for him to say how he feels and that it might help if he could use the dolls and the dolls' house. He said that he couldn't. However, when I told him that we had only five minutes left he fetched the house and pulled it apart. The whole house began to collapse and he said 'This is a useless house, it's just like a house in (the town where he lived)'. I said, 'Is this your house?' and he said 'Yes'.

In our next session he went straight to the broken house which was virtually as he had left it. He began to pull the furniture apart and then spent a long time trying to mend it, refusing my offers of help. He took the grandfather doll and put him in a bed. He then took several other dolls, pulled their legs apart and put them on the bed too. He hurled the grandmother doll to the floor and was very angry with her. He also pulled the feet off the girl doll (his attempt to stop her going away perhaps?). He then balanced the furniture all over the place, putting beds on the roof balancing over the edge of the building. He put the toilet in the bedroom. The whole scene was one of danger and chaos. He took a doll and said it was Spider Woman and made her try and fix things. I said, 'Can Spider Woman do anything right now?' He replied, 'She wants to but she can't'. Once again I was left feeling helpless. He then brought in Spider Baby (himself?) who also tried to sort things out but couldn't. I said, 'Do you think that if Spider Woman and Spider Baby work together they can do anything?' He tried this with the dolls but said 'No, they can't do it'. I asked if there was anyone who could help. He said 'Super Man can do it ... but he isn't here right now'. It was time for us to go. As we left he said, 'I'll need to use this again next time, I have so much to do'.

In the following session he used the sand tray and the dolls. He threw the family into the sand and said, 'This is quicksand'. I asked how they got there and he said 'The first dad did it'. He took the dolls and buried them, then rescued them. He did this over and over again. He then took the man doll and threw him into the sand with the rest of the family. I asked who this was and he said, 'It's the bad dad'. I asked if this was the real dad, he said 'Yes it is'. I asked who put him in the quick sand and he said, 'I did'. I said, 'You feel it is the real dad's fault and you are very angry with him'. He said, 'Yes'. He then took out the boy doll and the woman doll (Phillip and myself/mother?), washed them and put them in a jar of clean water; they were naked and upside down (quite a disturbing sight). He took the second dad figure and the girl doll, washed them, wrapped them up and put them in the top of the jar. Phillip put the jar on top of the cupboard 'where no one can touch them'. He was unable to do more with them and as we left he said, 'They'll have to stay there till next time!'. In fact those figures stayed up there for many weeks. He occasionally went to check that they were still there and to top the water up if necessary.

It is only very recently that Phillip has been able to remove the figures from the jar and it is obvious that he still feels very angry with them, throwing them into the sand tray and saying 'They stink'. As he did this I gently removed the boy doll from the pile, washed him, wrapped him in a paper towel and said to Phillip that I would look after this boy doll because I thought he was a very special doll. He seemed delighted at this and almost unbelieving. Since that time, myself, a teacher or a member of the care staff has taken care of the little 'boy'; Phillip chooses who. He has made the boy some clothes, a bed and blankets and he is at present building a model house. These actions reveal that despite all Phillip has developed some self-worth.

So ... there is no 'and they all lived happily ever after' ending to Phillip's story and play therapy has not cured all his problems, but he is less aggressive, he is able to cry (something he did not do before), he will allow himself to be comforted by a trusted adult. He talks, however tentatively, to those caring adults around him about how he feels about what is happening at home. I believe that our time together has given him a consistency that was so lacking in his young life and an opportunity to express his innermost fears and feelings in a safe way. I would hope that this space and the materials will be available to him for as long as he needs them.

Christine Froude's moving account shows non-directive play therapy at its best. Her whole approach indicates a willingness to be receptive to how Phillip is feeling and to what he might have a need to express, even when she is not sure she fully understands what is happening. She survives the period of chaos and feelings of being useless, offering real 'containment'. The strict time limits of the session help in this. When Phillip has difficulty in focusing on a medium for expression she acknowledges that feelings are difficult to talk about; she directs his attention to the doll family but accepts his initial rejection of this, leaving him free to return to it when he chooses. She works within the symbolism, using the third person to talk about the feelings of the boy doll and his family. There are echoes of Axline in the account of the quicksand. In a crucial intervention, still using the symbolism of play, she intervenes positively to take care of the boy doll. This taking care then becomes shared with other carers in the school, providing a wider therapeutic environment. Her intervention is particularly appropriate in a residential setting, where one of the school's roles is substitute parenting, if only in term-time. This work has a parallel in Christine Bradley's symbolic intervention to take care of a boy in residential care (see Chapter 9). Above all, Christine Froude's work reinforces the conviction that there are no short-cuts. Work must go at the child's pace and may take a long time.

PLAY FOR CHILDREN IN HOSPITAL

Hospital care for children has changed dramatically since John Bowlby and the Robertsons first demonstrated the harmful psychological effects on children of separation and loss. The importance of parents' presence is now much more widely understood (Robertson 1970). It is also recognized that the stress of a hospital stay can be further reduced and a child's recovery hastened by the provision of play. The Expert Group Report on the Role of Play for Children in Hospital (1976), the Platt Report, recommended play staff on every children's ward. Brimblecombe (in Weller and Oliver 1980) called attention to the value of professional hospital play specialists. Play work with children in hospital may also be carried out by nurses, nursery nurses (Dartington *et al.* 1976), hospital teachers or social workers (Crompton 1980). Play specialists are more common now but are still not found on all children's wards, and many children are still nursed in adult wards. A report from Save the Children Fund (1989) points out that most hospitals fail to provide adequate play facilities and calls for play provision to be a statutory responsibility.

Children's need for autonomy

Kathy Sylva (1986 and 1990) showed that children who suffered least stress from a hospital stay were those who felt that they had retained some control over what was happening. Their coping strategies were information seeking, securing and maintaining comfort, initiating and maintaining social control, and maintenance of their autonomy through play. Susan Harvey explains the importance of play provision which supports children's autonomy in helping them cope with their anxiety about what is happening to them. She stresses the need to avoid diversionary play.

Play which takes the initiative from the child, and gives him a passive role – play which becomes a diversion and a denial of what is happening – does not help him to come to terms with current experience. This is one important reason why the adult does not impose his own ideas, but takes all his cues from the child.

(Harvey 1984: 279)

Reducing anxiety through familiar play

Play is a normal developmental need of all children when they are in hospital, as well as a means for coping with the specific emotional stress of their stay. Children who may be in hospital for long periods have a particular need for adequate opportunities for play so that their normal development is not interrupted. Play specialists, whose training includes normal child development, the role of play, and communication with children, can provide this. Jean Gregg, hospital play therapist at Lord Mayor Treloar Hospital for children with physical disabilities, describes her provision of sensory play, based on the Snoezelen idea, for both stimulation and relaxation. Children explore the magical environment at their own pace.

My most recent development in the playroom was to set up a special cubicle to stimulate the senses, especially for mentally handicapped patients. It grew from work I'd read about in Holland and began with a soft area, flashing lights and a bubble machine. I began to find the area could be used with soft music for calming and relaxing, so it is great for babies on traction, with womb music, and without bubbles for pre-meds. Just recently the bubble machine has come into its own for encouraging mobility after plaster removal, and I'm about to start introducing smells. It has all been a surprising experience.

(Gregg 1988)

Play specialists may use play to welcome children, to help them to come to terms with the hospital environment, and to manage their fears about separation from parents and from familiar surroundings, as well as to prepare them for stressful procedures and to cope with their consequences, and to aid recovery. 'Play specialists do far more than occupy children. They can reduce uncertainty by providing play that is familiar, a welcome relief after all the strange sights, sounds and bodily discomfort' (Lansdown and Goldman 1988: 557). Even when parents are with the child in hospital the child is separated from familiar aspects of life at home. Play can make a link between hospital and life outside. Children need their normal play activities. Allowance may need to be made for the fact that their illness may lead to some regression in play; children often need play materials that are familiar rather than challenging.

Numerous ideas for normal play activities, from babyhood to adolescence, are found in the series of leaflets, *Let's Play*, produced by the National Association of Hospital Play Staff (NAHPS), and in publications of the National Association for the Welfare of Children in Hospital (NAWCH), such as *Messy Play in Hospital*. (Other sources of information and ideas on play provision in hospital are Lindquist (1977), Weller and Oliver (1980), Noble (1967), and Harvey and Hales-Tooke

(1972).) Play with unstructured materials such as sand and water can be soothing and relaxing for an anxious child. It enables regressive play without the child worrying about appearing 'babyish'. Sand and water play can be adapted for bed-bound children or children immobilized in plasters, or for children in isolation. Mobile children may have more autonomy in a playroom offering a variety of play materials and activities. It is, of course, important that the play materials reflect the different cultures of the children in hospital.

The role of parents

Children may find that their parents do not have the same role in hospital as at home and they may be confused by parents' loss of authority. Parents may find coping with their children and their illnesses in the hospital environment, where the normal parental roles are removed or modified, both frightening and exhausting. Whilst they need other forms of support too, their involvement in their child's play can give some relief and also give them an active role in helping their child, restoring their own autonomy and self-esteem as well as their child's. Respectful recognition of the parents' role is important. For example, 'Members of the oncology team can help parents by reassurance or by suggesting appropriate play techniques and approaches, but frequently we can stand back and learn from them' (Lansdown and Goldman 1988: 558). The play specialist can have an important role in enabling this, including recognizing differing attitudes to children, play and illness in families from different cultures. It is crucial that the attachment needs of mothers and children are understood. For example, 'mothers in special care baby units should hold their babies and talk and sing to them as they would at home' (National Association for the Welfare of Children in Hospital 1984).

Siblings

Play may also help siblings who often experience loss of attention and 'containment' because of their parents' focus on the sick child. They may pick up parents' feelings of confusion and anxiety. They may also feel guilty, believing, through 'magical thinking', that they have caused their sibling to become ill. Group work, particularly for siblings of children with long-term illnesses or disabilities, can be helpful in reducing their fantasizing and their sense of isolation.

Focused play in preparing children for medical procedures

Focused play techniques are often used to prepare children for surgery or other unpleasant procedures. The aim is to give children information about their treatment and to reduce their anxiety of the unknown. In play preparation programmes, sometimes even before admission to hospital, children are encouraged to play with nurses' uniforms, gowns and masks, anaesthetic masks, bandages, stethoscopes and syringes. Lynda Weiss, in 'Preparation for Surgery and Unpleasant Procedures'

(NAHPS *Let's Play* series) suggests that children up to six years old can be prepared in a group with their parents. Individual preparation is also possible, and for older children it is usually more appropriate. A teddy, puppet or doll is introduced as the patient who has arrived for an operation, and used to go through the pre-operative routine. The children are then invited to dress up and play with the equipment. As the children play it may become clear what they have understood; misconceptions can be picked up, as well as some idea of what questions and fears remain. Weiss emphasizes the need to speak to each parent and child individually after the group, encouraging the children to talk about the operation so that the worker can correct any misconceptions and help work through anxieties. The following example from Joy Pearce, hospital play specialist at Amersham Hospital, shows how the worker may need an empathic and imaginative approach to find a way into preparation for surgery.

> James was flitting from one end of the playroom to another in an almost frenzied state. I tried to get him to settle down by showing him some of our more interesting toys, and I tried to talk calmly to him but he could not keep still for a moment. After a while he walked over to the blackboard where there were some felt-tip pens and he began scribbling on a large piece of paper that was attached to the board. I took this opportunity and asked him what he had drawn. He replied, 'My dog'. I then asked him if he would like to see a picture of my dog and he said 'Yes'. I drew a picture of a large dog with huge paws and said that his name was Carlo. I then proceeded to tell him how Carlo had once needed to have an operation and he had come into hospital and the doctor had put Emla cream on his paws to make his paws numb. So when he had to have his injection he would not feel the needle, only a small scratch.
>
> James had become completely engrossed by this time and had relaxed considerably. We both drew the Emla cream on to the paws, and then we drew another dog and pretended that he was the doctor, drawing in his white coat and stethoscope. As I was drawing I was explaining to James that what had happened to Carlo, the dog, was going to happen to him. He was calm enough by this time to assimilate what I was saying to him. I tried to back up my preparation with the Operation Book but James refused to look at it, so I decided to leave well alone. After James had gone to theatre I asked his mother how he had reacted to all the medical procedures and she was quite relieved to say that he had coped quite well.
>
> (Pearce 1990: 16)

Other preparation techniques include the use of a home-made 'operations book' or short video illustrating the procedure, the use of drawing of body outlines, and the use of anatomical dolls and puppets. Anatomical dolls whose bodies can be opened should not be used unsupervised as they can frighten children unnecessarily. They are sometimes used to illustrate simple procedures beforehand but are probably more useful in post-procedural play. Procedures, such as injections or the insertions of lines, drains or catheters, may be best demonstrated on an ordinary teddy or doll. For example, 'A teddy bear with a ... catheter inserted in the appropriate place, in the hospital corner of the playroom, allows children to go through the event in anticipation and thus to have some sense of mastery over it' (Lansdown and Goldman 1988: 557).

Children often have a great fear of needles. Much play repeating a child's experiences involves injections. Crompton (1980) warns that the use of techniques such as practising injections on a 'scape-teddy' are only really valuable if they also permit the child to express fears rather than be offered bland reassurances. Lansdown suggests a number of techniques to avoid children feeling pain over injections. His suggestions include singing to and stroking the child to enable relaxation, using counting games, puzzles, games, jokes and stories, video and Walkman tapes, to help them to create a mental barrier to pain. Young children might be asked to help their 'sick' doll to overcome its fears. He describes the use of some of these approaches to help Sarah.

> Sarah was a six-year-old who had to be held down by three adults before a doctor could take blood. In conversation with her parents it was discovered that she wanted to be a nurse and that she liked the song *Yellow Submarine*. She was encouraged to sit on her mother's lap and listen to the story about a girl who became a student nurse. She had worked very hard to pass all her exams and she enjoyed her first day in the hospital but she did not like the second day at all because she had to learn to give injections. That meant that one of the student nurses had to practise on her, because all of the students had to practise on each other. And the girl in the story hated needles. The ward sister helped by explaining that there was a magic submarine in the basement of the hospital, and that once in this magic, yellow submarine, people could still feel a needle but it was nothing like as bad as it usually was: there was just a little feeling of pressure.
>
> Sarah's mother told this story a couple of times before the next appointment and on the day of the next blood test it was arranged that there should be a nurse's uniform in Great Ormond Street colours just the right size for her to wear. Her parents brought a Walkman with a Yellow Submarine tape and she sat on her mother's lap, listening first to the story and then to the tape. She put her arm out with some apprehension, but was able to have blood taken without a murmur.
>
> (Lansdown 1988: 16)

Deeper fears of pain and damage, separation and loss

Lynda Weiss (NAHPS) reminds us of Anna Freud's understanding that 'the response of children to surgery does not depend on the type or seriousness of the operation but on the type and depth of the fantasies aroused by it, mutilation, castration, abandonment and punishment'. Younger children are more likely to fear separation, older children pain, mutilation and even death. Play therapist Jean Gregg anticipates some needs by having kinds of play available, such as plastering dolls, but she is aware that the real need may turn out to be, for example, in a family where the parents' marriage is breaking up, the child's fear that mother will never return. She describes how one child, whose mother had died, had lain very still on the floor with his arms crossed. She did the same and role played his mother; she 'tried out' feelings with the child, saying 'I didn't want to leave you. I had pains in my head but they've stopped hurting now', and explaining that it was not his fault she had died. With another child she knew that his grandmother had recently died in hospital and was aware of the implications that this might have for his feelings about coming to hospital. Sinason (1990) describes how ten-year-old Jonathon's grandmother, who lived with him and his parents, suffered from headaches and told him his noisiness would be the death of her. She happened to go into hospital at the same time as he was having a tonsillectomy, which he saw as punishment for his speech organs. He became mute until helped by a child psychotherapist. In another example,

> Ten-year-old Mary needed a heart operation. In her drawing and plays she expressed the fear that she would lose her insides. Being shown educational diagrams of the heart did not help. She angrily tore the stuffing out of her teddy bear so that it lost its shape. Then she burst into tears. The hospital teacher helped Mary put the stuffing back in and sew the teddy up, showing how the stitches stopped the teddy's insides from falling out. After that Mary was able to face the operation more calmly.
>
> (Sinason 1990)

Drawing and painting often provide a ready means of emotional communication when other forms of play are less available, as with a child immobilized in bed. A seven-year-old with his leg in plaster after being hit by a car was refusing to eat or talk. He drew several small cars and one large car. Asked why one was large he said that that was the one that had knocked him down, and went on to explain what had happened and how he blamed himself for running across the road without looking. After this he became more lively and started to eat (Harvey 1987: 5).

Crompton (1980) gives a poignant account of using drawing with a dying child, a most painful area of work recently explored by Judd (1989). Recognition and 'containment' of children's feelings and fears require a worker who can bear to experience them. In a hospital setting it can sometimes be difficult to provide the worker with the containment which they in turn need to do this. Denial is an emotionally more comfortable response for staff constantly faced with potentially overwhelming distress. A team approach to dealing with the stress which all workers experience can be vital.

Dealing with anger

Children's anxieties and fears may, however, be more readily accepted than their anger. One hospital play therapist worked with a very angry child where the hospital's mismanagement of diagnostic tests had meant that the child was having to go home and to return at a later date. The child had been told off by a nurse for banging her hand repeatedly to such an extent that she had made it sore. The play therapist took the child into the playroom for an hour's anger session. The child used throwing, jumping and banging to express her feelings, which were acknowledged by the therapist. The session ended with music and a story, and a cuddle together. Whilst this was helpful to the child, the staff were angry with the therapist for pandering, as they saw it, to the child. The therapist was able to recognize their projected anger and guilt at the hospital's role in mismanagement.

This situation illustrates the particular difficulties of providing emotionally therapeutic play in a setting whose main purpose is other than this. The playroom is usually the play worker's main base, different in tone from other clinical areas, containing perhaps the comfort of familiar toys, sagbags, music and the clink of cups in the background. There, play can be provided within a safe physical boundary, with an adult who is alert to a child's signals of unhappy feelings which need to be acknowledged and worked with. Yet children mostly come into the playroom for a non-specific time, even if they regularly spend much time there. They may be alone, with parents, or part of a group of children and parents. Workers in this situation may not often plan individual play sessions with a child. Rather they will use their knowledge of the child and the family to help them to be responsive to needs as they are expressed. There has been some debate about how inviolable the playroom should be as a sanctuary for the child. Many workers feel that nursing and medical interventions *should* be allowed to take place in the playroom because there is a greater possibility of minimizing the child's anxiety in familiar surroundings. It is also necessary to work closely with other staff, especially where children cannot come to the playroom and need play taken to them in bed. The boundaries of play can often best be provided by the worker's presence.

Sometimes it is possible to negotiate uninterrupted individual play sessions with a child, in the playroom or in bed. Rosemary King (1988) describes her use of a specific uninterrupted playtime each day for children isolated in a bone marrow unit. She uses this time to give them some feeling of normality and a link with the outside world, providing a variety of activities to stimulate learning but also to help them to express emotion and cope with what is happening. Of messy play she writes:

> It is a positive way for them to 'unwind' from the stress caused by being on a unit such as this. I have found that a lot of children need much reassurance to use paint, dough and water as they normally would and still feel 'safe'. Messy play provides an excellent opportunity to use many of the threatening pieces of medical equipment in a non-threatening way, for example, syringe painting, water play, collage and printing. This also gives children a sense of control over these items, something which has been taken away in other respects, and gives them permission to express anger at the way the equipment has been used on them.

> (R. King 1988: 12)

Again we return to the need to allow expression of anger within the safe boundary of play. Play provision for this can include dough and clay, materials which can survive a child's anger, helpful in allowing a child to realize that anger can be expressed without destroying things, and people, that matter to them. Dressing-up, doll play and hospital equipment allow children to play at being doctor or nurse and 'treat' dolls and teddies, re-enacting their experiences and working through their feelings of anger and fear. The account of play therapy with Mark, earlier in this chapter, shows how a worker can support this healing process.

In conclusion, focused play techniques, used imaginatively and flexibly, provide children with information and a sense of the familiar, relieving anxiety and increasing their autonomy and their ability to cope with a stay in hospital. Reflective non-directive methods can reach much deeper feelings of fear and anger, and may help children to heal themselves through play.

Chapter 7

Play for children in bereavement and divorce

THE EXPERIENCE OF BEREAVED CHILDREN

When a child's parent dies the grief of the remaining parent is often so overwhelming that this parent is unable to recognize or cope with the grief of the child. It may be thought that children do not really understand about death and that it would cause unnecessary pain to involve them in the parent's grieving, whether through going to the funeral or seeing the parent cry. Because a child is not showing overt grief it may be assumed that the child gets over it quickly. In fact the evidence abounds that children have the same reactions to loss as adults (Bowlby 1980). These are initial shock and alarm, followed by numbness, denial and disbelief. Then follows a time of yearning and pining, and searching for the lost person, feelings of intense anger or guilt, mental disorganization and despair. If all goes well some kind of reorganization and reintegration is reached (Kubler-Ross 1970). The tasks of grieving are to accept the reality of the loss, to experience the pain of grief, to adjust to an environment in which the dead person is missing and, finally, to withdraw emotional energy and invest it in a new relationship (Worden 1983). The period of intense grief may be shorter for children than for adults, but the whole grieving process may take many years and is renewed at the milestones in life, such as changing school, birthdays or having their own baby, when the parent is again deeply missed (Hemmings 1990).

Whilst children have the same needs as adults they also have some additional ones. Younger children have a limited understanding of time. They also may not have grasped the irreversibility of death, and may expect the person to come alive again or to come back from hospital. This is more likely if they have not been involved in the death, through seeing the body or coffin, or sharing in other people's grief. Young children, generally those under eight years old, are likely to use 'magical thinking' to make sense of incomprehensible events. This may lead to intense guilt as they come to believe that some perceived misdeed or angry thought of theirs, which is linked in time with the death, is the cause of it (Wolff 1973). Feelings of extreme insecurity and anxiety are likely. If one parent has been lost then the child fears that this could happen again.

The death of a parent not only causes direct feelings of loss but often results in an upheaval in the child's world. At best the surviving parent has a changed role in the family. The child may be expected to take on a more responsible adult role, being told 'Look after your dad now', or 'You're the man of the family now'. For some the disruption may be more severe, involving new carers, such as a house-keeper, perhaps eventually a step-parent, or a foster family. These are likely to intensify a child's sense of grief and loss, and to involve a loss of identity and self-esteem.

The death of a brother or sister often results in the surviving child feeling guilt that it was not the one who had died. Brothers and sisters are always in competition with one another at some level. Death gives the survivor an unfair victory and a feeling of guilty triumph, as well as of loss, sometimes so severe as to lead to emotional disturbance (Sinason 1990). Again 'magical thinking' may lead children to blame themselves for their sibling's death. Before the death, siblings may have felt confused and isolated. Normal life disappeared and parents were often pre-oc-cupied, yet many have pretended all was well, fearing their own loss of control. Because of their own grief, parents may either not notice or not be able to bear their child's equal need to grieve. The parent may be unable to provide 'containment', whether in the short or long term, for their child.

Bereaved children are likely to have feelings of confusion and bewilderment, of insecurity, of guilt, of anger, of isolation, and of loss of identity and self-esteem. These can be expressed in a number of ways, from nightmares, enuresis and crying, to angry and difficult behaviour. Children have usually learned that they are expected *not* to talk about their feelings. In any case, many of their feelings are not experienced and thought about at a conscious level. Thus play methods have an important role in helping bereaved children to acknowledge and express their pain, in order that they may be able to cope better with their lives now and in the future.

A number of children are bereaved by one parent killing the other. These children are at severe risk of post-traumatic stress disorder and should be treated immediately, and only, by skilled child psychotherapists (Black 1990).

THE USE OF PLAY IN HELPING BEREAVED CHILDREN

All About Me is a game to help children to talk about their feelings about death and bereavement, devised by Peta Hemmings, a project worker based at Barnardo's Orchard Project in Newcastle, a support service for bereaved families and people with terminal illnesses. The game was initially invented to help one child. Hemm-ings writes:

> Michelle's mother recently died of cancer. She had major problems dealing with the intense anger she felt at her mother's death and released that anger by punching people. She was keen on board games and this was the way she felt able to articulate the anger and frustration she felt inside.
>
> (Hemmings 1990: 16)

The game is based on Snakes and Ladders, using a dice to indicate how far each person should move forwards or back. On landing on a square the player picks up a card, on which is written a question or sentence to be completed. These range from simple questions such as 'my favourite programme' or 'my favourite colour' to more complex and painful feelings. Hemmings' experience is that children find this game unthreatening and they quickly relax and start to talk about feelings which may have been bottled up for some time. The game gave Michelle permission to feel angry and to express her anger. She became able to talk about her mother. 'She visits her grave with her father and they cry together. The punching has stopped. Michelle and her dad have learnt to share the emotions they both feel over their loss' (Hemmings 1989: 11).

Young children who cannot conceive of the irreversibility of death can come to understand it better through a powerful technique used by Marion Burch, a professional foster parent in Hull. She sits with the child in a darkened room lit by a lamp, talking about how life is like electricity or light. She switches off the light and plunges the room into darkness, showing how life is cut off by death. Following this she finds that a child can visit the cemetery much more easily and accept that there is nothing living there. It is important that any worker using this approach is ready to accept strong feelings which may be unleashed, whether of sadness or anger.

Eve Banks and Sarah Mumford (in Aldgate and Simmonds 1988) show how the expression of anger enables the process of grieving. Mumford used a set of small knitted dolls to represent the family of a bereaved four-year-old boy who was living with foster parents. She wanted him to know that it was not his fault that his mother had died and that it was safe to express his anger at her leaving him, which she had not wanted to do. John named the dolls spontaneously and spent much time putting the mother and John dolls together and then separating them. A doctor doll was told off and hit for his failure. John once expressed his anger by tying up the mother doll and dragging her round the floor. The worker listened and repeated back to him what he was doing, with some questions for clarification and, later in therapy, occasional suggestions. By the last session John had worked through his anger. He sadly kissed the mother doll goodbye and put her away in the bag.

This example is of relatively early intervention, in accordance with crisis theory; sound intervention at a time of crisis may have long-lasting effects since patterns of response established then are likely to be repeated. The child who is helped to face grief will not only be better equipped to cope emotionally from day to day but will also not be quite so vulnerable to future loss.

Unresolved mourning in a surviving parent which affects the ability of that parent to help the child to grieve can lead to angry behaviour from the child, a projection of the parent's anger, which may then be punished. A four-year-old boy with 'behaviour problems', who had witnessed his father's accidental death, was given help in six individual sessions, whilst his mother watched through a one-way screen. He used a frieze with illustrations of monsters from Sendak's *Where the Wild Things Are* to help to express his anger at his father's death. The mother's therapist then used the same story to show the mother that angry feelings could be safely expressed in fantasies provided they have a secure boundary (Muir, Speirs and Tod 1988). In Sendak's story, Max is angry at being told off by his mother for his wild behaviour. In imagination he sails off to the land of the 'wild things' where he becomes their king, only returning when he becomes lonely, to 'his very own room where he found his supper waiting for him and it was still hot'.

A ten-year-old boy had repressed his grief at the death of his much loved grandmother three years previously to such an extent that his ability to read and write were affected. The therapist's focused drama and play techniques included drawing a picture of the grandmother, burying her in the sand, and writing a memorial album using memories and photographs. The boy became free to mourn, freeing the family to mourn too and visit the grave for the first time (Nilman and Lewin 1989).

Group work with bereaved children

Group work may often be an appropriate way of helping bereaved children. The similarities in children's experience may be greater than the differences. Children may therefore find it helpful to realize that their experience is not an isolated one and they may draw support from one another. Children's groups have been set up by the bereavement organization Cruse (Johnston 1990). Accounts of two other groups, one for children whose parent had died, led by social workers, the second for children whose sibling has died in a cot death, led by a clinical psychologist and a health visitor, illustrate the way in which play techniques can help children in groups.

Margaret Pennells and Sue Kitchener (1990) have run groups in Northampton-shire for children aged seven to ten whose mother or father has died. They wanted to help the children to grieve, and to express and deal with any fears and concerns, enabling them to adjust positively to their changed life. After introductions and ice-breakers the first sessions start with positive memories of the parent who has died, using stories and painting, as well as a memento of the parent. Later sessions look at more painful memories, as each child tells about what happened and its feelings about it. These include feelings of responsibility – for example, 'If only I didn't go to school and helped mum more she wouldn't have died'. The leaders continue:

> They draw faces of how they felt, act out their feelings and give each other support through their sadness and anger. Most children feel anger at not being allowed to go to the funeral or not being told what was going on at the time. They felt outsiders.
> Some have a confused idea as to what a funeral is, mixing it up with paying a visit to the graveside. So we ask them to act out a funeral and with the aid of a dressing-up box, they produce a play of what they think went on.
>
> (Pennells and Kitchener 1990: 14)

Ideas and fears of heaven and hell, ghosts and angels, dreams and nightmares, are explored, often helped by drawing. Children role play how to cope with nightmares, so realizing they have common fears. They also role play ways of coping with angry feelings as well as coping with thoughtless children at school. These led to increased confidence. Finally they draw how they will see themselves in a year's time, leading to a positive discussion of 'how they will cope and go forward'. After a last session of fun and goodbyes they leave with a poster which they have been working on throughout the weeks. Follow-up indicated that the children were suffering less from crying, nightmares and enuresis.

The group for children whose sibling has died in a cot death (Sudden Infant Death Syndrome) consisted of five children aged four to seven, younger than in the other group. The group leaders were concerned that through normal jealousy the children might have 'wished away' the new baby, resulting not only in guilt but in terrifying feelings of power. They might have fears that they too might die. The eight group sessions, at Kingston Hospital, took place after school.

In the first two weeks getting-to-know-you games, drawing each other and round each other, were intended as a gentle introduction. In fact the children quickly announced 'We're here because our babies died', and wanted to talk about why they had died. Two further sessions explored distressed and confused and, above all, angry feelings. One child 'repeatedly drew pictures of black monsters who would "kill everyone", including, it was made clear, the therapists'. Anger directed at the leaders in physical attacks was re-directed to hitting or punching an 'angry cushion' which every child used at some point. The next two sessions were devoted to the theme of loss, and the pain and fears which result.

> The children drew pictures of their families, and several of them described spontaneously that their families were 'looking for something that they've lost ... but won't find it'. They drew pictures of their dead siblings, and, again spontaneously, each child related where she/he had last seen the baby and how the baby had died. This was a very sad session, and.... following these accounts of the babies' deaths, the group ALL *en masse* decided to go to the toilet, leaving the two therapists alone: thus we all had 'a break'.
>
> (Krasner and Beinart 1989: 14)

With only little help the children made up a story about a princess whose cat had died. They said she would be sad for a long time although her parents had told her to try to forget her cat. One child was frightened that the princess would fall down and die too, but was reassured by a child less recently bereaved that the princess would grow up and become a queen. The children returned to the story in the next session, wondering if a good fairy could bring back the dead cat or 'magic' a new one into being the dead cat. With help, the children decided it would be better for the princess to love the new cat for itself. The children seemed to reach the concept of the irreversibility of death as they decided that 'this kind of magic "couldn't really happen", but that the princess would never forget her old cat'. The last session was a party with games.

Through the lives of these two groups the needs of bereaved children become clear, both the needs which they share with bereaved adults and their particular needs as children. Play techniques, especially drawing and painting, and the use of stories and fantasies, often drawing inspiration from Oaklander (1978) and Jewett (1984), help children to express their feelings, of profound anger as well as of sadness, and to begin to accept the irreversibility of death.

CHILDREN IN DIVORCE

Children whose parents divorce suffer a form of bereavement. The loss of a parent from the family through divorce gives rise to similar feelings and a similar process of grieving to loss through death. The loss in divorce may not be final as in death, although many children do lose touch with one parent, but it involves loss of familiar patterns of roles and relationships in family life. It certainly involves separation and the anxiety which results from loss of an attachment figure. Divorce often entails conflict and intense acrimony between the parents which complicates the emotional situation for the child. It often leads to a change in circumstances, sometimes a move away from familiar places, away from friends and relatives, and a change in standard of living.

Children's reactions to divorce are likely to follow the general pattern of reactions to separation and loss, with initial shock and disbelief, confusion, fear, anxiety about whether they will be looked after, extreme anger and great sadness. Young children, using 'magical thinking' to explain situations which make no immediate sense often feel guilty, blaming themselves for their parents' divorce. They may pick up notions of blaming, placating or rescuing their parents and punishing themselves. '"The two walls of the house are collapsing and I am left trying to hold the roof up" is how one 12-year-old described his parents' divorce' (McFerran 1989). The divorcing parents, embroiled in their own conflicts, may be unaware of how their children are feeling and may under-estimate their children's distress. Their own distress may mean that they are unable to give their children appropriate help. When one in three marriages ends in divorce the scale of the problem is immense.

Children in divorce need an explanation of what is happening and why. They need to know that the divorce is not their fault. They need a reassurance, if possible, of continued love and care. A complete and clean break with a parent has been shown to be the most damaging. Children need to be free to maintain a relationship with the absent parent and to have a means of keeping in touch. They need to have their feelings recognized, especially by their parents, and to have these feelings kept separate from their parents' conflicts. These are the findings of research studies, described in Mitchell (1985), Walczak and Burns (1984), Lund (1984), and Howard and Shepherd (1987) in Britain, and by Wallerstein and Kelly (1980) in the United States. Garwood (1989) includes an invaluable summary of research about children in divorce.

The role of conciliation

The involvement of children in conciliation offers a way of meeting some of their needs, by helping children to express their views and by improving communication between parents and children. Fiona Garwood, of Family Conciliation Scotland, carried out a study of the Lothian Family Conciliation Service (Garwood 1989). She found that a conciliator sometimes saw children with their parents but more often children were seen separately, sometimes in preparation for a family session or a meeting with parents. Children were usually seen with brothers and sisters, and some children later said that they would have preferred to have been seen separately. The setting was informal, with drawings and paintings by other children on the walls, which some children said had helped them to realize that they were not the only children involved in divorce. Conciliators first explained or discussed with the children why they were there – for example, 'to have their say' or 'to help parents with their plans' (Garwood 1989: 30). Whilst sessions consisted mainly of discussion some play methods were used, particularly with younger children where toys, books, drawing and painting, charts and diagrams helped them to relax and encouraged them to talk and raise questions. (Family Conciliation Scotland is now producing *Me and My Changing Family*, a special workbook for children.) The need for appropriate methods for communicating with children is clear from the comments of some children who later said that they could not always understand what the conciliator was saying.

Garwood writes:

In some cases the material used in the conciliation sessions made a very clear impression. One seven-year-old girl remembered a book, *Dinosaur's Divorce*, containing a calendar which she had subsequently copied at home and used to mark the days when she and her sister were due to visit their father. Two boys recalled how they had drawn a picture of their family home, before explaining to the conciliator about the changes that had taken place in their home.

(Garwood 1989: 32)

Subjects raised were access arrangements, children's feelings about the separation or divorce, and their relationships with parents and their new partners. Garwood continues:

Children sometimes asked the conciliator to take some sort of action on their behalf or convey a message to their parents. One five-year-old boy, whose father sometimes travelled by plane to visit him, drew a picture of a plane ... He carefully signed it and asked the conciliator to have it in the room when his parents next met to discuss access. A boy of six used Lego to build the house where he visited his mother. He demonstrated some of his fears through his play and this helped his parents to understand his feelings and they subsequently modified the access arrangements.

(Garwood 1989: 34)

Garwood emphasizes that the success of involving children in conciliation depends on parents being committed to take joint responsibility for the issues their children raise and for making ultimate decisions about their children's future. Children need to be willing to come, and to be clear about why they are being seen. Conciliators should avoid secrets between themselves and the child. For example, a nine-year-old who was reading *Dinosaur's Divorce* with his mother 'stopped at a page about people who can help and asked if he could speak to someone'. He came with his younger brother and drew pictures whilst a conciliator noted the questions they raised. The brothers wanted to know what a divorce was, whether they would still see their dad when they moved house, if mum and dad would still be friends, and who would look after them after school. The conciliator helped them to ask their questions at the family meeting the next week, and the parents responded positively (Garwood 1990).

The benefits to children from being involved in conciliation, Garwood concluded, were children's relief at being able to talk to someone about how they felt and improved communication in the family, including better access arrangements.

Play techniques in divorce court welfare work

The divorce court welfare officer, who is a member of the probation service, may be asked to make an assessment for the court of the feelings and views of children whose parents are separating, especially where questions of access/contact and custody/residence arise. The 1989 Children Act requires that the child's welfare should be the paramount consideration 'when the court determines any question with respect to the upbringing and property of the child'. The court must ascertain the child's wishes and feelings without putting 'undue pressure on the child'. This is not a straightforward task of asking children with whom they would like to live. Children, above all, want their parents to stay together. As we have shown they may have confused and guilty feelings about their role in the separation and about what they should do now. Once they have reached the point of feeling that they would be happier living with one parent rather than the other, it is still the parents' task, with help if necessary, to decide on the future care of their children. Children may be seen on their own or in family sessions. At the same time as establishing children's feelings and views a court welfare officer can be engaged in conciliation to help the parents to make the best possible arrangements for their children and end their marriage in the least harmful way.

The court welfare officer is unlikely to have time for more than the bare minimum of sessions with children in which to establish communication and to come to some understanding of how they perceive the situation and how they feel, hence the need for a means of establishing rapport quickly. Lisa Parkinson (1987) describes how a friendly play environment can help children to feel secure enough to share feelings, which they may be unable to put into words, with people they hardly know. Carefully chosen play materials can help children and parents to discuss problems and possible solutions. Even pre-verbal children can absorb a great deal through the tone and manner of what is said, and parents may learn from observing their reactions. For example, Garwood describes how a young child's play in the room where his parents were meeting became more frantic when their voices were raised. His parents were able to notice and recognize this; it proved a useful point. Parkinson suggests play materials, including Uniset stick and peel houses, play people, finger and glove puppets, and paper and drawing materials. These can be used, for example, to rehearse with a family how they will manage an access visit. Jigsaws, with figures that fit into a wooden frame, can help children and parents to look at who fits where in the child's daily life and to realize that each has something different to offer. This can be helpful to separated fathers who often have no clear role in the divided family.

A roundabout, with figures flying out of their seats, might trigger discussion of the family coming apart (McFerran 1989). Pulling one part of a hanging mobile and asking what happens is a technique used by family therapists O'Brien and Loudon (1985) to help a family to understand that everyone in a family is affected when one member is disturbed. They also use balloons to demonstrate the effects of stress, and weighing scales to illustrate emotional imbalances in families. Parkinson recommends these techniques for work with separating families. She also adopts their idea of using a model family and wooden rods of differing lengths 'to illustrate a child's need for firm links and boundaries, as well as showing who is in contact with whom' (Parkinson 1987: 67).

Rosemary Gordon (1986), at the time a divorce court welfare officer in Leicester, used play in therapeutic work with individual children of separating parents. Whilst recognizing children's need for explanations and information she believes that they need, above all, to express their grief. She used a wooden mosaic set to represent the family of ten-year-old Jenny, making patterns showing how the family used to live together and helping her talk about moves away, close relationships and new family members. Asked to show how she would like things to be Jenny put her mother back in the family, despite reports that she did not think about her mother whom she had last seen five years before.

With 12-year-old David, Gordon used a graffiti wall. They drew a wall covered with all the words or slogans associated with family separation, such as tomorrow, school, being alone, fear and death. They played the Faces Game, drawing what the face feels like when it thinks about ... making a meal for the family, the past, facing a new family. She asked David to show her how he would draw the family in shapes and colours, explaining that we all have our smooth sides and our jagged bits. He drew a perfect orange circle for mother; sister was almost a circle with points or 'grumpy bits'; dad was a few harsh strokes in the far corner of the paper. Gordon saw this as alignment with mother, showing David's need to sacrifice one parent for his dependency on the other.

With seven-year-old Wayne, Gordon used the Faces Game to ask 'What does the face look like when mum rings up?' Its confused and partly neutral expression suggested that he was distancing himself from the choice of one parent or the other by displaying little emotion.

Jewett (1984) and Oaklander (1978) provide the inspiration for many of Gordon's play techniques in helping children to cope with their grief at the loss of their family. As well as the techniques described she uses role play, body sculpturing, music, and talking about angry or sad feelings as shapes or sounds. Anger is invariably a part of grief, which children need to be able to feel and then express physically. Suggestions include punching a pillow or cushion, tearing up newspaper, kicking a can, hitting a bed with a racquet or bat, writing all the bad words they can think off, drawing, painting or modelling their anger. They also need to put their anger into words and to say them to the source, such as speaking to the figure in a drawing, or to an imagined person sitting in an empty chair. At a later stage, children need to be able to reflect on their anger, on what causes it, how they feel and how they express it. Gordon finds that children are already actively involved in seeking ways of coping with their problems. She aims to re-direct this problem-solving activity into ways that might reduce stress and induce change.

In working with a child, Gordon emphasizes the need for comfort, quiet and privacy, with play materials carefully selected and attention given to cultural and environmental influences in the child's life. The worker begins where the child is and follows the child's cues, whilst establishing mood, purpose and pace, providing direction without intrusion. Direct questions are avoided and 'show me' is preferred to 'tell me'. The child's confidentiality is respected. It is important to be responsive to distress or withdrawal, and not to push the child too far. The worker should 'remember every child's right to know "Who am I?", "Why am I here?", and "What's going to happen next?"'(Gordon, in *What About Me?*, a booklet produced by Leicestershire Court Welfare Service).

Court welfare officer, Jackie Kiggell, in Leicester, usually sees children initially in the context of a family interview. She tells families that the court makes decisions but does not have solutions, and she helps the family to work out a solution for itself – for example, over access and custody. Normally she reports back to the court after ten weeks. Where the family cannot reach agreement she puts forward 'assessed alternatives'. She uses a variety of play activities in her work with families, finding that sometimes parents play as much as the children. For example, parents and children who have not seen each other for a while might be encouraged to draw and discuss their respective environments. She helps them to ask questions about each other's drawings and find out information. Most frequently she uses mosaics, small wooden brightly coloured diamond and triangular shapes, obtainable from toyshops. She describes her approach in *What About Me?*

> Ask the children to select a wooden mosaic to represent each relevant family member (or involved party) and suggest the larger diamond shapes for the adults and the smaller triangular ones for the children. Then show them how these pieces can form many different patterns – they may be cohesive, or have the points of one sticking into the sides of the other, or maybe partly touch, or not touch at all. Next explain how each family has its own pattern and ask if they will show how they usually see their own family pattern. Then point to various

pieces and explore how 'comfortable' or 'muddled' that piece may feel and that piece's perception of the other mosaics.

If there is a lot of discomfort and distress in the pattern ask the children to select a duplicate set of mosaics and arrange them in the pattern they think would feel most comfortable. The visual impact frequently has a catalytic effect on the family, and then together you can explore various avenues of movement from the present pattern to the preferred pattern. The mosaics have a visual impact which ... helps to keep the participants task-oriented and more objective as they seek to re-define their family goals, (and) facilitate children's abilities to communicate their emotions.

(Leicestershire Court Welfare Service, undated: 20)

Jackie Kiggell describes the use of mosaics in helping one family to decide where the child should live. She writes:

I was asked to do a wardship report for Billy, aged seven, who was living with his grandmother (the plaintiff). His mother (the defendant) was claiming custody. I saw the grandmother and her sister, and Billy's mother and her fiancé all together at the office, the two others being invited by the family as they were involved with Billy. Billy had been invited to that first meeting but his grandmother chose not to bring him. At that meeting mother and grandmother's sister suggested that I saw Billy alone, the latter offering to bring Billy to the office, to which all agreed. It was also agreed that I would then see Billy at both his mother's and grandmother's homes to share our session together with him present.

I duly saw Billy. After some general chat and exploring the room I explained, in terms he could understand, that lots of people had different family patterns and asked him to show me his. I used the mosaics to give him some examples. He made a pattern, alternating himself between his gran's and his mother's. He moved himself freely between both households, but each time put himself firmly into his mother's and into gran's more peripherally. He did this however many times we might come back to it and look at different possible shapes (Figure 7.1).

We looked at the first pattern he could remember, which was mum and Billy close together. He took the patterns through, remembering that when his mother had taken him to his gran's she had said 'for three days', and gran had said 'for ever, not three days'. He then explored with the patterns how things might be. His preferred option was to be based in his mother's household and to see his gran frequently, but he did not want to hurt anyone.

With some reluctance but amazingly accurate recall, Billy subsequently shared the patterns he had shown me with his mother and then with his grandmother. From the outset Billy was aware that any final decisions as to his future would be decided by his family or, failing that, the court. His mother and gran's sister were concerned that gran was denying Billy's love for his mother and his wish to spend more time with her. Gran was anxious that she would not

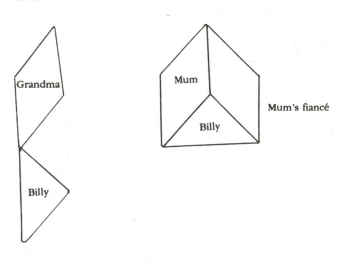

Figure 7.1   Billy's mosaics

see Billy if he went to his mother's because of the animosity between herself and his mother. Since Billy was able to show that he wished he could be with mum but wanted to see gran regularly the family agreed to a trial period in which to do this.

Jackie Kiggell and Rosemary Gordon used focused play techniques to help children to express feelings and to help their families understand these feelings and make decisions about their children's future, in the short time available. Some children, seriously disturbed by their parents' divorce, may benefit from a longer period of therapy. Such was the need in the following account of a less focused form of work.

Play in the work of a children's divorce counsellor

Lesley Aberdein, an educational psychologist, is Children's and Young People's Divorce Counsellor for Aberdeen Voluntary Service. She offers support and help to children of school age (between five and sixteen years) who are experiencing difficulties as a result of their parents' separation or divorce. She illustrates her non-directive methods of work in the following case study.

Jason, ten years old, was referred to me by a learning support teacher who had been concerned about him for some time. He often had not completed homework and had several times revealed that he was distressed by his parents' arguments. Interviews with parents separately showed that arguments frequently involved physical violence, during which Jason and his younger sister were often present. Jason would try to stop the rows by creating a distraction, usually something particularly naughty. His sister would go upstairs, open the windows and scream. Counselling was offered to both parents and children.

I saw Jason weekly in the playroom. He had a free hand to choose any of the play materials available, which included paint, crayons, clay, chalk, puppets, punchbags, dolls' houses, toy telephones and sand. During many of the initial sessions he chose the same items again and again, sand, paint, puppets and the punchbag. Jason's parents split up, eventually divorcing and each setting up house with new partners. I continued to see Jason over the next two years. Two sessions in the playroom after the parental split are summarized here.

Jason arrived with mum who said he was desperate to talk to me about the situation; she added privately that he had behaved very badly that morning. Later Jason told me about it and added that mum had told him he was just like his father and complained that he did nothing but think of his dad. Jason chose to make a mask and spent the rest of the session painting and cutting out a horrific, ugly, monster-like face, which he finally finished and put on. I asked if he ever felt like the monster he had painted and he said he did. He felt sure mum saw him as a monster because he was always doing naughty things at home, and because he wanted to be with his dad. For the last few minutes Jason thwacked the punchbag with venom. I asked him if there was anyone he would really like to thump, and he replied, 'Everyone in my family'.

A week later Jason came in with dad, holding his hand tightly. He was smiling and clearly delighted to be with his father. Dad left, promising Jason he would see him soon. Today Jason wanted to paint. His painting looked like a cracked window and I reflected this back to him. He agreed, then began to colour in one of the cracked pieces a different colour. I asked why part of one window was different and he replied that that was dad's. Like the window his family had split but it was dad who had left, causing the break-up. It was his fault and so dad's part was to be a different colour. I suggested that just as broken windows could be replaced by new ones a broken family can also be replaced. The new family, like the new window, would not be the same as the old one but it could eventually be as good as before. Jason looked at me long and hard, then said, 'We had a window which got broken once. We got a new one, and' (here he paused, then continued in a definite, set tone) 'it was exactly the same as the old one!' Jason was not ready or willing to accept the parental split and remained very angry with dad for some months.

After this, Jason began to paint again. I looked at it and confessed I found it difficult to make out what he had drawn. 'Look, there's the flowers round about. Does that give you a clue?' I admitted it didn't. 'Look, it's a coffin. Those are all the flowers round it.' I asked what was in the coffin. 'My family. My family is dead.' We talked about how he felt about the break-up. He expressed anger towards mum who had a boy-friend and would not consider a reconciliation, despite dad's wish to return. He moved to the sandpit and began to bury every single toy. I suggested that there were times when he felt like burying himself away from all the unhappiness around him. He agreed and said 'Sometimes I just feel like hiding so that I can't see or hear what they are saying. Then when I come out I'll find the family is like it was before.'

Jason at first used the opportunities in the playroom to express his anger at the loss of his family. His monster masks also suggest some feelings of guilt, although this is not explored further. Children in divorce often wrongly believe that their own bad behaviour is the cause of break-up. Although Jason's talk also showed his anger with his parents, his paintings revealed a profound sense of grief and loss as he recognized the death of his family. This grief needed recognition and acceptance rather than assurance that all would be well. This account shows how in a long-term relationship with an accepting counsellor Jason was able to make use of symbolic play to help him to integrate and express his feelings, eventually becoming able to put them into words where they could be thought about.

Group work for children of separating parents

Many children in Garwood's Scottish study were interested in taking part in a children's group, where they could meet others in similar situations. Leicestershire Court Welfare Service have regularly run a children's group as part of their divorce experience course for parents. Their booklet *What About Me?* suggests guidelines for these groups. Their aims are to help children to realize that they are not alone in their experience of divorce, to give them an opportunity to talk about things that may be difficult, forbidden or taboo elsewhere, in the presence of an attentive and accepting adult, to act out situations and to empathize with others, and to learn that it is not their fault. They can learn too that they are not passive victims but can make choices and act on them. Since children only come on one occasion, the last evening of the course, the aim is for the evening to be enjoyable and not 'open wounds that you haven't time to heal'.

A session begins with introductions, 'Who are we?'. For younger children, clapping and ball-catching naming games, making badges, or using action songs such as Five Currant Buns make good ice-breakers. For children aged eight or over, paired introductions based on pets, pastimes and parents can be added. Trust or relationship games are suggested, some derived from the I T Resource Centre's *Youth Games Book*. The next stage, 'Where are we and what is it like?', encourages children to explain their present situations and how they feel, breaking down their sense of isolation. Using a play street map (or cardboard houses), a bus, and play people, children are asked in turn to demonstrate who they live with, where the other parent lives, and what they do when they see them. (This can be written up and illustrated on the wall.) Or children might draw the two homes showing the people in them. Older children can draw a genogram or family tree, showing who lives with whom. Mosaics can be used too.

In the Faces Game, children are asked to draw faces to match how they feel 'when I think of school', ... 'when my parents don't know how confused I am', ... 'when I feel lonely inside', ... 'when my parents fight', ... 'when I go to bed at night'. Younger children can be given outline faces and asked to add a mouth to indicate happy, sad, angry or puzzled feelings for different situations. Drawings are shared and used to stimulate discussion. Older children can use sentence completion games to explore feelings, using phrases such as 'I get angry when ...', 'My biggest fear is ...', 'The trouble with dad is ...'. Listening or moving to music, using musical instruments, using clay or play dough, or drawing feelings in shapes and colours are suggested as other ways of expressing feelings. Children can make each other into shapes – for example, ' the sad shape she feels when dad doesn't turn up as promised'. Older children may be able to use the group members to 'sculpt' their family. Oaklander's guided fantasies may be used.

The third stage of groupwork continues the process of exploring feelings, but goes on to explore 'What can we do about it?' It aims to help children to realize that they can make active choices and are not passive victims of the situation. Using the 'faces', children are asked 'What can we do with angry/sad/happy feelings?' and how to tell a parent how they feel – for example, saying 'Mummy, this is my sad shape'. Group worker Maxine Costelloe suggests a group story or role play, such as the divorce of The Three Bears. Ways of dealing with anger, described earlier, may be explored. The 'empty chair' can be used not only to express anger with someone but as a way of practising anything that needs to be said to the person. Children can also pretend to be the parent or person responding, which is a useful means of getting some insight into their feelings too.

An interesting exercise about making choices is My Goal. The meaning of a goal is discussed, using general goals such as reading, passing music exams, getting a swimming badge or making the football team. Then together group members choose a goal and write up the 'benefits' of achieving it and the 'burdens' or consequences of not achieving it. The group leader suggests applying this to situations at home, such as those already described in using the 'faces' or the 'empty chair'. *What About Me*? gives the following example:

> My goal is to tell dad next Saturday when I visit that I don't like baked beans any more. (They used to be my favourite.)

> Benefits – I won't have to eat them any more, I won't feel sick at dinner-time, I won't worry about going so much.

> Burdens – I will have to force myself to eat them and feel sick, I will probably look upset and dad'll wonder why, I will start to put off going until after dinner even though I want to see him.

The final stage of the group, 'Endings? What now?', is important and not to be rushed. A shared activity, such as collaborative drawing, reinforces the idea that children are not alone. Children might be read a story, such as Althea's *I Have Two Homes* for the youngest, *When Gemma's Parents Got Divorced* for older children, and excerpts from Townsend's *The Diary of Adrian Mole* for teenagers. The session ends with goodbye games. These and numerous other ideas are included in *What About Me*?

We have seen how play methods are used in work with children and families at different stages in separation and divorce. At the point of separation, conciliation, whether in a voluntary or statutory organization, can help families to make the least damaging arrangements for their children. Play, using mainly focused techniques, gives children an opportunity to express how they feel and facilitates communication in the family. If difficulties arise later – for example, over contact and residence – similar methods may be used. Some children who become emotionally disturbed may benefit from individual non-directive play therapy and counselling. The large numbers of children involved in divorce make group work a feasible way of supporting them. The Leicestershire Court Welfare Service provides a valuable model for group work, using many play techniques, which could be followed more widely.

Chapter 8

The use of play in helping sexually abused children

Recent awareness of the sexual abuse of children has caused considerable anxiety among workers as they search for appropriate skills in communicating with children who may have been abused. Workers' own reactions to abuse are invariably strong. Feelings of anger, disgust and revulsion may cloud initial judgments of the best way to help the child. The child who perceives a worker's shocked reaction will beat a rapid retreat, confirming its impression that the subject is not acceptable and cannot be discussed. Therefore the workers' first task is to become aware of their own reactions to abuse, so that these cease to take them by surprise. Many training courses use experiential methods which can help with this. Then workers are more able to offer an open and accepting response to children's communication, able to empathize with a child's pain, guilt or confusion without being overwhelmed by it. Support and consultation need to be available as a matter of course for any adult working with abused children.

COMMUNICATION THROUGH PLAY WHERE ABUSE IS SUSPECTED

Workers, usually under-fives workers and teachers in schools, who are in daily contact with normal children are in a good position to be alert to signs of distress in a child. Children under five who have been abused are likely to be extremely confused and unhappy, sometimes with feelings of shame and guilt. Bentovim *et al.* (1988) notes that pre-school children tend to show sexualized behaviour, and regressive behaviour, such as wetting, soiling, eating problems and sleep disturbance. They may have fears of specific rooms, such as the bathroom, or of particular people, such as men of a given size or hair colour. Older children have much stronger feelings of stigmatization and shame, of having a terrible secret to hide, of feeling dirty, and of feeling powerless and betrayed. They have found that the most important adults in their lives are not to be trusted. Worse, they come to believe that it is their fault that they have not been looked after; their self-esteem is extremely low. Sometimes their school work may be poor as they find it difficult to concentrate. Their feelings may be variously expressed, in 'acting'-out unmanageable behaviour, in withdrawn and depressed behaviour, in tummy pains or illness, or in highly conformist 'good' behaviour, perhaps staying close to the teacher. Girls are likely to end up as typical 'victims'; boys are more likely to identify with the aggressor. However, factors other than sexual abuse can cause these sorts of behaviour and a worker or teacher is simply alerted to the possibility.

Familiarity with normal development and play in under-fives leads workers to notice a child whose response to adults or whose play is unusually sexualized and goes beyond normal mummies and daddies, or doctors and nurses, play. Four-year-olds are interested in sexual differences and may explore them in play, but a detailed enactment of sexual intercourse or of sexual variations is unlikely and should raise questions as to the source of their knowledge. With children of school age, as well as being alert to more general signs of distress, teachers may become concerned if they observe sexually explicit play in the playground or if a child behaves in a sexualized way – for example, a boy getting out his penis and pulling down a girl's pants in the toilets.

Whilst children's play may also give warning signals it may give the worker a way of listening to the child and finding out what is wrong. The under-fives worker can use reflective listening techniques as the child plays spontaneously – for example, play about monsters who come in the night. Thoughtful play provision, however, can make the child's communication easier. Occasionally more focused play techniques are useful.

With older children it may be helpful to create a play situation in which the adult can be involved alongside the child, perhaps using drawing and painting, clay, puppets or stories (such as Rouf's *Mousie* for young children and *Secrets* for older children), to show a readiness to accept whatever the child's communication may be. (Appendix 4 includes suggestions for books to use.) Direct disclosures are less common with school-age children than drawing attention to their plight through drawing or stories, such as a story about an abused friend. For example, a ten-year-old girl had been attending a primary school unit for maladjusted children for some time with no apparent suspicion of abuse when her teacher, Rose Larter, suggested she drew her dream house. She drew a house with windows, with lovely patterns of dots and colours. In the garden to the left of the house she painted mum's towel and her sister's swing (she had not mentioned her sister before). On the right she painted a big black rectangular towel which she labelled 'dad'. On an intuition her teacher started to talk about her having her own bedroom where you don't have to let anyone in; people have to knock on doors and ask to come in. She asked 'Does anyone come into your room when you don't want them to?' The child replied 'I've got a terrible tummy ache' and put her head down in her hands. Her teacher sat quietly with her on the cushions and read to her for the rest of the session.

If the child uses an allegory or third-person story it can be less threatening for the child if the adult keeps to the symbolism in the story. Educational psychologist Anne Peake (1989) tells of a child's story about a princess who had to kiss the prince and did not want to. She suggests saying 'It sounds like the princess needs some help, let's talk about how she could get some help for herself and stop the prince' and telling the child 'I would be unhappy and frightened if that happened to me ..., I'm glad you told me this story so we can discuss what to do'. This supports the child in planning how to cope and who to tell (the princess's mother?), and may help a direct disclosure. After some discussion the adult may ask directly 'Has anything like what happened to the princess happened to you?'

Workers in family centres are increasingly aware that they may be the first people outside the family that a child gets to know, and therefore also the first people to have a chance to recognize when a child may have been abused. Nomony NCH Family Centre for under-fives in Plymouth is equipped as a normal under-fives nursery, with home corner, sand and water play, painting, dough, cutting and sticking, miniature vehicles, construction toys, and a dolls' house and family. (The dolls' house converts to a flat or a single room, essential for some children.) Observation of a child's spontaneous play often alerts nursery workers to the possibility that something may be wrong. A boy's frightened reaction to the television set in the home corner led to finding out that his father had made him watch video nasties. His mother had not understood why he was frightened to go to bed at night and the centre's explanation meant she could protect him in future. A girl's play led to workers discovering that she had been encouraged to watch a horror film and was too frightened to go to bed, so her father went to bed with her.

Project leader Anita Edwards and family care worker Mary Stone, inspired by a course from Madge Bray, have prepared a special toy box to help young children to communicate about sexual abuse. It contains 'nice' and 'horrible' toys, snakes and worms, a knife, scissors, spiders, a crocodile, a plastic winged bat with a big mouth, a big tongue monster, a hammer, a mask, telephones, crayons and paper, a Fisher-Price medical kit, a piece of sheepskin, two pandas 'hugging' each other, puppets, dolls with a happy face on one side and a sad face on the other, a big-mouthed doll, a Red Riding Hood granny doll that turned upside down becomes a wolf, and anatomically complete dolls, including grandparents, parents and children, with day and night clothes. The toy box is used to give a special one-to-one playtime to a child for whom there is some concern. Usually this is not in a separate room but in a quiet corner of the nursery. Other nursery workers recognize what is going on and subtly minimize interruption or distraction. Ordinary nursery activities may also be used in communicating with children, as the following example illustrates.

Lisa's mother was worried by her nightmares and agreed to one-to-one play therapy sessions. Using the toy box Lisa said spiders had frightened her and 'I don't like willies by my face'. In a cooking session making jam tarts she gave further signs of abuse. The nursery nurse announced 'You can lick it in a minute' (meaning the spoon). Lisa said 'I don't want to play the licking game'. However, it was when she was playing with play dough, making pastry men, that she disclosed even stronger indications of abuse. She made a pastry man (Figure 8.1) with a big mouth, a belt with a huge buckle and a long stick 'to make you do it'. She insisted that the man had a big willy 'cause they're always big ain't they'. The worker copied the pastry man in a drawing and Lisa blacked in the eyes and the big mouth. She drew black squiggles at the bottom corner which she said was 'the mess, cause you see

Figure 8.1   Lisa's pastry man

there's always a mess after'. The worker later took the pastry man to show to the members of the case conference.

Disclosure of abuse came relatively quickly for the child described. Very often it takes many months and sometimes years for children to show clearly what has happened to them. The family centre workers emphasize the need to respond to the child's overtures in spontaneous play. All workers stress the importance of going at the child's pace and of recognizing that disclosure does not happen overnight but only after a long process of building up trust between adult and child. Young children may not be aware that the abuse is wrong although, like Lisa, they may know they do not like it. Older children are often torn by conflicting feelings. They may feel it is their fault, especially if some pleasure has been involved in the abuse.

They may feel it is all they deserve. They have been sworn to secrecy and told of the terrible consequences for the family if the abuse is found out. Sometimes the abuser is the only person in their lives who gives them any kind of nurturing, however distorted. They have experienced adults with enormous power over them, their trust has been destroyed and they are not likely to trust readily *any* adult.

It is important that the worker is able to take control and relieve the child of responsibility for the consequences of what it may reveal. Like Madge Bray, workers may sometimes need to say 'Some secrets are too big to keep'. An anxious child may need constant reassurance. An over-sexualized child may ask the worker personal questions or touch them inappropriately. Workers need to be prepared and not thrown off balance by this, maintaining their control of the situation.

Case study: Concern about a three-year-old in a family centre

Work with Nina at the Nomony NCH Family Centre had been going on for some weeks before she began to reveal signs of abuse, and it was many more months before these signs began to add up to a significant disclosure. Social workers were already anxious about her and the health visitor asked for the centre's help in observing her. Her mother was alcoholic and had a volatile relationship with another man as well as Nina's father, and was often bruised, comatose or absent. She also had lodgers. Nina's mother seemed fond of her, and gave her clothes and presents. At the family centre Mary Stone used one-to-one play with Nina and the following is based on her account.

Mary drew a sad and happy face and asked Nina what made her feel like that. For the happy face she said 'ice-cream' and 'dad'. But then she said for the sad face 'No one loves me ... dad hits me ... under the arms ... knife in my tummy' (the latter is a typical indication of sexual abuse in a young child) and then 'Dad is pissed ... he broke the big window ... dad is crying'. Nina was later playing with the dolls' house and family, and was asked to name the dolls. She put the mother on the roof saying she might hit her. Dad went on the roof next and had a fight with mum. Another male doll she put aside saying 'I don't want Rob in my house'. Whilst playing in the nursery she told other workers about dad's attacks on mum.

Nothing significant was revealed for three months, when workers became concerned about the changing situation at home. Mary again drew sad and happy faces for Nina, who said that 'the sun ... birthdays ... mum' made her happy. The sad face was for 'when mum smacks ... when mum cries ... Rob was hitting her (mum) ... she was naughty, Rob doesn't want her anymore'. She added 'I like Rob but he doesn't like me, he says I'm horrible'. Asked 'Where do you sleep?' Nina said 'In my bed'. 'Where does Rob sleep?' 'In my bed ... there's no room for him in my bed.' Nina did several drawings. She drew big eyes, with 'big drips', saying 'Rob makes her sad', and 'Rob's long face with all his mouths' (also highly suggestive of abuse).

Workers were finding Nina's behaviour with other children and staff increasingly manipulative and unpleasant. Playing with the toy box she said the big soft owl who likes children was 'crying ... afraid of the dark ... Jack Frost killed him ... there are witches in my bedroom'. Later she said, 'There are snakes in my bedroom, they sleep behind the chair'. She was not interested in the anatomically complete dolls, but another doll was 'crying cos no one loves me'. She used syringes, playing at making people better. Another time Nina was playing with the dolls' house with Mary, telling the Rob doll 'Get out of my bedroom' and putting him in bed with mum. Then she put the mother doll on the roof,'cause she doesn't like Rob', followed by the Nina doll saying 'Rob killed me and mum'. The dolls all fought and then Nina squeezed all three dolls tightly in her hand. She took a man doll and tried to take off his trousers, saying 'He goes in my bed and wakes up in the morning and puts his trousers on'.

Amidst mounting concern all staff were made aware of the need to listen carefully to what Nina was saying. A YTS worker reported the following conversation. Nina talked of her dark house with monsters, and then said, 'The goblin touched my mum and mum's mary.' ('Did he?') 'Yes.' ('What did he do?') 'He touched my mary.' ('Mm?') 'Yes, he scratched me.' ('Who was this goblin?') 'He had a mask on but it was my dad.' Later Nina told the centre leader, 'I've just told Tina my secrets'. ('Have you?') 'Yes, I've told her I've got a goblin in my house.' Then her mind went off at a tangent and she chatted about a little dog. Nina's drawings continued to show mum crying or not well, and everyone being sad.

Through these months a series of case conferences involving the network of agencies working with the family monitored the situation closely, aware of the indications of sexual abuse but lacking real evidence on which to act. This is a common situation which causes great anxiety for all concerned.

PLAY IN THE ASSESSMENT OF YOUNG CHILDREN WHO MAY HAVE BEEN SEXUALLY ABUSED

The Report of the Inquiry into Child Abuse in Cleveland, 1987, affirmed the importance of the child 'as a person and not an object of concern', and recommended that 'professionals should always listen carefully to what the child has to say and take seriously what is said' (DHSS 1988: 245). It also focused on the need for a high quality of evidence in assessment and stressed the need for training in techniques of interviewing children, as well as in child development and the use of play. In the wake of the report, guidelines for formal investigations of sexual abuse have been established everywhere. A joint investigation involving police and social services departments is usual.

The Cleveland Report expressed concern that there should not be a 'disclosure interview' in which the child was either disclosing or believed to be in denial – that is, inhibited by internal or external pressures from revealing the truth. The interviewer must have an open mind as to whether abuse has occurred. Whilst there can be no disagreement about the need for an open mind there is no doubt that disclosure of abuse is a painful procedure for the child with painful consequences. Therefore the process of assessment must be conducted in the least threatening and most helpful manner. One-way screens can be helpful in making sure that there are not too many people present in the room and overwhelming the child. The interview is often recorded on videotape, preferably with the child's consent, and may be used later in the legal process.

The Report was concerned that assessment and therapy should be kept separate. Whilst the purpose of interviews with a child is assessment, the process at best may be therapeutic as well. At least the interview should be so conducted as not to cause further damage to the child. There is also the problem that the quality of evidence required for the courts may be greater than that which convinces the interviewers of the existence of abuse. Another problem, particularly for the police, is how to decide when preliminary investigation by a social worker might be more fruitful before proceeding to joint interviewing with its inevitable pressure. A further question concerns the sex of the interviewers, and, at a later stage, the therapist. Whilst woman police constables are invariably involved in interviews the available social worker may be a man, and this may be inappropriate when abuse by males is suspected.

Whilst there are no easy solutions to these dilemmas, play can be an effective method of communication with children where abuse is suspected or where children have already informally disclosed abuse to another child or adult. Even older children who may be able to talk about their experience can use play to reduce the pressure of the situation. With younger children, pre-verbal children, and some children with learning difficulties or communication disorders, communication may not be possible without play. Vizard found that play 'proved to be the key to disclosure' with many inhibited and frightened children. She writes:

> Sometimes disclosure takes the form of simple words after the child has been helped to communicate by the process of earlier play. On other occasions disclosure does not involve the use of words but emerges through the child's drawings, the way the child positions the anatomically correct dolls and so on.
> (Vizard *et al.* 1987: 21)

A combination of non-directive and focused play techniques may be most useful both in helping the child to feel comfortable and in exploring the specific question of sexual abuse. As with all communication with children the ability to use reflective listening or re-capping techniques is crucial. Repeating what the child says or providing a commentary on what the child is doing shows that the interviewer is listening carefully, is not in a hurry, and is neither shocked nor frightened by what the child has to say.

Using knowledge of child development–children's memory, and pretend play, including anatomically complete dolls

Interviewers of young children need an understanding of the stages of a child's development, including intellectual and language development and play (see Chapter 1), if they are to assess accurately what a child is communicating either in words or actions. The quality of children's memory is an issue of particular importance. The evidence suggests that what children remember is not essentially different from what adults remember, especially for central events in their lives. In recognizing pictures and faces, young children under five do as well as older children. There is evidence that children can remember things from their earliest years, even abuse which they were not aware was such at the time. Fundudis (1989) gives an invaluable summary of research relating to children's memory.

Young children may have difficulty in remembering details of events, such as places and times, if these are asked as abstractions and out of context. They do much better if given the opportunity to relate a familiar sequence of events (using 'script memory'). The interviewer can start the sequence – for example, saying 'What happens when daddy puts you to bed?' – with play materials available which enable the child to show as well as tell this. Reflective listening and further questioning may then follow the child's spontaneous version of events. The questioning *must* be open-ended, with no hint of a suggested reply. Young children do seem to be more likely than older children to agree with an adult's suggestion, probably simply because of their experience of the power of adults. Even then they seldom go along with major suggestions that they know to be incorrect.

A common concern is that children may be unable to distinguish fact from fantasy. Some of this dates back to Freud's dismissal of women's accounts of sexual abuse in childhood as wish fulfilling phantasies, although it is now thought he often ignored real sexual abuse.

As discussed in Chapter 1 it is important to recognize that young children cannot fantasize about events completely outside their experience. On the other hand, they may make wrong interpretations of real situations. Nina's goblins, in the preceding example, are a case in point. Whilst the goblins, known about through books or television stories, are fantasy representations of unpleasant people, touching her 'mary' is most unlikely to occur in stories and more likely to be based on experience. Her statement cannot, therefore, be dismissed as fantasy and needs further investigation.

Children under five are unlikely to lie deliberately. They have not learned how to 'hedge' and usually respond honestly to the question as they perceive it. However, if they are able to anticipate the answer the interviewer expects they may give this instead.

Older children are more able to resist suggestions but are capable of lying, and may do so for many reasons, including fear and guilt. Hesitant and confused accounts are more likely to be true than a coherent, unemotional account told 'pat'. There are numerous pressures on children *not* to be truthful. An accusation of sexual abuse leads to immense pressure on the child, within and without the family, so that denial and retraction commonly follow. Whilst each individual situation must be carefully evaluated, children are far more likely to lie in retracting and denying abuse than in making an initial accusation.

Anatomically complete dolls

The use of anatomically complete (or correct) dolls has been widely debated. These are male and female rag dolls which have sexual parts, a penis and scrotum, or vagina and breasts, body hair, a rectum and an open mouth, sometimes with a tongue. The name, as Glaser points out, is a euphemism since they do not have ears! Dolls are available representing three generations, children and teenagers, parents/adults and grandparents, and with different racial characteristics. (There is also a mother doll which can 'give birth' to a baby.) The Cleveland Report warned against the use of the dolls as a routine prop in initial interviews by inadequately trained interviewers. However, used wisely they can be helpful in assessment of possible abuse.

Workers themselves need to be familiar with the dolls' appearance and to have handled them, so that they will not be caught by surprise by their own reactions. They need to know too how children normally react to them. Glaser and Collins (1989) observed how normal children, from age three to six years, played with the dolls. They found that children were clearly aware of the dolls' difference, with responses ranging from giggling to shyness. They were generally more interested in excretion than in sexual functions. Once children were familiar with the dolls they tended to ignore their sexuality and used them in everyday pretend play situations, such as meal-times, bathing and putting them to bed. They were often undressed and left undressed, typical of a pre-school child with any doll, as any nursery worker knows from the frequency with which they need to re-dress a collection of naked dolls after a session. Sexually abused children are often anxious to dress the dolls again and show relief when they are dressed.

Contrary to what some have supposed it does not seem as if the dolls alone encourage the children to sexual play. The 'overwhelming majority did not show any sexually explicit play'. For the few who did 'it appears that explicit sexual play with the dolls may well arise from the child's pre-occupations which are based on previous exposure to explicit sexual information or activity' (Glaser and Collins 1989: 559). They may have observed sexual activity, in reality or on film or video, or been abused themselves. Lack of sexual play does not mean the child has *not* been abused, neither does explicit sexual play mean the child *has* been abused, but used with other indicators they can help to build up a picture of the child's experience.

Anatomically correct dolls are most helpful in the assessment of abuse of pre-school and other children whose language and cognitive skills are still developing. Children can use the dolls to show things for which they do not have the words or even the concepts. Older children, unless they have specific difficulties in communication, may have little need of them and prefer to use ordinary dolls or drawing. Jones and McQuiston (1988) feel that the dolls can be intrusive and frightening. They would rarely use them with children over the age of seven. Occasionally children may find it helpful to portray a situation with the dolls which they are too embarrassed to describe in words.

The interview procedure

In interviewing children where abuse is suspected it is important to go at the child's pace. A single interview is rarely enough and a series of interviews may be needed. This approach may compete with other urgent demands, such as having to complete an investigation with a view to criminal or civil proceedings. This causes acute conflict for many workers who feel that quick results are expected and who yet feel sure that children's emotional needs dictate a slower pace. The Cleveland Report recommended no more than two investigative interviews. Whilst agreeing that this is right if the sessions consist of focused probing for abuse, David Jones, consultant child psychiatrist at Park Hospital for children in Oxford, finds that 'children sometimes require an extended period of assessment either because their mental state is disturbed or because they are extremely reluctant and fearful'. He suggests it can be useful to set up a series of six sessions in order to understand the child better, 'knowing that sexual abuse is a strong possibility as one of the factors that may be creating disturbance for a child' (Jones 1988: 16). Many interviewers use between one and three interviews, as suggested by Bannister and Print (1988).

Occasionally careful preliminary work can lead to a rapid disclosure in a first interview. Fine tuning to the meaning of children's play in the Nomony NCH family centre, whose work with Nina has been described, made for a rapid disclosure in a joint police and social services investigation. In the centre Suzy was 'odd', withdrawn and sad. She would hide when it was time to go home. During play conversations on a toy telephone she said several times 'I'm going home and I'm going to bite Ed's willy'. (He was her mother's cohabitee.) The worker echoed the child, 'You're going to bite Ed's willy', showing that she was listening and not shocked, affirming what Suzy said so that she could say more if she wished.

The investigative interview took place in the child's house with a police woman present. Centre leader Anita Edwards brought the toy telephones, the child's photograph album (put together for every child in the nursery), and 'show and tell' (anatomically complete) dolls. Suzy repeated her telephone conversation and named the dolls, taking off their clothes, and again said 'I bit Ed's willy'. Anita asked, 'How did you bite his willy?' Suzy, indicating the doll, said 'Hold him up a bit', and then re-enacted the situation, biting with her teeth. The mother then disclosed that she too had been abused as a child, by her grandfather. Because of lack of corroborative evidence the case did not go to court but the mother received help and so was able to help her child.

The interview room and play materials

A comfortable welcoming room can help a child to feel more relaxed. Carpet and floor cushions mean that the interviewer can get down to the child's level and play on the floor. Play materials need to be selected carefully as an over-abundance can distract children. The following minimal materials are all that some interviewers use: drawing materials appropriate to the child's age, a dolls' house (two houses can be helpful) and furniture, which must include beds, a bath and a toilet, with doll people, such as Lego or play people, including a baby and grandparents. Additional materials may be helpful. Toy telephones enable the child to talk to the adult indirectly, often easier for the child. Play dough, clay or Plasticine allow a child to model an abusive situation. Doctor kits, toy cars (especially police cars, fire engines and ambulances), and soft toys or puppets representing 'good' and 'bad' people are often added (Jones and McQuiston 1988). Puppets are also useful for indirect communication and may be suggested to a child when 'it's hard for you to talk'.

Anatomically complete dolls need to be available, if not in view initially. Ordinary rag dolls, rather than miniature ones, and domestic furniture which matches them in size, such as a baby doll with a cot, help children whose capacity for symbolic play has been impaired (as Sinason (1988) found was often the case with sexually abused children). Larger dolls more nearly represent real people and the feelings that go with them. The dolls should have removable clothes.

A tape-recorder, an old camera (useful in identifying pornographic use), a jigsaw puzzle of interlocking bears (fighting, sexing or cuddling? wonders Madge Bray), a whoopee cushion (giving permission for 'rude' things), sets of farm and zoo animals, and toy soldiers may also be available. Books, such as Rayner's *The Body Book*, containing anatomical drawings, special drawing and colouring books, and jigsaw puzzles of people whose clothes can be removed are often useful.

As Jones and McQuiston (1988) emphasize there is no cook book approach to interviewing children. However, the following stages can be identified, even if there is some overlap and moving forwards or backwards between stages.

The interview assessment

The first stage of assessment – showing the child you are listening

The interviewer must first decide where the interviews are to take place, bearing in mind what the place means to the child. The child should be shown where parent or carer is waiting and given access to them if necessary. The interviewer should sit at the child's level, usually on the floor, mentally marking out a personal space not too close to the child and keeping to this to prevent re-enacting an abusive situation. Beforehand the child may simply have been told it is coming to talk about 'things in the family'. Depending on the age of the child the interviewer may say something like, 'This is a place where you can say anything. I'm someone who talks to children who have worries or are sad.' They might enact a telephone call. For example, Madge Bray sometimes reassures children by role playing a telephone conversation with a 'police lady', explaining that 'we're here to get to the bottom of muddles ... no, I won't be asking lots of horrible questions'.

The child is often given an opportunity to play freely with the play materials. The interviewer can say 'You can do whatever you want to do with the toys. I'll be here with you.' The aim at this stage is to make the child as relaxed and comfortable as possible and for the interviewer to start to understand the child's level of development and the child's view of its world. If the child does not start to play spontaneously the interviewer can start playing, and the child will usually join in. The interviewer observes carefully without directing play and describes aloud what the child is doing as it plays, repeating the child's words so that the child knows they are acceptable to the adult. The interviewer may quietly join in play, perhaps demonstrating some of the toys.

Madge Bray, social work consultant with Sexual Abuse: Child Consultant Service (SACCS), whose sensitive training has helped and inspired numerous workers, has a collection of toys which help children to express how they feel. The wise hedgehog puppet understands a lot and has a badge which says 'I listen to children'. If a child picks up a little sheep which baas, she may say 'It's a very sad sheep. You can hear him crying. I wonder where it is hurting.' Or with a tiny battery-powered trembling rabbit, she says 'This is a very frightened rabbit; you feel him shaking and trembling. I wonder why?' A musical doll has a head which goes round and round. 'This little girl has so many muddles in her head. Do you know anyone like that? Maybe we could draw a picture of the muddles.' She finds that the child may start to tell her about her 'doll', or draw a picture of her muddles, 'the mummy's telling the daddy off, 'cos the little girl was naughty' (Bray 1991).

Later in this first stage the interviewer can start to find out information about the child's view of its family. They may use drawing, asking the child to draw itself and its family, perhaps doing something together, or making a model family with dough or Plasticine (sometimes helpful with reticent children), or playing with dolls. Jones and McQuiston (1988) suggest these and also Winnicott's squiggle technique, described in earlier chapters. Children can be asked to talk about their drawings. It is important to know the names the child gives to each family member (especially where there are more than one possible 'daddies') and its feelings about each person (Bannister and Print 1988). Elizabeth Wright, social worker for Oxfordshire Social Services, often uses drawing with pencil and paper as a tool for communicating with children. After introducing herself as someone who helps children with worries she may go on to ask, 'What do you think a worry might be? What might make you sad or worried?' She might then draw the child's family tree, with leaves, or faces of family members, asking the child, for example, 'Does mum have a sad or happy face? What makes mum angry?'

Non-verbal or frightened and inhibited children may be more comfortable in playing with dolls. If anatomically complete dolls are used they should start dressed at this stage. The interviewer should refrain from naming the dolls. For instance, the interviewer should not say 'Is this doll Daddy?' but 'Is this doll like someone you know?' and the child should be allowed to change the dolls' identity in the course of play, as young children often do. Play often reveals useful information, including areas the child avoids in play. Frightened children may refuse to touch all or specific dolls. Very sexualized children have shown quite explicit behaviour, such as sucking male or licking female genitals (Bentovim *et al.* 1988), unlikely in non-abused children. The interviewer should similarly note whether the child's drawings include or emphasize the genitals.

The second stage of assessment – the question of abuse

The second stage of the interview is concerned more directly with the question as to whether the child has been abused. Some interviewers lead up to this by getting the child to identify parts of the body on drawings or dolls, including anatomically complete dolls. Others make use of the play situation and gradually lead the child into play which involves situations in which the suspected abuse might have taken place.

Jeannie Wells (in Blagg, Hughes and Wattam 1989) explains how she uses pin people drawings. After a respectful introduction she sits with the child at the same level, with paper and coloured pens, saying 'I don't know very much about you yet. Perhaps this will help me to find out, and for you to help me. If you choose a colour then I will start' (p. 55). She draws a circle for the child's head, and adds hair and features, asking the child to suggest colours, shapes and sizes. She continues drawing from top to bottom of the child's body asking as she draws what each part of the body is called. Outline clothes may be added. Then the child is asked which have been the hurting places and she draws on a small oblong plaster, for small hurts, and a large double one for a bandage, for big hurts, as the child decides. Open questions about what happened can follow naturally.

The anatomically complete dolls are best introduced as dolls that look like people really do underneath. To make use of young children's 'script' memory the interviewer can suggest using these or ordinary dolls to enact situations such as bedtime, bathtime, watching television or babysitting, if possible using previous information about suspicions of abuse, as in, for example, Shamroy's (1987) suggestion 'Let's pretend that you and dad are home while mum is at work'. A distressed child may need time, reassurance and the interviewer's skill in finding a way to communicate. Baker (1986) gives the example of a pretend game he devised in which the girl doll has a secret to tell her granny when the daddy doll has been put out of the room. In arranging the dolls many children reveal their sense of isolation, putting themselves alone. Sometimes they enact very clearly their sexual abuse. Anatomically complete dolls may be used as a matter of course by some interviewers but many experienced people find that they use them quite rarely; rag dolls are usually adequate. Some interviewers do not present the dolls until the child has expressed something in an abstract or symbolic way which the dolls might clarify. Only then they may say 'Show me with the dolls what happened'.

Using a soft toy or puppet, Madge Bray might use a story of the wise owl who looks in the windows of the house and asks what he sees. A child's fearful reaction such as 'Don't look in there' (the bedroom) is noted and respected; the adult takes the attitude that 'If it's important you'll find a way to tell me and I'll find a way to understand'. A rabbit puppet is not very clever so he just has to listen more times than other people, 'so can you tell him again please'. A big bear puppet may be used to represent benign power, a strong person who will hear the child and look after them, 'so we'll tell him shall we'. A monster doll with an inflatable tongue, who makes rude noises, helps children to explore what is 'rude'. A clockwork licking mouth may get a strong reaction. Magic pens can be used to draw secrets. These and other uses of play are shown in Madge Bray's (1988) videotape *Monsters and Rainbows*, and in Bray (1991). She may use part-completed drawings, such as Striker and Kimmels' *Anti-colouring Books*, with 'My nicest dream', 'My worst nightmare', or 'Look through the keyhole and see what upsets me most'.

A projective technique for older children might involve both interviewer and child looking through an imaginary window and picturing a traumatic scene (Jones and McQuiston 1988). Or a child may be asked to draw a plan of its home showing rooms the child likes and dislikes, perhaps indicating where the abuse happened. A child's drawing of itself or others may also reveal much about the child's perception of its own body and what it knows about the bodies of others. A silenced girl drew herself with no mouth. Another girl drew a confused picture of her mother, and of her cohabitee's 'long willy' with something coming out, a surprising thing for a four-year-old to emphasize and certainly raising questions as to how she knew. Rather than ask the child why the drawing is like that it is a good idea to ask what is happening or how the child in the drawing feels.

Sometimes suspicion of abuse is very strong but children avoid talking or playing about their family. They seek any chance of distraction, such as talking about a picture in the room. Elizabeth Wright plans beforehand for these children by using a small plain room with minimal opportunities for distraction, providing little but crayons and paper, and dolls, and a strong and friendly lion which the child can hold when telling something hard. She uses play to try to hold the child's attention but if this does not work she may put play aside and say gently 'I know it's hard to talk'. If necessary, she may ask 'Can I see you again and we'll talk another time?' She avoids long silences, aware that they may feel to the child like uncomfortable pressure.

As at earlier stages the interviewer listens and re-caps what the child is showing and saying, using the child's words, to show that the interviewer is listening and is not shocked or frightened by what the child may be saying. Questions need to be open (usually beginning with 'which', 'what', 'where', 'who' or 'how'). The child may show anger and frustration at some point and the child needs to be shown that it is safe to express this, perhaps by hitting a cushion or banging hammer pegs. Bannister and Print (1988) suggest the adult joins in and loudly repeats any 'rude' words the child is saying to give permission for their expression. If the child is very fearful they suggest asking the child where it feels safe and then putting itself in this 'safe place' in play. Then it is up to the adult to find a way of reaching or rescuing the child, using the child's metaphors revealed in earlier play, such as a police car, ambulance, angel puppet or building a block bridge. They also suggest that the interviewer joins in role play with puppets or dolls, maybe suggesting a scene such as 'Mummy cat and her kittens' or following the child's suggestion, such as playing the sleeping baby doll frightened by the child's 'monster' puppet. The child can be helped to kill or lock up the monster. They describe this process of 'harnessing the child's resistance' as follows:

The dynamic is similar to the use of paradox in family therapy. For example, if a child demonstrates why it is impossible to tell, agree with them, act out their fear with them and ask them for suggestions to overcome the 'power figure' that they have chosen to illustrate their fear. Sometimes it takes several suggestions from both the child and worker and several failures before the 'power figure' is sufficiently subdued to allow disclosure. This acting out and confirmation of fear, however, is much more powerful than simple reassurance.

(Bannister and Print 1988: 9)

In a somewhat different approach the Great Ormond Street structured interview (Bentovim *et al.* 1988) follows initial free play with dressed anatomically correct dolls by the interviewer asking the child to undress the dolls and then to name all the parts of the body. The interviewer repeats the child's family or slang words for body parts. The child is then asked to say or show with the dolls what sort of touching is 'nice' and 'not nice' ('bad, icky, funny or confusing'). If the child refuses the interviewer demonstrates stroking and smacking with the dolls. If the child spontaneously names the abuser and identifies a doll with that name at any stage then the interviewer uses this named doll in further re-enactment. If not, the child is asked to pick a doll with the name of the suspected abuser, or the interviewer does so. (Some useful suggestions for phrasing questions are also found in Glaser and Frosh (1988). For example, to find out who the abuser was, if a child has mentioned soreness, they might say 'Which of my dolls made the little girl sore?')

The child is asked about the room, furniture, clothes and time of day of the suspected abuse. Then the child is asked to 'show me if something rude/sexual happened with the dolls'. If the child does so it may be asked to show 'if anything else happened?' The child may be asked direct questions about types of abuse, whether anyone has touched it in a place it did not like, and if so, where. The child is asked to use the dolls to show it. For example 'Did he touch you? ... Where? (pointing to the dolls) ... What with? ... Can you show me on the dolls?'

The child is asked to say in words what was done to it and by whom. The interviewer repeats this and asks 'Is that right or not?' This interview approach is based on the belief that it should not be assumed 'that a silent or uncommunicative child has nothing to say'. Apart from the first ten minutes of free play the interviewer is directing the child in quite specific play themes and moving rapidly to identify the dolls with specific people. The drawbacks of this method are that it does not make use of the young child's 'script' memory, and the pace is set by the interviewer rather than the child. However, it may facilitate disclosure in children reluctant to reveal abuse.

Child psychiatrist Anthony Baker describes a similar though less structured approach. The child plays with the anatomically correct dolls, the interviewer suggesting that the child names them and finding out the child's names for body parts. Baker uses reflective listening, judging his pace and approach by the child's responses. He may ask the child to 'pretend that this doll is you' and show him what happened. Keeping within the symbolism he might ask, 'What did this child doll do then?' Only afterwards does he ask 'Did something like this happen to you, like you showed me with the dolls?' He describes a four-year-old girl playing freely with dolls when he heard 'This one winkles that one'. He asked what someone did when they winkled someone and she showed him with the dolls, saying the babysitter pulled down her swimsuit on the settee and 'pulled his trousers down and winkled himself ... then when it was all big he put it in my winkle. I wet myself with sticky stuff, and he wiped it off everywhere. We didn't tell 'cos mummy will be cross I wet myself, and daddy would smack me. Mummy's not cross any more 'cos daddy's naughty now' (Baker 1986: 15).

If a child at any time makes a direct statement about abuse this needs to be followed up by collecting as much specific information about the abuse as possible. Direct but open questions are asked about what happened and where, and what people said, and how the child felt. If the child is too anxious to say any more then the interviewer can go back to earlier stages of expressing feelings through play. Leading questions, such as 'Did he touch you there or there?', are only used at the end of the interview if the child has been unable to respond spontaneously. These can be helpful to the child but are likely to be inadmissible as evidence.

The final stage – re-capping and recognition

The last stage is for the child to express the abuse in words – what was done and by whom. The dolls, for example, 'are used to encourage recall and speech in preference to the demonstration of events remembered by the child' (Jones and McQuiston 1988: 35). The interviewer re-caps what the child has said, 'So he did that to you. Is that right or not?'

It helps if the interviewer acknowledges how hard it has been for the child to speak, a recognition of the child's feelings, which may be more helpful than simply telling the child the abuse was not its fault. If the child tries to retract or asks to keep it a secret it is important not to accept, but to say that 'I believe what you told me' or explain that some secrets are too big to keep. As the Cleveland Report (p. 245) recommended, 'Professionals should not make promises which cannot be kept to a child, and in the light of possible court proceedings should not promise a child that what is said in confidence can be kept in confidence'.

Bentovim et al. (1988) ask the child if it would like to say or do anything to the perpetrator and let it vent its feelings on the appropriate doll. Assertiveness techniques may be introduced through play, with the victim yelling 'No. Go away'. At this stage, however, they are more helpful as a vindication of the child's feelings and its courage in telling someone than as a means of protection. Some kind of winding-down play or activity can help the child to end the interview comfortably.

The child is reassured that it has done well. If there has been no sign of abuse the child's helpfulness is still recognized. The abused child needs to be told what is the next step for its protection. Some interviewers involve the child, asking 'How can we stop this?' or 'Who can stop this?' Bannister and Print (1988) stress the importance of having found out from the child's play or talk who is the child's most supportive ally. They also explain to the child that several people may need to be told for the abuse to stop. Jeannie Wells (in Blagg *et al.* 1989: 58) summarizes the five important things for the interviewer to have communicated to the child during the interview: I believe you, I am glad you told me, I am sorry this has happened, it is not your fault, and we are going to do something together to get help.

The child as witness

The Cleveland Report recommended that 'the views and wishes of the child should be placed before whichever court deals with the case' (p. 245). It often seems as if the court process itself ignores the child's feelings. At the time of writing, although videotape interviews are admissible as evidence, the child may still need to appear personally in court to be cross-examined. This can be a frightening enough experience for the child without the added terror of a personal confrontation with the alleged abuser. Screens offer only limited protection.

Any preparation of the child for its court appearance can only reduce but not take away the child's acute anxiety. Whilst, of course, what the child might say cannot be rehearsed, it is possible to use play methods of explaining what a court is for and what happens there. This can be enacted in role play with puppets and dolls, or with drawings or models. Madge Bray has written *Suzie and the Wise Hedgehog Go to Court* (1989) to explain the court process in a way that children can understand. The Children's Legal Centre has a useful information sheet on *The Child Witness*, and produces *Being a Witness* designed for use by children with an informed adult.

THERAPY THROUGH PLAY FOR SEXUALLY ABUSED CHILDREN

Play therapy for the sexually abused child can never be the sole intervention. Work must take place with the family as well as with the child, especially where the child remains with the family or may return at some point. Mothers have often themselves been abused and not been helped in the past. Wright and Portnoy (1990) found that the mothers' over-identification with their children got in the way of therapeutic work with the children. They found that group work with mothers was helpful in giving them support and reaching the 'child' within, so that they could in turn protect their children. Other sorts of preventive work are with potential abusers. When a new man enters the family in which a child has been abused in the past, social worker Elizabeth Wright may warn him quite strongly of the risks and educate him to take the responsibility not to collude with a sexualized child but to value the child for itself. The family must change if the child is to remain and be protected.

Equally, work with the family is not sufficient to help the child, who needs a personal form of therapy. The aftermath of disclosure may sometimes be as traumatic for the child as the original abuse, often involving separations and loss of a member of the family, and therapy may need to address both. Moreover, many sexually abused children have suffered other kinds of abuse, physical and emotional abuse, and neglect, and need a general form of therapy. Once the disclosure process has been completed many workers find that they 'change gear'. They are more able to go entirely at the child's pace. (One problem which sometimes arises is further disclosure of abuse. The worker may have to act, especially if another perpetrator is involved.) They often find that therapy can continue for a long time before the child is ready to play out any specific episodes of sexual abuse. They are dealing instead with the child's general feelings of lack of self-worth.

Looked at in terms of Erikson's stages of emotional development, instead of basic trust the abused child has learned mistrust, instead of autonomy the child has learned shame and self-doubt, instead of initiative the child has learned guilt, and instead of industry the child has learned inferiority. As the child reaches adolescence it experiences role confusion instead of developing a sense of identity.

Finklehor (1984) analyses the damage specifically caused by sexual abuse and the related needs of the child which therapy must try to meet.

1 The child has been betrayed – by father, mother, family or friends. Therapy must restore the child's trust in people.
2 The child is stigmatized, feeling 'different', and developing a negative self-image and negative ways of communicating with others. The child wonders 'Why me?' and 'What did I do?' The child feels guilty for not stopping the abuse and equally guilty for disclosing it. Loss of self-esteem is pervasive and extremely damaging. Children need to know that they are not to blame for what happened, that they are right to tell, that they are not responsible for what happens to their family, and that they have a right to protection. Therapy must restore children's feeling that they are normal.
3 The child feels powerless, having lost what little control children have over their bodies and over their lives. Whilst some remain passive and frozen 'victims', others exert what power they can and become bullies of other children or abusers themselves. (A child's figures of the 'monster' and the 'ballet dancer' (Hunter 1986) illustrate how an abused child internalizes her parents. Father is a menacing sexual gorilla, while mother, the dancer standing on one leg with arms raised, is both seductive and helpless.) Therapy must increase the child's feelings of control to that approprate to its age and stage of development.
4 The child has suffered sexual trauma. Children may feel dirty or suffer from a conditioned fear of sexuality, or become inappropriately sexualized. Poor relationships and inappropriate giving of love and affection are likely. They may cover up all feeling and eventually become devoid of any real feelings or sensations. Therapy must help to restore the child's capacity to feel, and to express and cope with feelings of anger, fear, disgust and sadness, enabling the eventual development of normal relationships of mutual sharing and care.

Therapy has parallels in bereavement work. It must deal with similar stages of denial, guilt (for allowing abuse, or disclosing), idealization (of the abuser), anger and sadness. The longer the period of sexual abuse and the older the child the longer the therapeutic work dealing with the specific question of abuse is likely to be (Glaser and Frosh 1988). Young children are prone to show other problems that require therapy. The following two examples of long-term therapeutic work illustrate some children's emotional responses to abuse. They emphasize the difficulty of the task of therapy and the slow pace which it may require.

'All the perfumes of Arabia will not sweeten this little hand'

Jenny comes to a play therapy session for an hour one afternoon a week with one other child in the resource unit at a primary school in Reading where Rose Larter is the teacher. Jenny is now aged nine and her sexual abuse over a long period of time came to light 18 months ago. She is a classic victim, isolated and bullied at school, although an excellent reader. For several sessions she spent most of the time playing with the dolls. She would lift the girl doll's skirt and belt it, giving it the beatings she used to receive. The baby was sent to bed without supper for being naughty. After the beatings Jenny would get the girl doll and bath it, washing the doll, her 'dirty' self, clean. She did this again and again. Her mother says that at home when Jenny is upset she fills the sink or bath with bubble bath and washes herself clean.

One day Jenny seized one of the two telephones in the playroom, calling 'Is that the WPC? I want you to come here because I am beating my children and I think I might kill them'. The teacher role played back on the other telephone, offering help. Jenny decided she would paint. (To encourage painting Rose Larter usually paints alongside the child, asking the child about the painting and if she may write down what it says and pin it to the painting.) First Jenny painted a large patch painting with black cloud of 'a Viking ship on a stormy sea. All the people have been blown off. They're going to die. Their families are upset that their sons are dying of cancer.' Later she painted a Slinx, a creature with thick red arms from a reading book. She explained 'My sister's like a Slinx. She grabs everything for herself. She gets the belt. Joe gives it her and she swears. Mum says I should get the belt but I don't.'

Another painting was her 'aunt's house'. The house was red and black, with a black roof. There was a small yellow sun and a garden full of black and brown flowers 'knocked off'. This sad painting was followed by a crude patch painting of a figure outlined in red with red arm protuberances, brown hair, a purple chest and abdomen, and a huge protruding purple patch 'pocket' (penis?), all on two pin legs on a black line. In the top corner was a small yellow circle. Jenny described it, 'Joe my dad, he's working, that's why he's got that suit on – his pocket is inside out – he's standing on tar – it helps him push his car more easily ... It's night, the moon is shining.' She sounds like Madge Bray's doll with her 'head full of muddles'. Rose Larter writes down Jenny's comments for her and feels that is as much as Jenny can take. If she tries further interpreting or reflecting Jenny abruptly changes activity. Jenny has been coming for several months. Now she enjoys the 'nurturing' start to the session when Rose sits on the floor cushions with her and they sing or share a story. Today she is painting stripes, pressing so hard with the brush that you can see the scratch marks in the paper. Rose expects her to be a victim for some time to come.

A child in a residential therapeutic school

Alice had been abused from infancy until the age of eight when she went to live with foster parents. She protected herself with a false-self. If her foster parents told her to go and play in the garden because she was noisy she would go out and run in circles with a fixed smile on her face, being 'good'. In the Caldecott Community she disclosed her abuse to her worker while buying Coca Cola in Sainsbury's; at home it was a reward for sex. She had also previously disclosed whilst at Sunday school! She tells people in a very matter-of-fact way, avoiding pain. Alice is so confused about her identity that in a game touching body parts she is not able to put her hands on her head or her nose. She does not know where she is or even *if* she is.

Her worker is Sarah Hemsby, whose magical playroom is described in Chapter 3. Alice loves the playroom and the idea that there she has that 40 minutes a week to *be*. Sarah described her first playroom session with Alice. Usually a very delicate child the first time Alice painted she slopped the paint on. When she had finished and was about to give Sarah her picture she checked herself, saying 'I don't have to give you my picture. It's my time', and kept it. She started singing and dancing. She dressed up for a while, then got out the tea things. She did not know what to do with them, and made 'baked potatoes' and 'sugar'. She got very excited, saying to herself 'No, I mustn't get excited', and got more excited. Similarly with a doll, she said fiercely 'I want to poke its eyes out', then checked herself and started loving it. She said the room reminded her of things in her past but then said 'No, I don't want to think about those things'. She made excuses not to tidy up at the end of the session and it became a battle. She kept trying to provoke Sarah to anger. Sarah said later that it felt like being with two people; it was quite uncomfortable and frightening. Although she was feeling Alice's projected anger she was able to contain it – that is, experience it but not act on it. The value of the whole session became apparent when Alice went back to her group and was fine for the rest of the day.

Alice's anger is expected to increase considerably and staff are planning how to cope. As well as seeing Alice in the playroom, Sarah works with her every day in the residential unit, as part of the care team. All playroom workers meet as a group with their training supervisor Christine Bradley for an hour or more every week so that they can share feelings, understand what is happening and respond to children appropriately.

Such planning and support for therapy with extremely disturbed children who have been involved in long-term incestuous relationships can be vital. Glaser and Frosh advise that profoundly therapeutic work should not normally be started unless the child is also living in an environment that can support the therapy over a prolonged period of time, including times when the child is rejecting the therapy and therapist. The process of therapy, as Moustakas's stages indicate (see earlier chapters), is likely to involve periods of extreme anger, at first generalized but later directed at specific people who may include the therapist.

Both Jenny and Alice showed signs of internal muddle and confusion. Feelings of being 'a mess' is often one of the earlier issues in therapy. Art therapist Carol Sagar explains why art and play therapy can be helpful.

> Using art and play materials, because of their tactile, physical nature which relates directly to sensation and emotional feeling, is arguably the most useful therapy for children who have been sexually abused ... as they can work with their feelings and experience them directly in the handling of materials used in the therapies. The process and results express clearly the confusion and damage which abused children suffer and reflect how they find ways in their work to bring about repair, change and growth from within.
>
> ... Often the way in which most satisfaction seems to be found in using art materials is by making a messy mixture which is then spread on any surface. Messy packages may be formed and given to the therapist to keep. Containers and packages of the mixture may have to be kept for a long time until the child emerges from the compulsive need to handle and examine the internal chaotic feelings where 'good' and 'bad' are indistinguishable. The messy package may represent the secret which the child has had to hold, often over a long time, which is now passed into the therapist's keeping. At some point later the package and the containers of mess will be asked for by the child who may decide that they can be disposed of – usually thrown away – or who may not yet be ready to let go of them. Later the child may begin to use the materials to represent and express present phantasies and the current relationship with external reality.
>
> ... A 12-year-old girl made a very large painting within the outline made by drawing round her body whose insides were represented by thick black paint. The painting was rolled up so that the paint, when dry, made it impossible to unroll the paper. This was trusted to the care of the therapist for some time before being undone.
>
> (Sagar, in Case and Dalley 1990: 92, 97 and 113)

The therapeutic approaches discussed so far have been non-directive, using play and art to help children to heal themselves in their own time, within the safe boundaries of play. For sexually abused children whose every conceivable boundary has been breached in the past these boundaries are vital. Regular time-limited sessions with a safe adult can begin to restore some trust. The therapist may need to place limits on behaviour in the session. If the child tries to touch the therapist inappropriately or exposes itself the child needs to be told that that is not permitted.

Many workers consider it unnecessary and wrong to direct or lead the child into giving any details of its abuse in therapy. One experienced worker said of a child used in ritual abuse, 'I've never asked her the details. I don't know if she ever will tell me as it was so horrific. After two years she's now told me some things.' Another worker said about a child, used in pornography, with whom she had worked for 18 months, 'I don't know what happened and I don't need to know'. They do, however, let the child know that they recognize the abuse has happened, avoiding collusion in keeping it secret, so that the child can raise the subject when it wishes.

Where workers differ is the extent to which they introduce some focused methods. One of the workers just mentioned uses Axline's non-directive play. However, her travelling play kit includes items which 'invite' certain kinds of symbolic play, such as a plastic collapsible knife, face paints, glitter cream, pretend blood (for a child who has suffered ritual abuse) snakes, a witch puppet, monsters (which can be got rid of into draw string bags), various friendly and stern soft toy animals, miniature people and animals, dolls and baby bottles, as well as a magic wand.

Social workers, who may have less time available for prolonged work, often use some focused methods in conjunction with a child-centred approach. Games may be introduced as a way for worker and child to get to know one another. Sara Dellar (1989) uses Harmin's *Got to Be Me* and the Catholic Children's Society *Finding Out About Me*. She goes on to introduce games, for older children especially, which focus on feelings. She uses cards which each name a feeling to help children to choose and talk about which ones are like them. Younger children can use drawn 'faces', described earlier. She uses a game of 'opposites' to help children to deal with ambivalent feelings about a perpetrator. Starting from the child's lists of 'big' and 'small', she works through 'nice' and 'nasty', to 'good' and 'bad', to 'good' and 'bad' things about 'George'. This helps the child to come to realize that the same thing can be good and bad, and so understand ambivalence.

Many workers use cathartic techniques. 'Action techniques may be very directive in that they use the material the client offers and then deliberately channel it so that a specific problem can be addressed' (Bannister 1989: 80). Many children are angry and need help in focusing this on the abuse rather than expressing it generally. Elizabeth Wright helps a child to write a letter (not actually sent) to the perpetrator. Madge Bray has many toys which children can use symbolically to express anger. A wooden jointed snake takes a lot of punishment. A Rambo puppet with a boxing glove both gives and receives a hammering. Vile disgusting monsters are often liked, however, and used to carry off the baddies! Children may be invited to draw a picture of 'horrid things', or feelings, then tear it up and put it in the monster box which goes in the bin. Then they can use a pair of rainbow specs to see rainbows instead. The child's medical examination or police intervention may be sources of anger; a medical kit, toy cars, police cars and ambulances (which crash) may help express this. (Other materials for cathartic anger work include sand and water, clay or Plasticine; further suggestions can be found in Chapter 9.)

Stories with which children can identify provide a symbolic mode for working through feelings. Older children may like fairy stories, such as *The Ugly Duckling*, *Snow White* or *Hansel and Gretel*, or modern stories of good triumphing over evil, such as *The Lion, the Witch and the Wardrobe*. Younger children need stories nearer to home such as *Can't You Sleep Little Bear*. Some stories have been specially written about sexual abuse, such as *I'm Glad I Told Mum*, Rouf's *Mousie* and *Secrets*. (These and other books are available from SACCS – Nightingale Books, see Appendix 4.)

Younger children may work through their feelings in doll play. Ordinary dolls (not miniatures) are used mostly, preferably with 'home corner' furniture, such as baths and beds. Many experienced workers find that anatomically complete dolls are not necessary. Social worker Elizabeth Wright does not probe for details about the abuse but recognizes that it has happened, and when appropriate may say something like 'Big people are naughty sometimes, they shouldn't do that', to help the child to understand that adults sometimes do things that are wrong. Therapy is child-centred and child-led, but she may use the doll to stand for the abuser and to help the child show how it *feels* about the abuser, either directly to the doll, such as throwing it, or by using some of the indirect techniques suggested earlier. Oaklander's Gestalt techniques can be used not only with dolls but also with drawing and painting, with the child asked to talk to a figure it has drawn or to be that figure or object and say how it feels. (This approach might help Jenny whose paintings have been described.)

Sometimes it is the child who becomes the doll baby. Anne Bannister tells how 'one little boy repeatedly placed a boy doll in a cradle and then attacked it with "a daddy doll"'. Because the child was tearful the worker picked up the doll to protect it, and the boy stopped playing. Bannister continues,

> It was suggested to the worker that next time she should allow the attack to continue but express sympathy with the baby. 'Poor little boy, he must be feeling very frightened and lonely' she said as the 'daddy doll' attacked the baby again. The boy began to cry, as he had not done before. He seemed to experience relief from his pain and was able to start to share his feelings.
>
> (Bannister, in Blagg *et al.* 1989: 90)

Regression play may occur and the provision of baby feeding bottles, with juice or squash available to put in them, enables some children to go back to infancy and grow up again (see abused 'Sally' in Chapter 5). Floor cushions, pillows or a cot large enough for a child can be useful. Food and drink offered in the session convey a feeling of being cared for.

Role playing, with role reversal, is often extremely helpful. The worker, sometimes using puppets or dolls, plays the role given by the child, usually the victim. The child becomes the powerful controlling monster.

> 'I'm frightened', I say (as the child), 'I'm going to tell mummy'. 'No you're not', says the child. 'Mummy will be cross, you're feeling mad' ... Because the

child has told me I'm 'feeling mad', I respond to the monster's attack with gusto and a battle (which did not happen in the real abusive situation) ensues. My child puppet may eventually lose the battle for this is the element of realism. But next time we play the game the child may want to play herself and actually express some of her anger that she could not do at the time of abuse.

(Bannister, in Blagg *et al*. 1989: 80)

Another worker was given the role of doctor to examine a baby who was ill because the monster had touched her vagina. The doctor told the four-year-old 'baby' that there was no damage, a message which the child needed repeated many times in play. The worker was then told to become mum who dealt with the monster doll and protected her daughter (Shires 1989).

Anne Bannister has found that five or six sessions can give many children enough confidence to continue with their daily lives, provided that they have continued support from the child's carers, and further help available at future stress points. Parents or foster parents may be involved in some parts of therapy to help them to understand what support is necessary. Many workers take therapy to wherever the child is living to make this process easier (Weinstein 1987). Longer periods of therapy for deeply disturbed children are more often held in some kind of sanctuary or neutral ground. Independent social worker Celia Doyle (1987) prefers all therapy to take place there, feeling that the child's home should not be the place where painful feelings are stirred up.

Another area over which there is disagreement is whether therapy should teach children to protect themselves through assertiveness, saying 'no' to inappropriate touching. Some experienced workers point out that it must never be forgotten that children often have great loyalty to adults who are able to exert power over them. Teaching about 'good touching' is of little value because children's safety ultimately depends on the adults around them. The focus of work should be on the role of the child's protectors. Work with the child is directed towards building the child's self-esteem – the child's belief in itself as a unique and precious person. This may include the message that sexual relationships can be nice. Some other workers *do* teach assertiveness and some of their techniques will be described. They are not appropriate in the early stages of therapy when the child's feelings are confused. Some workers use them as a final stage of therapy. However, any worker adopting these must bear in mind the ultimate powerlessness of a child.

Role play in which children eventually learn to shout 'no' or 'go away' to a monster or puppet which has frightened them gives children some sense of control. They have usually vented their anger first – for example, by being the policeman putting it in prison, or beating or 'killing' it. The therapist may have joined in play, helping the child, giving the message that there are adults who will help. 'A hand held by another through a puppet can be the first step towards the child learning that he or she can receive physical comfort without being expected to give anything in exchange' (Doyle 1988: 31).

Information books, such as *The Body Book*, can help to give information about children's bodies and clear up any misunderstandings. Other books, such as *A Very Touching Book* and *No More Secrets for Me*, help children to learn about what is appropriate and inappropriate behaviour. Colouring and activity books, such as *My Book, My Body*, are available. Madge Bray teaches children to say 'No. I don't like that' with a 'funny' spider puppet who says, 'I'll just go for a walk up Amanda's arm because I feel like it'. She asks her, 'Do you like that?' and if Amanda says 'no', she says 'He can't hear you, say it louder', until Amanda can give a loud clear message. A child who can proudly look at itself in a mirror has gone a long way in developing self-esteem.

Celia Doyle, using miniatures including play people and animals, gets a child to choose a figure to be itself. The child figure and animal friends in the farm are surrounded by threatening wild animals. 'The child is then encouraged to make a line of the remaining figures which he views as strong and reliable' (such as teacher, mum, foster dad, policeman, social worker) 'to protect him from the wild animals', so learning that there may be 'people who can help protect him in future'. One child put all the baby animals into a shoe box with two horses to look after them. 'I confirmed with her that it was no longer her responsibility to look after her younger siblings; that was a job she could now leave to adults' (Doyle 1988: 31). We return full circle to the need for work with the whole situation and not just the child.

PLAY TECHNIQUES IN GROUP WORK WITH SEXUALLY ABUSED CHILDREN

Belonging to a group of children who have experienced abuse can have the apparently contradictory effect of helping a child see itself as an individual and not just as a 'victim' of sexual abuse (Furniss, in Christopherson *et al.* 1989). It is often a great support for a child to find that it is not the only child who has been abused. For many children and workers, group work is a practicable and even enjoyable way of helping children to develop their confidence and self-esteem, to make choices where they are able to, and to learn how to assert and protect themselves, to the extent that this is possible, in the future. As in individual work they can be helped to find ways of expressing feelings and directing them appropriately, so that behaviour can become more constructive rather than self-destructive. Some workers with adolescents use group work to help children to explore issues of race and gender which contribute to children's powerlessness (Boyce and Anderson 1990).

Group work with young children is less common than for older ones. At Great Ormond Street Hospital, Eileen Vizard has pioneered a structured approach to group work with young children between the ages of three and seven. Groups of about eight children attend hour-long sessions, led by two co-therapists, over six weeks. (A caretakers' group meets at the same time.) Food and drink acts as an ice-breaker at the start, after which children are involved in playing a game giving their names for parts of the body. The children are

given a package of sex education information, positive alternative options for behaviour if molested in future, and specific training in assertiveness, using video feedback techniques, role play games and constant reinforcement of learning within the group ... A whole range of specific games, exercises and tasks are now incorporated into this programme, and we have found particularly helpful the use of picture cards, which depict familiar situations in which there might be an element of risk to the child. These provide a helpful focus for discussion of possible alternative options for ... what to do in these situations, and since one or two of the picture cards actually show a child being touched sexually, this has proved a very valuable way of breaking through the tremendous denial surrounding the whole subject ... Photocopies of these picture cards ... are supplied to the caretakers' group, so that they are informed about the material under discussion and are able to pick up on any comments relating to this made by the child.

Similarly we have used anatomically correct dolls themselves in the group work and these concrete teaching aids seem particularly appropriate when working with very young children.

(Vizard 1987: 18)

The dolls might be used to show examples of 'nice touching' or 'how mummies and daddies have sex'. During the final session of the group the caretakers join the children's group and together watch a video of the children. Further details of activities in these groups are found in Vizard (1986). Walford (1989) describes her use of this model in group work with young children in Belfast, including role play practising 'telling mum'.

Vizard considers this kind of group work most suitable for children who have ambivalent feelings about the abuser, rather than those subjected to severe threats and violence. She has found that the otherwise successful structured approach of the group 'leaves little emotional space or actual time in which to deal adequately with very painful feelings and experiences, and these need often to be taken up elsewhere'. Whilst individual therapy may be necessary for some children following group work, some children will not be ready to benefit from the group without some one-to-one work first.

Rosemarie Musgrave (in Silveira *et al.* 1988) describes her development of the GOS approach to one putting more emphasis on therapeutic play. Safe Ways project in Leeds runs groups which aim to prevent future abuse, while at the same time ending abused children's isolation and building their self-esteem. Role play and story-telling through puppets help children in saying no and telling someone (Webb 1991).

Practical advice on the detail of arrangements for running groups for older children are given by educational psychologist Anne Peake (1989). Play is only one of the methods used in group-work. Workers use other play-based techniques, including trust games to build confidence, Gestalt exercises such as expressing feelings in drawing and talking to the person or object drawn, or talking to an empty chair, as well as role play exercises. Some of these were described in Chapter 7.

Chapter 9

The use of play in work with children in care

Recent years have seen a renewed interest by social workers in direct work with children in care. This has been due to the move to permanency planning for children in care which requires social workers to intervene more actively, as well as the result of child abuse inquiries, court reports and the explosion in sexual abuse cases, all of which call for more attention to be paid to communication with children to find out their wishes and feelings and to consider their development. Self-advocacy of children in care as well as research studies pointing out failures in involving children in decision-making about their lives have emphasized this need. The Children Act 1989 requires that 'When the court determines any question with respect to the upbringing and property of a child – the child's welfare shall be the court's paramount consideration' (section 1 (1)). Among the items the court should consider in deciding how to ensure this are the ascertainable wishes and feelings of the child, as far as they can be determined without undue pressure on the child, and the child's physical, emotional and educational needs.

The skilled social case-work with children undertaken by the specialized child care officers of the fifties and sixties was diluted or neglected in much of the generic work which followed the Seebohm Report. Some workers, notably those in fostering and adoption, retained and developed their specialist skills. The chief medium for disseminating these skills, old and new, has been BAAF, British Agencies for Adoption and Fostering, through courses and specialized publications. Not only were the writings of teachers in Britain such as Clare Winnicott and John Bowlby kept alive, but also relevant literature from the United States was made known, notably the works of Vera Fahlberg, Violet Oaklander and Claudia Jewett, explaining techniques of effective therapeutic communication with children. BAAF produced a training pack *In Touch with Children*, devised by Daphne Batty and Nessie Bailey (1984), linked to their work on a specialist child care course for social workers at Goldsmiths' College in London. The pack is widely used on in-service courses on communication with children. Many of the course papers are included in Batty (1986).

Some workers use non-directive play as their way of opening communication with a child. They may continue in the same way or move to using more focused methods. Other workers make use of focused or directive techniques from the outset when they judge that the child can cope with them. The methods chosen depend on the workers' skills and resources as well as on the child's age and stage. They also depend on the aims of work and on the time the worker has available in which to complete it. For example, in carrying out an assessment for the court workers will often use focused techniques, either following a time of non-directive play or from the outset. Focused approaches are useful too when children are not so much in need of deep therapy as of help to clarify what is happening in their lives, and where there is a clear task on which worker and child are engaged, such as preparation for family placement. Non-directive play can be helpful when the worker does not know why a child is unhappy or when the child is extremely disturbed.

PLAY IN COMMUNICATING WITH CHILDREN INVOLVED IN CARE PROCEEDINGS – THE ROLE OF THE GUARDIAN *AD LITEM*

The guardian *ad litem* is a social worker who is appointed as the child's independent representative in care proceedings. Guardians have a duty to inform the court about children's wishes and feelings, and to ensure that they understand as far as they can what is happening and why. With the implementation of the 1989 Children Act the work of guardians *ad litem* can only grow.

Guardians need to be able to establish trust and to communicate with children quickly and effectively, over a short time period. Madge Bray recommends the use of a playbox (as described in Chapter 3). 'Adults need to find ways into a child's play world to obtain the information they seek' (Bray 1986: 19). Even though time is short, she feels that it is important for the first session to use non-directive play and reflective listening. Later the worker may be more focused, asking the child to draw or paint, or play a game. She wants to understand how children feel, what their fears are, how they perceive their family and what has happened to them. Other workers may take the lead more quickly, perhaps explaining to the child that they are 'a special person for you from the court', and then setting up an activity or discussion, such as drawing their own family portrait and inviting the child to do the same, or using the squiggle game. It is important to use things with which both guardian and child feel comfortable – for example, if the guardian finds puppets awkward, drawing may be preferable (Kerr *et al*. 1990).

Philip King, a guardian *ad litem*, at his Independent Child Care Agency in Birmingham, first writes a letter to the child, in an aim to equalize the relationship with the child who is normally powerless. At the first meeting he gives all his attention to the child, regardless of who else is present. He gives a simple introduction of who he is and why he is there, explaining that he sees many other children and telling the child what they are going to do together. He helps the child to relax by using silly questions, such as 'Are you married?' He often shows the child a set of scented marker pens, which help to relieve the child's anxiety and introduce drawing, an activity he finds more useful as an opening than a playbox. Later, ethnically sensitive play people or dolls and telephones can be essential triggers or props to help children with limited skills to tell their story. He uses open questions (how? what? when? why? where?) and emphasizes that there should be no pressure or probing, only encouragement. If children do not want to talk there is a reason; the guardian can only provide the climate and the opportunity. He points out that a court needs verbal evidence; play and drawing are a catalyst, a means towards this end. Observation of play may lend support to what the child says but interpretation of play alone should be avoided.

Suzette Waterhouse, a Northampton guardian panel member, in *Time For Me*, has collated information from different guardians as to what they have in their 'tool kit' for working with children. To determine a child's wishes and feelings the guardian must find out the child's needs, perceptions and attachments. Like King, she warns that a guardian should be 'cautious of interpretation, which may need a strong theoretical background' (Waterhouse 1987: 16). Relatively unstructured free play is needed with younger children. For older children, play materials, such as a telephone, or a tape-recorder for a pretend radio interview, foster communication by making it fun and minimizing adult pressure. Puppets and animal toys which 'don't understand' or which make mistakes encourage a child to explain everything; or the toys may be understanding, and good listeners, reassuring children that they can speak safely. Again, if they are like the child, perhaps a bit bedraggled or worn, the child can identify with them.

Materials to elicit the expression of feelings include flash cards with faces or feelings, trigger cards (I like my ..., I feel like crying when ..., I wish ...), dolls with sad and happy faces, and home-made games such as a snakes and ladders game with sad and happy caterpillars. A session may be used for the child to tell 'your story', perhaps using play people to create the distance which makes it possible to tell. The guardian observes how the child plays with a doll family. Animal families, families cut out from paper, plastic stick-ons, or modelling materials might be offered. Later the guardian can check back with the child to get a clear picture of what the child thinks had happened.

Children may be asked to draw or paint, 'the time you spend with mum and dad' or 'the presents you would give your family'; or they may draw 'the nice/nasty thing about dad/mum is ...'. In drawings of the family the guardian should observe the order in which people are drawn, their relative size and the child's position, often nearest to the preferred parent or adult. Is anyone omitted? Does the child see itself as central or peripheral? Isolated or involved? Part-completed pictures, such as *The Anti-colouring Book* (Striker and Kimmel 1978), *Moving Pictures* (Alton and Firmin 1987) and *Talking Pictures* (P.King 1988), can be a useful stimulus and provide a basis for discussion. Philip King describes work with a four-year-old girl. She drew a picture of herself, of the house she was living in with foster parents, and of her house before with mum. He asked open-ended questions about what happened at home. They talked about visits to her mum, using drawings of sad and happy faces. She drew a happy face for access visits seeing mum and a sad face for when it was time to go, saying 'I want to be with my mummy'. Further drawing gave a good description of stresses at home. In another case, using *Talking Pictures*, a boy drew his dad with long stripes down his front, explaining dad had been in jail for attacking his mother and added 'I think he'll be in jail again'. He was worried that, if he returned from foster care to live with his separated dad, his dad would get to hurt his mum again when she had access to her son.

Pictorial genograms such as family trees with roots and branches representing past and present families can be used. Time drawings or picture flow charts (Figure 9.1, see also Chapter 2) and ecomaps (Fahlberg 1988) can depict the child's point of view and be used to help discussion, which is important in helping the guardian to check out the accuracy of hypotheses based on observations of play and drawing. Later sessions may pursue the child's wishes and feelings about the future. Older children playing or drawing houses may be asked 'Who lives here?', or 'Who would you like to live here?' Boys who reject doll play may be tempted by a road map with transport between houses and people. An unusual idea, useful in adoptive situations is a collection of farm animal families, fences and gates. 'The fences can be constructed as boundaries around each family group and gates can be added that can be left open or closed as the child wishes (Waterhouse 1987: 33). Fantasy journeys to the moon or on a magic carpet ('Who is coming with you?') are suggested, or imagining being at a holiday camp and allocating family members to chalets. General books about family life can provide openings to explore important matters, sometimes more so than books with a special message or plot. Waterhouse's booklet offers a mine of ideas.

A guardian *ad litem*'s work often involves explaining to children about court procedures. Philip King has a model court room with small wooden figures. Many workers draw the court scene for the child or act it out with dolls. Some use role play. In civil proceedings, children are not usually involved in court, except for a brief appearance, but the guardian may help them to write or say something for the court themselves, as well as the guardian's report. The guardian needs to make clear to the child that it is the court that makes decisions, only promising to tell the court what the child wants. Contact with child, a visit or a letter, after the court case shows that the worker still has the child in mind, and can explain simply the court's decision.

The over-riding concern of guardians *ad litem* is to establish two-way communication with children which is both fast and accurate. Play can facilitate this communication. In so far as this use of play enables children to be informed about and understand the events in their lives, and to be given a means of expressing their feelings and views – to be 'heard' – then it can be therapeutic. Play is used to help children to express feelings of which they are already reasonably aware; it does not normally explore unconscious feelings, although ambivalent feelings may well emerge. Because the guardian's role in most cases is short term more prolonged work may be carried out by children's social workers. Many guardians are also social workers and are familiar with this work. Social workers in statutory work settings may themselves be asked to make assessments of children for the court. Social workers draw on a long and developing tradition of direct work with children in care, to which we now turn.

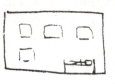

born in hospital

Mum and me live
with Nan and Grandad

Mum gets married
I stay with Nan

Go to live with Mum
and stepdad Jo

Stay with Jo when
Mum goes

Tina comes
to live with us

Stay with Tina
when Jo leaves

Go to live with foster
parents Brian and Sue
and their baby

Go to live with Pete and
Kathy foster parents

Figure 9.1   **Picture flow chart (2)**

FOCUSED PLAY IN LONG-TERM WORK WITH CHILDREN IN CARE

The understanding of a child's feelings following separation and loss is based on the theoretical framework provided by John Bowlby (1969 and 1982, 1973, 1980) and Kubler-Ross (1970), and their application in direct work with children by Jewett (1981), Fahlberg (1988) and Oaklander (1978). Jane Aldgate (Aldgate and Simmonds 1988) outlines the theory and gives examples of practice. The basic principles are that separation involves fear and anxiety which must be mastered, and that loss involves anger and grief which must be expressed.

Claudia Jewett's summary of the aims of work to help children to cope with separation and loss is widely known and constitutes an important and appropriate description of the aims of social workers in this area:

> Because every major loss disrupts the development of self-esteem, the smooth progression of life, and the sense that events are predictable and meaningful, recovery from such a loss requires that damaged self-esteem be repaired, continuity be re-established, and a sense of meaning be restored. To recover fully from a loss a child must satisfy five needs:
>
> First, the child must understand that he was born to a father and mother; he must know who they were, why he was separated from one or both of them (without blaming himself for the separation), and what, if anything, he might do to return things to their previous condition. He must experience and share any strong feelings of anger, sadness, guilt or shame that he has been holding back.
>
> Second, the child must know what persons or families have cared for him if he has lived away from his birth parents. Who are the people in these places he has lived, why did he go to those places, why did he leave (or why will he be leaving), and what, if anything, might he have done to make things work out differently?
>
> Third, the child must say goodbye, directly or symbolically, to past caretakers (and, if a change of caretaker is forthcoming, he must say hello to the new caretaker).
>
> Fourth, the child must receive permission from his caretakers to be happy, loved, successful and loving.
>
> Fifth, the child must get ready to face the future with increasingly diminishing concern about the past.
>
> (Jewett 1984: 129–30)

The use of play in this work includes communication through play, the use of play and games in focused work such as life-story work, linking feelings to people and events, sometimes in preparation for family placement, cathartic play and anger work, sensory and regression play, and in non-directive play therapy. Ken Redgrave, a family placement worker for the Boys' and Girls' Welfare Society, and whose book is a superb source of games and other play techniques, comments:

> In undertaking therapy work with deprived and emotionally damaged children the emphasis, particularly in early stages of treatment, will be on the use of non-directed play (or other free forms of self-expression) but I am conscious of

the fact that *most* of the children who are needing family placements or have been rehabilitated to their own families, or who have been adopted, are not in need of 'treatment' (e.g. psychotherapy) but are reasonably healthy kids who need to be able to talk and get things sorted out. I am also aware that many adult workers find it difficult to get the child and themselves exchanging ideas on some of these delicate areas. The 'games' I have spoken about have helped these conversations along.

(Redgrave 1987: 122)

Direct work with children should always take place within the context of work with others in the child's life, their families or carers and social workers. They may also be able to join in or independently provide therapeutic play. Foster parents, for example, can make an important contribution.

Planning focused work

Kate Burke, a family placement worker with the Catholic Children's Society, whose programme of sensory work was described in Chapter 2, sets out a detailed programme for her intensive work with children whom she is preparing for life in new families. Work often takes a year and may go on for two years. In planning work she considers: 'child's need', 'suggested work programme', 'time scale and monitoring', 'work to be carried out by'. The following programme is a condensed example.

- Child's need – 1. *Good primary care experiences and play*
  This covers all aspects of day-to-day care. Foster parents' pervading attitude should be one of care, giving a clear message of acceptance and value. Certain times of the day are particularly important: help in getting up and getting dressed, getting ready for and taking to school, food and meal-times. Provide opportunities for play with an adult as well as with other children. Include messy and water play with no goal other than enjoyment. Give individual time at bathtime for play and conversation. Make bedtime calm and read a story. Good primary care to continue indefinitely. It may lead to the expression of infantile behaviour. Foster parents to record significant play observations.
- Child's need – 2. *Sensory experience*
  Renew and strengthen the five senses which may have become dulled through traumatic life experiences – touch, hearing, smell, seeing and taste. Give a week to each sense, foster parents continuing each theme at home through the week (see Chapter 2).
- Child's need – 3. *Who am I?*
  Introduce and help her to work through the *'My Book About Me'* booklet (BAAF). Use sessions concurrent with sensory work.
- Child's need – 4. *Separation from birth mother*
  Why did I get separated? Use of pop-up houses, roads, cars, puppets and play people to represent carers and other adults and the various moves and changes

of circumstances. Use of dolls' house to re-enact or explore. Use of picture flow chart to help her to see the sequence of moves and events. Use of candle ceremony in relation to carers and attachment figures. Use Jewett's videotapes (from National Foster Care Association). Foster parents to be involved and to carry out some of the work, as well as keeping an observation diary to monitor feelings expressed in play.

- Child's need – 5. *What is happening to me?*
  Will this family really stay with me? When I do something naughty will they send me away? How perfect do I need to be in order to be really accepted? I know I have opportunities but am I loved, really loved? Reflect on attention seeking, lack of concentration and behaviour/survival pattern. Give careful consideration to the promotion of attachment behaviours within this family. What are the unspoken expectations? Where are the satisfactions? What must change for parents and child to gel? Share information with foster parents. Pace work according to child's needs.

- Child's need – 6. *Life-story work*
  To help child understand and live with the trauma of her life. Develop a fuller understanding of who she is, why she was separated, why her mother did not come, and what is going to happen to her. Use ecomap to show where father fits in the picture. Have photograph of and information on father. Explore how she feels about all this, including her fantasies, misconceptions and guilt. Fill in any gaps. Use sad, happy and angry faces to represent her feelings to adults. Use water play. Make a family tree. Help her make life-story drawings. What positives has she received from her parents (life itself, needs met in the womb, colour of hair and eyes)? Pace the work according to her needs.

- Child's need – 7. *Looking at legal documents*
  Show birth certificate, photographs of birth, hospital etc.
  Healing process/re-parenting courtship and commitment.

- Child's need – 8. *To know her worth and feel a sense of belonging*
  I am who I am and this is my family. Claiming each other, warts and all.

Using focused play techniques

Getting to know one another

Ken Redgrave (1987) recommends the use of a 'third thing' (Clare Winnicott's phrase) in establishing a relationship with a child. The child often uses something, such as showing the adult a toy car, as a way of making contact and to test the adult out to see if the person is safe. Redgrave suggests using the child's special interest or hobby, making a personal box for the child to keep its work in, using a tape-recorder or telephone, or using games and quizzes. Some workers use unfinished picture sheets or sentence cards, such as 'If I were a giant I would ...', 'I get really fed up about ...' or 'If I could do anything I wanted I would ...'.

A getting to know you board game with dice is suggested in the Catholic

Children's Society (1983) booklet of games for preparing children for family placement. Child and worker each draw important people or things in their life in numbered squares on a board. They use each other's boards, and as each lands on a square they ask the other about that picture.

Focused work on past, present and future

Ecomaps, picture flow charts, diagrams and drawings of how people fit into a child's life and how they were linked together at any one time, illustrated geno-grams or family trees, story-telling or enactment with dolls and puppets, all these can help children to understand what has happened to them. These ideas can also be used to introduce children to new families and involve them in the decision-making about their future. With a young child, Kate Burke might help them to name and cut out cardboard figures representing different people, attaching them with velcro to big cut-out houses stuck on to a large coloured cardboard sheet. Another worker uses a visual time line, a string on which pictures, photographs and objects are pegged in time order, and helps a young child name them. Redgrave describes a variety of techniques. He devised a board game called Marathon Walk; road blocks represent particular difficulties (such as 'mother can't get a house') which they can then discuss to see which can and which cannot be moved. He wanted 'to show the child that they could move forwards, towards a goal, even though when the game started we did not know what the end goal would be' (Redgrave 1987: 137). He also makes a game using Fahlberg's (1988) notion of three parent circles – birth, legal, and substitute or 'now' parents – to help children to talk about their expectations of each.

Trigger pictures to help children to talk about the moves in their lives are Alton and Firmin's (1987) *Moving Pictures*, and Macliver and Thom's (1990) *Family Talk. Finding Out about Me* (Catholic Children's Society 1983) suggests a board game, Moving Around. A road divided into squares with houses along the way represents each move a child has made, whilst question cards help the child to talk about past moves ('Do you know why mum and dad could not look after you?') and plans for the future. Children as young as three can use a people and places chart, depicting people in the child's life and the building each belongs to. Other ideas include home-made jigsaw puzzles, and other card and board games. Some people tell stories, sometimes telling the child's life story in the third person, or using symbolic stories, such as the story of the suitcase which became increasingly battered and got more and more labels stuck on it as it made more journeys. Published stories include van der Meers's *Joey*, Orritt's *Dennis Duckling, Going into Care*, and Thom and Macliver's *Bruce's Story*. Owen and Curtis (1988) offer play techniques such as 'loving and caring candles', described later, and 'brick-wall', the bricks and gaps representing the child's life and moves to a new family. All can be used as an adjunct to, and necessary foundation for, life-story work.

Life story work

The making of a life-story book is probably the method most used in helping children to understand their background and personal history. Much life-story work has been criticized for being carried out as a routine procedure for children in care, without sufficient sensitivity to the timing, pacing and depth of the work. When done well it can 'help take the child on a therapeutic journey through parts of their life that pose most pain and conflict' (Ixer 1988: 26). It requires warmth, empathy and genuineness. It must go at the child's pace, with the child in control of what it is sharing, allowing for times for respite; it should not take place when the child is in a crisis. Ixer recommends too that all workers should undergo their own life-story work first. Before starting the worker needs as complete information as possible about the child's life. They should then write it out, in the third person, to have an account to draw on in the course of work.

Skilled workers use life-story books as one tool among many, using a good repertoire of play techniques to help pace the work, as Kate Burke's programme shows. Redgrave describes the making of life flow charts to help the child to construct or retain a picture of past events as a first stage before going on to make a life-story book. The *process* of making the charts and books is as important as the end product, for it enables clarification of feelings about events and their causes, and the correction of possible misunderstandings – for example, about why a child was moved. Taking the child back to visit, photograph and record people and places can be a positive experience. It is helpful to remember both good and bad times. The worker must have all the information available about the child's past so that the worker can pass it on to the child. Pictures of the child itself might include a poster-size photograph, or a life-size drawing started from an outline drawn around the child lying on the floor. Helping the child to make its life book is often the last stage after the child has assimilated the information about its past and expressed and dealt with its feelings. Many workers follow the guidelines for making life-story books offered by Ryan and Walker (1985). All writers warn of the need for this work to be carried out in the context of a relationship with the child and not as an isolated task. Play techniques require creativity, imagination and, above all, empathy. Children leaving the Family Makers Home Finding Unit at Gravesend take with them three copies of their life story, 'the book they themselves worked on, a tape-recorded life history containing the recollections of significant people, and a more detailed life history which is given to the new family for safe keeping' (Catholic Children's Society 1983: 2).

An example of play-based work with very young children is Enid Hendry's (1988) account of how, as a family placement social worker, she prepared four-year-old Jamie and his two-year-old sister Jenny for their new family. The children were in a short-stay foster home, having come into care because of long-term neglect and abuse. At first neither could walk or talk but both progressed physically and Jamie was able to speak a little, but both remained withdrawn and showed little emotion. Enid Hendry wanted to involve them actively in understanding what had happened to them and what was planned next, and to help them to express some feelings. First she wrote out a simple script telling their story, making this into a book, illustrated with drawings. She hoped the foster parents would use this as a regular bedtime story. She visited the foster home with a collection of play materials, a teapot house with rooms inside, simple cardboard houses she had made, two cuddly hand puppets, cars and Playmobil figures of parents, children, babies, doctors and nurses. The children were at once eager to look inside the yellow teapot house where they found the figures. She told them she was going to tell them a true story about 'a little boy called Jamie and a little girl called Jenny'. She continues:

> I invited the children to choose a figure to be Jamie and one to be Jenny. Jenny observed quietly. Jamie got involved in choosing figures. I explained how 'Mummy Sue' and 'Daddy Jim' had lots of cross arguments, and how 'Mummy Sue' had gone away. 'Daddy Jim' had tried to look after them on his own. At this point Jamie took the figure that stood for 'Daddy Jim' and shut him in the teapot house, holding down the lid. I remarked that he had shut 'Daddy Jim' in the house but made no other comment. I continued explaining how they went to hospital – moving the figures about as I did so. Jamie said 'Sore tail'; the foster mother, who was sitting quietly observing, said this was his expression for his sore penis, which had been severly ulcerated when he was admitted to hospital. It seemed clear that he was not only able to follow the story, but was connecting it with memories he had of what happened.
>
> Encouraged, I continued the story of their coming to the foster home. Jamie then insisted on introducing another figure into the story – an elderly female figure – a 'grandma'. The foster mother told me that the grandmother rang from time to time to inquire about the children, and was important to them. It was clear that 'grandma' had to be included in the story and in any future plans that were made for them.

> (Hendry 1988: 4).

Enid Hendry went over the story twice, using the same phrases, and then watched as Jamie played repeatedly shutting the daddy in the house, ignoring the mother figure. She then gave them their 'book about them', including Polaroid photographs of the children and foster family, and adding mention of grandma and Jamie's sore tail. The book became extremely important to Jamie from then on, a symbol of continuity and his identity. (In retrospect, Hendry thought she should have made a book for each child.) On her next visit she told the story again and introduced the idea that the children needed a family that could look after them for a long time, as this family only looked after children for a short time. She continues:

> The prospective family had two children and a dog, so I made the family with play figures plus dog, and pretended to drive them along in a car saying that they could come and visit Jenny and Jamie. I had previously arranged with the current foster parents and the intended foster family a first visit to the foster

home to meet the children, so shortly after I had enacted the visit with play figures the 'new family' arrived, complete with dog.

The story was told again. The current foster parents helped Jamie to take photographs of the visitors, and helped him to put them in the book, thus symbolically giving him permission to include them in his life. Jenny quietly showed the visitors the yellow teapot house. The 'new' family were then invited to have a drink, and they settled down to play with the children and look at their life-story book.

(Hendry 1988: 5)

This simple but beautifully effective piece of work enabled the children to move happily and laid the foundation for much further work with the children. It was successful because it was attuned to young children's need for a concrete representation of their experience. Telling the story in the third person gave the children enough emotional distance from it to hear what it was telling them. Through play the children were actively involved and contributing important changes, such as the role of the grandmother. Young children's limited concept of time was recognized in the prompt arrival of the new family after play had introduced them. Foster parents were involved at all stages, of great value when the social worker's role is necessarily limited by time. Above all, although the work was structured this was done so as to receive communication from as well as to give it to the children. Enid Hendry's empathic relationship with them is evident throughout.

Cathartic play and the expression of feelings

In order to grow and develop children must be able to face and feel pain, so that they can deal with it. Life-story work needs to be preceded or accompanied by work which helps children to express and cope with painful feelings. Many hurt children deny their feelings and find it hard to talk about them. Faces showing sad, angry, happy, scared and lonely expressions, drawn on cards which are used in games, can provide a way in (Jewett 1984). Many social workers use, adapt and extend these ideas – for example, using puppets, dolls and paper bag masks for depicting and enacting feelings. Redgrave (1987) uses a slider card, revealing one feeling at a time to talk about. He also draws pictures of sad or angry children encased in a 'holding in' skin, contrasting this with feelings coming out, and asks the child which way it feels better. Professional foster parent in Hull, Marion Burch (1990), has designed posters which she uses to help children to express feelings, such as a fire with no coal (love) so that it could not burn. Some workers use a water analogy to show children how they protect themselves. Coloured water, representing good feelings, is poured into a glass, representing the child, but most is spilled. The little remaining water in the glass is covered with cling film which protects it but means that no one can pour in any more (Owen and Curtis 1988). The technique can show that the child was not 'born bad' but started as an empty glass, waiting to be filled with good feelings which their parents were unable to do.

When a child's basic needs have not been met in the past then anger is inevitable, often either directed inwards at the self or towards inappropriate people. Children may first need help to recognize the source of their feelings so that they can direct their anger appropriately. Jewett (1984), a valuable source of ideas for anger work, suggests becoming aware of the part of the body, hands, feet or mouth, which a child uses to express anger and then directing the child's attention to safely discharging anger accordingly through, for example, yelling or writing expletives, thumping clay or tearing newspaper, kicking or stamping on a cushion. Owen and Curtis (1988) emphasize the value of carefully conducted anger work. They offer many ideas from hitting cushions or images of the object of anger using a rolled up newspaper, throwing paper balls at a specific target and foot stamping, to drawing, painting or modelling feelings or the object of anger and then destroying them or it, role play directed by the child, and 'hot seating', talking to a person imagined in an empty chair. They recommend that objects resembling real weapons should not be used. They have found that once anger is discharged other deep-seated feelings, of hurt, or sorrow, or loneliness, often start to emerge.

Many family placement workers make use of a cathartic technique to express grief, the candle ceremony. Different forms are explained by Owen and Curtis, and by Jewett. The child may be helped to light candles, signifying loving and caring feelings, for each member of the family, and to express sorrow as a candle is moved away, still alight, representing loss of that person but showing that loving and caring feelings remain as a good memory. The child may need a cuddle or some physical comfort. This is a powerful ceremony and not to be used lightly. It should also come at an appropriate stage. Anger work may often need to precede it.

The need for anger work becomes very clear in the following case study from the team providing the parents/carers and children's progamme at the Children's Society in the Wrekin. An important part of their work is with abused children, referred by Shropshire Social Services, with whom the team works closely. The context in which their demanding and difficult work with abused children takes place can be crucial. The Children's Society team sets out the following working principles.

Teamwork is important in creating, sharing and adapting each other's ideas, and in building a pool of knowledge about communication with children, and in planning sessions. We work in pairs or even threes in carrying out direct work with children. Work with children takes place, where possible, on our own premises, where an environment can be created to help the child feel safe and special. Children are often seen in school hours because we believe our time with them is important and special. (Schools usually strongly support this. One school said that a child would not be able to develop academically until the child's pressing emotional needs were met.)

We allow children to express what they really feel, however angry they are. For example, they may throw bricks (polystyrene!), or draw pictures showing dreadful punishment for a parent, or act out punitive roles such as being a policeman locking up an abuser. We find out what each child sees as important and we do not assume that a child feels the same as we might ourselves feel. A child may see abuse differently from the way an adult sees it. We respect the importance of each child's life. (For example, the eldest child of five children had often fulfilled a parental role in looking after the younger ones, and when in care missed being needed. When we were working with her we encouraged her to share her feelings about what she had given up.) We are not afraid of being truthful with children about the past. For example, we do not invent signs of love from an absent parent. Above all, we give children the time they need. It may take months, or even years, before they are ready to show some of their feelings. We do not pressurize a child to use a session in a particular way if they are not ready, although we always try to end a session positively, such as with a game, or a good memory.

The Children's Society team, Pam King, Julia Selley and Sarah Smith, describe their work with Paul.

Eight-year-old Paul had been physically abused and had witnessed his brother being sexually assaulted by their father. Both children had been threatened with knives and had been locked in dark rooms without any carpets or furniture. During his year in care Paul has had four different foster homes whilst his brother has been placed separately. We work with both the children individually. Although Paul was able to talk quite freely about events he spoke in a very matter-of-fact tone, reasoning everything as though it had happened to someone else. At first Paul rejected the opportunity of play therapy, not being able to cope with free play where he felt out of control. He preferred the structure of expressing his thoughts through drawing, writing or questionnaires.

After a year of talking about different issues this way, Paul became ready to share his true feelings about his dad. At one session the words started to come flooding out and Paul became oblivious to any other work. Using a large floor cushion to represent dad he climbed on a cupboard to jump on him, stabbed and shot him, bound him up like a parcel and hung him from a curtain rail. He tied the toy guns, knives, snakes and spiders around the cushion with a camera placed to take pictures if dad tried to escape. He wrote on the cushion 'Dad Jones leave him here', and on a paper to his brother wrote 'This is for you I hate dad, bastard, wanker'. Another time he used the cushion to fight with on the floor, throwing it around the room and then pushing it into a dark box.

It was important for Paul to let his brother know how he felt about his dad. To be able to do this Paul chose to include his brother's keyworker for part of the session. He left his display as it was until he came again next week so that his brother could see what he had done. When he came again Paul inspected the display and wanted confirmation that his brother had been informed. Paul and his worker both took photographs of the display, which may lead to further discussion.

Paul can display troublesome behaviour but the attractive side of his personality is emerging. He often tests his foster mother and our own rules. He has learned that in his special sessions here it is acceptable to express angry and destructive feelings in ways which are not allowed at school or at home, where they disrupt other children or the family. We have frequent discussions with his foster mother about our work with Paul and she understands that what he does with us is quite separate from what she provides for him.

It is immediately striking that it took a year of structured work before Paul felt able to reveal his angry feelings. It emphasizes the importance of going at the child's pace, however slow this may seem. It also makes clear the need for continuity of work, in the 'sanctuary' setting which was provided. The involvement of foster parents was important so that each could understand the other's role and then set appropriate and different limits for Paul. Dockar-Drysdale's stages towards integration illuminate the process of Paul's anger work. First he had to *experience* and *realize*, or become aware of, his anger. He then *symbolized* it in his display construction. Finally, by taking photographs he was able to *conceptualize* it – that is, put it into a form in which he could think about it and talk about it.

NON-DIRECTIVE PLAY THERAPY FOR CHILDREN IN CARE

Some children in care are deeply disturbed by a long-term continuous series of damaging events in their lives, particularly when they have not had sufficient help at the time, such as that provided by Kate Burke's intensive family placement work, to make sense of the changes and moves that have happened to them. They tend to ricochet from one placement to another, and, as they grow older, become increasingly hard to manage, even ending up in prison. They also become harder to reach, blocking off all painful emotions in withdrawal, shallow friendliness or aggressive acting-out.

Therapeutic work is likely to be long and arduous, for both therapist and child, but offers a possibility of change and growth for the child which may not be possible in any other way. Most of these children are in residential care, either in residential homes or schools. Few people are available to do this work. They are mainly psychotherapists and art therapists. However, there are a few other workers, who have learned their skills in varied ways, who provide non-directive play therapy.

Social worker Janet West, in what appears to be a unique post, is employed as a play therapist by Nottinghamshire Social Services Department. (Play therapy in this kind of setting is most often carried out as sessional work by independent play therapists.) Formerly student training organizer in Leicestershire Family Service Unit, she described her work there in 'Play Therapy with Rosy' (West 1983). This is not only a case study of her work with a very disturbed six-year-old girl, then in residential care, the daughter of deprived and disturbed parents, but also an exploration of the theoretical background of non-directive play therapy. It constitutes an invaluable introduction to the subject. Janet West's approach is influenced by Rogers's and Axline's belief in the child's immanent potential for healing and growth, and by psychodynamic principles drawn from the work of Freud, Jung, Erikson and Winnicott. She offers non-directive play, recognizing that play is not automatically therapeutic without the therapist's sensitive, accepting and respectful response. Whilst giving interpretations using advanced empathy she recognizes that the child may reject them and, with Winnicott, notes that significant development occurs when the child surprises itself with an insight or under-standing.

In her play therapy with Rosy, Janet West used a well-equipped playroom, free from interruptions and available for regular sessions. Equipment included sand and water, a home corner, soft toys and dolls, jigsaw puzzles (often used when a child is puzzling over and trying to integrate parts of itself), blankets, feeding bottles and dummies, big cushions for regressive play, materials for drawing, painting, mod-elling and sticking, books, Lego, miniature animals and cars, musical instruments and dressing-up clothes. Ground rules were set concerning leaving the playroom and limiting damage. Sessions were for one hour a week, for over a year. She worked only with Rosy, as she felt it was important that play therapy offered a unique relationship which was not affected by any disclosures that Rosy might make.

Janet West describes the themes of Rosy's play. One of the most significant was 'a regression to babyhood, and regrowing to the little girl of the here and now' (West 1983: 652). The mother-baby relationship was a major theme with Rosy initially being the domineering mother telling the therapist/baby what to do. Later Rosy was able to become the baby herself needing comfort and love. Food was a related theme. Negative mother themes involving witches and ghosts were played out together until they became less frightening. Sexual themes followed, fraught with difficulties for the child but also for the therapist who needed to deflect Rosy from explicit joint role playing to enactment through doll play. Sublimation in music making followed. West describes Rosy's gradual growth towards age-ap-propriate activities in books, drawing and puzzles, and her improved behaviour and performance at school as therapy progressed. Termination was planned extremely carefully as the therapist was aware she carried a lot of mother transference and she wanted to pass this on to foster parents. She gradually changed her role from being therapist to becoming a real person in Rosy's life. Rosy had photographs and a promised special rug to keep, and the offer of future contact if she wished.

Janet West has found that a child's carers and school are frequently impressed by the changes which play therapy can bring about. Her pioneer work as play therapist in a social services department should encourage the development of opportunities for more work of this kind.

Role play and the worker's role

Occupational/play therapist, Pauline Little, describes some of the situations which children create in role play in therapy sessions and the ways in which the therapist can respond and participate. Her work is in child and family psychiatry in Carlisle. She writes:

> Any therapeutic work with children involves a sincere attempt to try and understand how the world, and the child's experiences, appear to the child. Children will often give vivid glimpses of this through their play and behaviour. I try to create a space where this becomes possible. My aim is not to collect evidence, pass judgment, or change the child's behaviour to something more acceptable. I attempt to accept the child unconditionally and to respond with empathy and honesty. I often fail, but children forgive adult failings if you seem to be making a genuine effort to understand. Within that relationship the children I see are frequently keen to tell their stories and to show me how they feel. Here are a few.

> Cindy, aged five, and her younger sister recently came into foster care. From the start Cindy set up games involving the dolls and the playhouse. Sessions would start with Cindy stating 'You're my little sister and we have lost our mum', and ended with her taking me by the hand and saying 'Come on, we're not good enough, we've got to find a new family'. On one occasion in the playhouse Cindy made great play about shooting people with the gun. 'I'm going to shoot mummy x (foster mother), I'm cross with her, she's bad, she won't throw the boys out' (foster mother's own children). Cindy then turned on me, demanding to know why I didn't throw out the hats that didn't fit her. I acknowledged how angry she was at having to share mummy x and also share me with the other children. Underlying this was her fear that she was not good enough for anybody and would ultimately be rejected.

> Another time Cindy directed me to come to the shop (playhouse) with a particular doll, which appeared to stand for her, and say that the doll had lost its mum and Cindy was going to look after her. Cindy as foster mum became more and more impatient towards the doll and then, yelling 'I can't cope, I can't give her what she needs', called me to the shop again. Another version of this involved Cindy alternating between being a child, who tried and failed to be good, and a foster mum who got crosser and crosser for no apparent reason. This culminated in Cindy as foster mum shouting down the play telephone, 'I can't look after her any more, I can't go on, she's got to go. They've got to find a new family, I don't want her, I've chosen the wrong one, the other children don't want her.' Cindy looked sad and said 'No one wants us, we're not good enough'. I empathized with her feelings. She had at this point just moved foster placement and the sentiments expressed were, from her point of view, essentially accurate. To try and give false reassurance, to tell her it was not true, or not to worry, would have denied her feelings and implied that the sentiments she expressed were unacceptable. That would have further compounded her belief that she was 'not good enough' for anyone to want to keep.

> She then made an idealized family, Cindy being a loving foster mum to the dolls. She made the telephone ring 'Brr brr – hello. Yes, they're having a meeting

to decide if she can stay.' (This undoubtedly referred to a review meeting she supposedly knew nothing about.) Cindy was not sure what the answer would be. She sighed and said tiredly 'It's going on years'. (She had initially been received into short-term care.)

Patsy was eleven and unsettled in her foster placement. She expressed initial interest in playing in the playhouse but seemed a bit self-conscious. I introduced the puppets into the game and Patsy seemed to identify with a benign crocodile puppet who was all mouth, a rather infantile character with an insatiable demand for food. A bit later Patsy replaced the crocodile by a little girl puppet who made demands. As the girl's mum Patsy acceded to these demands, but then she became 'the authorities' and said the girl was being made ill by all the sweets and had to go to hospital. After initial objection the girl's mother agreed. The hospital turned into a 'care' situation, which the girl liked but she also wanted to go home.

She was sent home on a special diet. I was given the role of the girl's mother. Patsy encouraged me to fail in my attempts to give the girl what she needed. Two boy puppets were introduced (Patsy had two brothers) and I was told that they fought and that I was unable to control them. Patsy became a nurse/social worker who came round to 'check up on all the children'. She plotted secretly to take the girl back into hospital/care and said that the girl had to be angry at first then go willingly. Once at the hospital the girl rang up her mum and said that she wanted to go home, which she was allowed to do. Patsy, as a nurse/social worker, desperately tried to sort out her inadequate mother. As her mother I was given money and food so that I could look after the children. She sorted out the boys, kicked out the no good dad, and took back money the boys had pinched. Mum was still not able to cope and Patsy became increasingly exasperated with her. When I gave the five-minute warning for the end of the fortnightly session Patsy said with resignation 'We're closing for two weeks, the kids will have to go into care'.

Mary, aged eight, lives happily with her grandparents. In early sessions she made a story in the sand tray. She created a home for a family of seals, father, mother and baby. The baby got separated from its parents and was put into a different enclosure, where the parents can see her. The parents try to get in but the baby doesn't want them to. 'She likes it living away from her mum and dad.' The mother later gets in but Mary said the dad wasn't allowed to see them at all as 'the Government wouldn't let him'. (He had spent some time in jail.)

Another time she chose Playmobil figures and made the child hit the mother. I verbally stated this action, and when that elicited no response, wondered aloud what might be happening between the mum and the child. Mary said 'You've got to guess'. (Mary was going through a stage where she was quite angry with me for being unable to understand all her unspoken needs.) I commented that the girl seemed very angry with her mum, to which Mary replied emphatically 'yes'. I speculated that maybe the girl thought that her mum didn't want her.

Mary replied, 'Well you've got that right at least!'. Recently Mary, now a year older, has spoken more directly of her family and the person she refers to as her 'ex-mother'.

These are three angry children. Cindy shows both her anger and her underlying fear at not being wanted by her mother, although on the surface her play is about rejection by foster parents and therapist. Patsy's play seems to be about her mother's inability to give her the right 'food', a sign of her inability to provide 'containment'. Despite all the support mother is given, she cannot cope and eventually gives up, to Patsy's anger and sorrow. Mary is angry with her mother for not wanting her and not being able to meet her needs for mothering. Like Cindy she projects some of this anger on to the therapist. The role of the therapist with these children is either a direct empathic reflection of the child's feelings or an acknowledgment of the child's feelings through playing roles assigned by the child.

Play therapy in a residential setting

Workers in residential settings, including foster homes, have the opportunity of providing a therapeutic environment, a more complete therapeutic experience than may be possible otherwise. The demands of near-continuous contact with a disturbed child put extra strains on a residential worker, but with appropriate support a worker may offer a child an invaluable accepting and supporting relationship. Sometimes play can be the key to reaching children.

Curtis (1982) tells how play was used to reach six-year-old Malcolm, in a children's home preparing for adoption. He was a quiet withdrawn child, unable to play with other children or to settle to play on his own without an adult. His keyworker joined in his games of shutting people in jail, houses burning down or monsters coming to get people. She let him take the lead but set limits, such as not allowing him to hit her. Something 'bad' always happened in his games. As he began to express his anxieties in play, Malcolm became able to use other parts of his relationship with his worker. He allowed himself to regress, playing with baby toys, asking to wear a nappy and becoming clinging, even wetting and soiling for a brief time. This re-parenting, making up for past deprivations, allowed him to start to grow up again, to learn new skills and to play (snowballs) with other children, and 'to become alive again'. Eventually, after using play people and making a life flow chart and a life book to understand his past, he was able to transfer his attachment to his worker to a new adoptive family. This work took two years, a significant reminder that work of this kind cannot be hurried.

Provision of a therapeutic environment is the aim of residential special schools which take children with severe emotional disturbances. The crucial contribution that play provision can make to this is recognized by Christine Bradley, training officer for the Caldecott Community. Herself a psychotherapist, she draws on the ideas of Erikson, Winnicott and Dockar-Drysdale concerning the value and use of play. She writes:

One of the ways it is possible to communicate with disturbed and deprived children is through playing. One can use this medium to help the child express the horror of his original trauma, and to progress from that until he discovers his own creativity and eventually is able to establish his identity. I believe that in residential care, if we are able to provide the child with a suitable structure inside which he is able to initiate his own play, and the grown-up can respond to him in a sensitive way, then it may be possible to reach a level of communication which could not happen in any other setting.

(Bradley)

Christine Bradley finds that many children in residential care are stuck at the early stages of narcissistic and pre-oedipal play. They have not reached integration and are rarely ready to make use of symbolic play. At the Caldecott Community, children who are not ready to benefit from attending school during the day may go to a nurture group, where play activities such as sand and water are freely provided, with a high adult–child ratio. Here children may meet their needs for sensory and regressive play. The school has small ponies for the children to ride and cuddle which meet a similar need. The living room for the younger children at Laxton House has a sunken floor filled with huge cushions.

All the children live in small care groups with their residential staff. Christine Bradley has been working with these staff, helping them to provide a therapeutic playroom in each of their 'houses'. She trains one play specialist in each care team. Her aim is that children should be given the opportunity of a special time to use play to deal with their anxieties, rather than acting out their phantasies at inappropriate times, as often happens. The playroom is kept as a special place and is locked when it is not in use. Each child has 40 minutes a week in the playroom with their keyworker. The playroom is equipped for domestic and imaginative play with a variety of materials, but without it becoming so full that it becomes unclear to the child what the playroom offers. (One of these playrooms is described in Chapter 3.) The children are told that it is a time when they may play as they like. They must not damage or break things and they must clear up afterwards. These rules are generally respected as children do not want to damage 'their' room.

Some initial difficulties needed recognition and working through. Some keyworkers were uncomfortable with the idea of spending time alone with a child. With experience the structure of the session with its beginning, middle and end became reassuring. Sometimes the concern came from the remaining worker who was left in charge of seven or so children. More generally the potential role of a special playroom was not always understood, or led to jealousies, only changing as its value to the children became apparent.

In the playroom Adrian put on a cape and made cakes from play dough, playing the king's tea party. He threw the contents of his teacup (water) all over his worker and stuffed a biscuit in her mouth, to her dismay. Yet before the end of his session he wanted a story read to him. Christine Bradley describes him as a frozen child, a narcissistic king. Normally he eats five dinners. After his playroom session a sandwich was enough! Emmy repeatedly built towers from blocks and knocked them down. After a visit to her home town she played tipping and pouring sand and water, threatening the worker by doing it very close to her face. After this expression of anger she relaxed and talked for the first time.

A favourite game is burying and finding. Gordon played for 40 minutes burying and finding people and a dog in the sand tray, getting very excited and using a baby voice. Vicky, an integrated child, has a doll beside her all the time and plays sorting out animal families in the sand, burying, finding and re-grouping them. Sometimes she cries for hours, wishing things had been different. Her worker allows and accepts this but finds it painful. Steve complains that the toys are babyish but still plays with them, annihilating objects in the sand. Winston's play reflects his day-to-day-life; if it is chaotic outside it is chaotic in the playroom. He enacts telephone calls from his social worker who is ending his mother's access. Kathy pours sand through the wheel whilst talking about her future, a source of much anxiety. Kelly plays repeatedly with a doll, always telling her worker to be the mother and giving her explicit instructions, such as to be cross and shout, or be loving. (This has echoes of Janet West's play with Rosy.)

A worker may not always know or understand what a child is doing in play, but the worker's accepting presence and willingness to try to understand can be enough containment to help a child to start to heal itself. The opportunity to share their experiences with other workers, with supervision and support, provides the containment which workers also need.

Sometimes even some profoundly disturbed children, perhaps those who have lost the integration they once had, or 'archipelago' children with islets of ego integration, are able to make use of symbolic play within the context of a relationship with a nurturing adult. Christine Bradley records a moving account of her use of therapeutic play in helping an adolescent boy reach integration, in her previous work in the Cotswold Community. It is important to note that play was part of an overall therapeutic environment. What took place in play sessions was shared with and had the support of care staff and teachers. Discussion with a consultant outside the whole situation provided important support and objectivity in understanding what was happening.

Tom was a quiet withdrawn 15-year-old boy. His mother had been severely depressed during pregnancy and made several suicide attempts after he had been born. She left Tom and his father when he was a few years old. Before she left it was reported that she had sometimes locked Tom in a room on his own all day without food. Although the father had struggled after the mother's departure to provide Tom with the care that he needed, he became quiet and solitary, and at seven years he was stealing from shops. The father eventually remarried and Tom found this particularly difficult to accept, even though the step-mother tried hard to relate to him. He gradually became more and more difficult to handle, continually running away from home and being delinquent. This was followed by his running away from the children's homes and community homes where he was placed.

When Tom arrived at the Cotswold Community he was fifteen but looked only twelve. He could barely communicate and when you so much as said 'hello' to him he shrank away as though you were going to hit him. Yet in spite of his quiet withdrawn manner there was another side of Tom which would spiral into excitement very quickly. He would 'merge' in with other boys' delinquency and only by physically separating him out from the person he was involved with would he quieten down at all. He could not distinguish between what was himself and what was other people. For most of the time he lived in total merger with his environment and was deeply unhappy. Occasionally one would see bits of real ego functioning, but in between there lay total chaos and despair. He attempted to prevent grown-ups from getting in touch with this part of himself, by using his quiet withdrawn self as a survival technique.

After some time we became very concerned about Tom and wondered if we would ever be able to help him at all. He could not communicate and the only time he seemed to make contact with the other boys was when he was involved in some form of excitement with them. The grown-ups could not discover what it was that he needed; all we could do was manage his life in such a way that he did not get into serious trouble, that is, by making sure that somebody was looking after him most of the day. It did not seem possible to help him emotionally.

One evening, when I went to say goodnight to Tom in his bedroom, he asked me to read him a story, something he had always rejected when it was suggested before. I read him the story of the little red fox who was constantly finding himself in trouble. He listened intently, and after a while he began to play with a little toy car which he had. I asked him if he had ever really played and he said he had not. I suggested that perhaps he would like a sand tray in his bedroom, so that he could play with it at bedtime or whenever he felt the need. He said he would like that very much and asked me if I would provide him with some animals to play with. He said specifically that he would like mothers and babies.

I discussed what had happened with the rest of the team and the following day we provided him with the sand tray. I bought him a selection of farm animals, a cow and a calf, a horse and a pony, hen and chicks, and some others. Tom was thrilled with these and immediately went into his room to play. He was very quiet for the rest of the evening and when I went in to see him he was in the corner of his room completely absorbed in the sand tray. I asked if I might join him and he nodded. I went over to where he was and saw that he had split the sand into two sections, with a river in-between. I noticed that the mother animals were on one side of the river and the babies on the other, neatly tucked into individual holes which he had made for them. I asked Tom what was happening. He told me that all the babies were going to run away as the mothers had left them alone and gone to play bingo. They were going to steal the mother hen's eggs and run away with them. At this point I felt I should intervene; it was clear that Tom was expressing something he was feeling at that time but I did not know what. I asked Tom if I should go over to the other side of the river and bring the mothers back, as perhaps then the babies would feel safer and not need to run away. He said I could but he did not think they would return. I pretended to sail across the river in the boat that he had made and tell the mother animals that their children were planning to run away as they were feeling so neglected. I brought all the mothers back just as Tom had lined the babies up ready to run away. I told him that the mothers were coming back, saying they would not leave their babies again. Tom immediately put the babies back in the holes with their mothers and said they would be all right.

By now it was getting quite late and I said that Tom should get into his bed too, now that he knew the babies would be safe. When he was in bed he asked me if I would make him a milky drink and a hot-water bottle, the first time he had done so. As I was tucking him up he told me he had planned to run away that night with another boy but now he had decided not to. I said I was glad that he had been able to tell me, and that perhaps at last he was beginning to feel more secure with us in the unit. He settled down to sleep. I had not mentioned the sand play, although it was now clear to me that this was what he had been acting out through the animals. It is quite likely that had I not been there and responded in the way I did, by being a 'concerned' mother, he would not have been able to ask for the provision that he did. He symbolized what he was feeling and then was able to turn that into verbal communication.

After this breakthrough the sand tray came to be a focal part of Tom's treatment with us. I realized that we had been able to provide him with something through which he could communicate. I arranged with the rest of the team that I would always be available to spend 15 minutes every evening playing with Tom. The time never varied, 9.15 to 9.30, just before he went to sleep. The sand tray became deeply important to Tom and when I was not there he would not use it, nor would he ever allow any of the other grown-ups to play with him, even though they all knew what was happening. As he came to depend on the time that I spent playing with him, so he was able to use the care and help offered to him in the unit. He seemed to be more at peace with himself and would often come to be looked after, developing aches and pains which needed attention. Eventually he felt secure enough with us to be able to show the more vulnerable unhappy side of himself. It became clear that he needed to be in a room on his own; up to that time he was sharing with another boy. Immediately he moved into his own room he was ill, so that he had to stay in bed for several days. During that time he was able to be helpless and dependent. At times he said he was too ill to eat, and had to be fed. He needed to be washed and his hot-water bottle had to be filled almost hourly! Much of the time he was ill he played with the sand tray. I kept to my regular time to play with him.

After four or five days Tom began to get back on his feet. When I went to play with him one evening I found that he had separated the animals into four groups, one in each of the four corners of the sand tray, the very small ones in one corner, slightly bigger ones in the next, and so on. The river was still in the middle. I asked what was happening. He told me that some of the animals were beginning to grow up and as they did they moved up a corner until they were properly grown, when they went into the river on their own, as they were by then big enough to look after themselves. This seemed to be the beginning of Tom's recovery. He seemed stronger inside and looked much more alive than he had done before. He was able to avoid other people's excitement by going off to his room to play with his sand tray. Sometimes he would go off on his own accord and sometimes at the suggestion of a grown-up.

The sand tray became more symbolic. He bought a milkmaid who looked after sick animals. This seemed to represent myself, as after a day's illness I returned to be told that the milkmaid had been given the sack for having a day off without permission. Only after Tom had made a lot of heavy demands on me and needed much looking after was she re-instated. He made a small pen which he said was for the animals who got over-excited, so that they would feel safer and would not disturb the other animals. Daily I would notice that some of them had moved up a corner. At the same time Tom was developing a sense of his own identity and was beginning to relate more substantially to other people apart from myself.

After some time he became attached to the unit cat whom he would spend a great deal of time cuddling; the cat became his transitional object. He was much more creative than he had been before. He painted pictures and brought in plants. One afternoon we spent some time picking shrubbery for the sand tray, which Tom now called 'his real world'. At the same time he was also becoming much more real. Tom was almost at the state of integration when I had to leave the unit to work elsewhere in the community. He was able to survive this break without disintegration or acting-out. He could verbally communicate his anxieties to other staff and was able to transfer his dependency from myself to them. After my departure the sand tray ceased to be used; eventually he asked for it to be taken from his room altogether. He no longer needed it. By now he was relating to other objects and was able to distinguish between what was himself and what was the outside world. He went to a unit for more integrated boys where he was able successfully to use the cultural opportunities which were provided for him there. He had enough 'inner world' to be able to relate to the outside world.

Reflecting on what had happened Christine Bradley continues,

If I had not been able to find a way of communicating with Tom through playing it might not have been possible to make a relationship with him. He made his first real contact with me through the sand tray, after which he was able to establish a primary bond and me to provide him with adaptations, the hot-water bottle and the milk. There followed a short period when he became totally dependent on me. During this time it was imperative that I was reliable and trustworthy, always keeping to the time I had arranged to play with him, never being late and never exceeding the boundary of 15 minutes. This way Tom knew exactly where he was. He was then able to separate out from me slowly and use the cat as his transitional object, the bridge between his inner world which his play experience had enriched and the external environment. Slowly he was able to become more creative and use the cultural opportunities of another unit. Through play Tom had moved from a state of non-being to being. After he became integrated he used his play as a space between himself and the outside world. Initially he communicated symbolically about his plans to run away. Later when I was leaving the unit he could talk about his anxieties and could describe how he was feeling to other people.

It is important that we are receptive when a child first tries to make contact with us. This can come in all sorts of strange ways which we may not even recognize. As long as we respond sensitively then it will allow him to feel that it is all right to carry on. If I had told Tom, when he attempted to make his first contact with me, that I did not have time to read him a story he might never have taken the risk again.

Appendix 1

Training for play

NEEDS IN TRAINING

A theory base

A play therapist needs knowledge of human growth and development and the role of play in development. The theoretical underpinning of training comes primarily from study of the work of Donald Winnicott and Barbara Dockar-Drysdale, Melanie Klein, Erik Erikson, John Bowlby, Carl Rogers and Virginia Axline. Their broadly psychodynamic and non-directive approaches are developed in much recent work in theory, research and practice.

Baby and child observation

Training in observation of children is crucial and should provide the core of any study. Infant observation in particular makes the observer aware of the early expression of raw emotions, before their existence is covered up in various ways, and so can offer a way of learning about the inner world of the child. It also helps understanding of the process of 'containment' in mothering, and awareness of how far the mother is herself contained. Learning to hold the role of the observer means learning to be emotionally present and at the same time able to preserve the ability to think about what is going on. Observation of children at later ages and stages is necessary to put flesh on textbook accounts of child development, as well as to understand how children are affected by different contexts. Observation is helpful both to workers who are not parents and lack an intimate acquaintance with children and to those who are parents but need reminding that their own children are not a yardstick for measuring everyone else's.

Experiential work and personal therapy

Experiential work in helping workers recall their own childhood memories and feelings is vital in developing a real understanding of how children may be feeling, perhaps particularly in recognizing the intensity of children's emotions. Memories of playing can be a positive way in to reaching past feelings and at the same time revealing the creative power of play. As well as being a way of understanding how children feel, exploring personal memories and feelings can enable a worker to become able to sort and separate their own feelings from those of the child or adult with whom they are working. This is essential for working with the counter-transference and providing containment. It is important to be aware that some memories may be extremely painful. Experiential exercises should not be undertaken lightly or without appropriate support being available at the time and afterwards. Training for child psychotherapy involves a full personal analysis; play therapists in training can benefit from their own personal therapy.

Developing skills

Whilst study of academic research and writing provides an essential framework, only practical and experiential work can bring this to life. Opportunities for the student to experience play themselves and to discuss their experiences need to be built in to any course. Adult education students joke about receiving lectures on running discussion groups; teaching about play must not fall into the same trap. Experiential methods need to be used to teach the skills of reflective listening and non-directive play. Practical role-playing is a good way to do this. Focused play techniques can be demonstrated and practised similarly. Students need an opportunity to try out new skills in supervised work with children and families, and to have opportunities to share and learn from one another's experiences. They need to be able to explore and reflect on the application of play therapy approaches in the particular context in which they work.

TRAINING IN PLAY THERAPY AND THERAPEUTIC PLAY

When this book was first written (1991) there was no specific qualification for play therapy in Britain, and play therapists arrived at their skills through a variety of idiosyncratic routes. The 1990s have seen a surge of interest in play therapy and there are now (1997) several training courses in play therapy, as well as the formation of a professional organization, the British Association of Play Therapists which validates courses as providing a qualification to practise.

Various kinds of training are available in which skills in using play therapy and therapeutic play form a part. Training for specific professions may involve some study of therapeutic play, either on courses leading up to initial qualifications or on post-qualification courses, often multi-disciplinary.

Child psychotherapists, especially those influenced by Winnicott and Klein, may use play to understand the inner world of and communicate with highly disturbed children. Some child psychotherapists are passing on some of their knowledge and skills to others working with children and families through multidisciplinary courses in child observation and therapeutic communication with children, offered by some centres to experienced workers.

Social workers and occupational therapists may specialize in therapeutic work with children, often learning by 'apprenticeship' and adding to their knowledge through post-qualifying and in-service courses. Hospital play specialists have a specific play training. Teachers, nurses, nursery nurses, playgroup workers, playworkers, speech therapists, educational and clinical psychologists and psychiatrists may receive a limited amount of information about therapeutic play in their basic training and add to this through post-qualification courses. Art, dance, movement and drama therapists, and music therapists have their own specialized training.

The following lists of courses may not be complete and details of courses and their validation may change. Interested students should seek further information for themselves.

COURSES IN PLAY THERAPY AND THERAPEUTIC WORK WITH CHILDREN

A list of courses in play therapy is available from:
British Association of Play Therapists, PO Box 98, Amersham, Bucks HP6 5BL. This list includes courses validated by BAPT as a licence to practise, such as the York and Roehampton Diplomas in Play Therapy.

Post-Qualifying Training in Non-Directive Play Therapy, University of York
The programme aims to provide training in non-directive play therapy at an introductory and clinical level within an educational framework which encourages the highest possible standards of academic achievement and professional practice. Students are trained in the method of play therapy developed from Rogers and Axline but there are links to other therapeutic approaches. Therapeutic work undertaken in a statutory context receives particular attention.

This is a modular programme for qualified professionals who normally have at least two years' experience in working with children and families and who wish to train as play therapists. It leads after a minimum of one year part-time study to a *Certificate in Play Therapy* and after two years to a *Diploma in Play Therapy*. The course is accredited by the International Board of Examiners of Certified Play Therapists as a professional training programme, and by CCETSW as an Advanced Award. Course director is Kate Wilson and staff include Virginia Ryan and Janet West.

The Certificate includes modules on normal and abnormal child and adolescent development and child observation (both requisites for proceeding), non-directive play therapy, supervised clinical practice and theoretical and clinical issues. Teaching is through a combination of two block weeks, fortnightly sessions, some distance learning work, assignments, individual supervision (offered in London, Leicester, and possibly Oxford, as well as York) and support group meetings.

The Diploma is similarly structured and includes advanced theoretical and practice issues (3 modules), clinical practice in non-directive play therapy, with children with more complex problems (2 modules, and individual supervision), and personal counselling (arranged by the student, minimum 30 hours).

Contact the Post-Qualifying Programme Secretary, Department of Social Policy and Social Work, University of York, Heslington, York YO1 5DD.

Courses in Play Therapy, Roehampton Institute, London

The programme views play therapy as based on the essentially human quality of imaginative and dramatic playfulness – communicating through bodily expression, projective images and improvised role play. Training is open to those with an appropriate degree, professional qualification or experience. The programme takes place at weekends and in summer schools. Teaching staff include Ann Cattanach and Brenda Meldrum.

The *Certificate of Play Therapy* course introduces students to the creative basis of play and its communicative potential, and to basic theories fundamental to the use of play as therapy. This is an introductory programme and does not constitute a licence to practise.

The *Diploma in Play Therapy* is part-time over one year and is a professional qualification. All candidates must demonstrate a basic understanding of the theory and practice of play therapy, normally obtained through satisfactory completion of the Certificate in Play Therapy. Modules include clinical theory (2 modules), play therapy method (working with abused children and children with illness or disability – 2 modules), play therapy practice and supervision and personal therapy.

There is also a *Certificate in Art and Play in Therapeutic Work with Children*.

For the Roehampton Institute courses contact The Faculty Registry Office, Faculty of Arts and Humanities, Digby Stuart College, Roehampton Lane, London SW15 5PH.

Certificate in Play Therapy – Kairos

The two-year course, eleven days a year, aims to encourage the use of play therapy which recognizes the full creative potential of the child, and to develop the therapeutic potential both of play in all its forms and of the course participants. There is emphasis on experiential learning, skills development and on archetypal material – 'restorying' through myths and legends. The play therapy course may become a module of a full programme of Diploma, Degree and MA courses in Counselling Development. Kairos also offers a variety of workshops related to play therapy.

Contact Kairos, 53 Ferriby Road, Hessle, Hull HU13 OHS (Director: Ted Wharam).

Lowenfeld Projective Psychotherapy with Children and Adolescents
Therese Woodcock, Developmental Psychiatry, Douglas House, 18b Trumpington Road, Cambridge CB2 2AH. Margaret Lowenfeld's original non-interpretative approach to play therapy is the focus of a planned MA modular course (not before 1998). Initial training includes experiential work, seminars and group supervisions.

Certificate in Therapeutic Play, Caldecott College
The Paddocks, Smeeth, Ashford, Kent TN25 6SP. Tutor: Christine Bradley. This part-time short course draws on the long tradition of psychodynamic play-based therapeutic work at the Caldecott therapeutic community for children and young people. It provides an introduction to symbolic communication through play and the skills involved in the therapeutic use of play.

The Play Therapy Trust
Ann Cattenach and Brenda Meldrum offer a variety of workshops, seminars and residential week-ends, through The Play Therapy Trust, Scotts Lodge Cottage, Cudham Lane South, Knockholt, Kent TN14 7NY.

Play for Real
Day workshops and short courses are available from time to time from Play for Real, 16 West End, Witney, Oxon OX8 6NE.

Postgraduate Diploma/MA in Play Therapy and Therapeutic Play, Leeds Metropolitan University
Faculty of Health & Social Care, Calverley Street, Leeds LS1 3HE. This course draws on the college's experience in playwork and therapeutic play.

PSYCHODYNAMICALLY BASED COURSES IN THERAPEUTIC WORK WITH CHILDREN

MA in Therapeutic Child Care, University of Reading
This is a two-year part-time post-qualifying course. It is a broadly-based course open to experienced workers in a wide range of settings. Students attend one day a week plus two residential workshops. The structure of the course day is intended to match the demands of practice; particular features are the use of opening and closing meetings, and the experiential group. The course includes study of the therapeutic community for children and

adolescents, therapeutic communication with children, philosophy for practice, understanding organizations, management issues. Students write a dissertation in their second year. The theoretical basis of the course is psychodynamic, particularly drawing on the work of Donald Winnicott and Barbara Dockar-Drysdale. Practical approaches include 'milieu therapy', and provision of 'primary experience', as well as play therapy. Course leader is Adrian Ward, and Linnet McMahon is a tutor. Contact Department of Community Studies, Faculty of Education and Community Studies, University of Reading, Bulmershe Court, Earley, Reading RG6 1HY.

Certificate and Diploma courses in Therapeutic Child Care, Caldecott College

The Paddocks, Smeeth, Ashford, Kent TN25 6SP. The one-year foundation Certificate course is accredited by the University of Greenwich. The two-year part-time Diploma course for qualified social workers and others is accredited by the University of Exeter and CCETSW. 'Managing or doing therapeutic work with children is the conscious exercise of a combination of skills – play, provision of food, clear boundaries, everyday routines, coping with transitions, assessing needs, making attachments, communication (verbal, non-verbal, symbolic), professional and ethical relationships, creating a culture – all of which reach both the conscious and unconscious worlds of the child' (course brochure). Other venues may include Stephenson Hall in London, Birmingham, Exeter and Newcastle. There is the possibility of progression to an MA at the University of Greenwich.

The Forum for the Advancement of Educational Therapy and Therapeutic Training (FAETT)

Organizes part-time training, with both academic and clinical components, in *Educational Therapy* for experienced teachers and educational psychologists. Contact FAETT at Canonbury Child Guidance Unit, Health Centre, River Place, Essex Road, London N1 or 3 Templewood, London W13 8BA.

Department of Child Psychiatry, **St George's Hospital**, Lanesborough Wing, St George's, Blackshaw Road, Tooting, London SW17 OQT, has a two-year part-time *Diploma in Psychotherapy Skills with Children and Adolescents.*

The Institute of Psychiatry, De Crespigny Park, Denmark Hill, London SE5 8AF, offers short courses as well as a one-year full-time *Diploma in Child and Adolescent Psychiatry.*

The Tavistock Clinic, Belsize Lane, London NW3 5BA, offers numerous courses including:
Postgraduate Certificate in Therapeutic Communication with Children (one half-day a week for a year), in London.

Postgraduate Diploma/MA in Psychoanalytic Observation Studies, with the University of East London.

Equivalent *baby and child observation courses* are available in Birmingham (Birmingham Trust for Psychoanalytic Psychotherapy), Bristol (United Bristol Hospitals Trust), Leeds (Leeds Psychotherapy Unit), Liverpool (Dept of Child Psychology and Psychiatry, Alder Hey Children's Hospital), Nottingham (Nottingham Psychotherapy Unit), London (Lincoln Centre) and Oxford.

Postgraduate Certificate Counselling Aspects in Education: Emotional Factors in Teaching and Learning, for teachers especially.

Psychodynamic Work in Learning Disability.

An Introduction to Working with Children Under Five and Their Families (10 sessions).

Working with Disruptive Adolescents (one week).

British Association of Psychotherapists, 37 Mapesbury Road, London NW2 4HJ, offers the following external courses:

Therapeutic Communication with Children and Adolescents: the contribution of psychoanalytic thinking.

From Infancy to Adulthood: an introduction to working with psychoanalytic concepts.

Infant Observation seminars – a Jungian approach.

The BAP also offers joint courses:

Understanding Emotional Life from Infancy to Adulthood, with the Specialist Psychotherapy Services, Leeds, Dept of Psychotherapy, Southfield House, 40 Clarendon Road, Leeds LS2 9PJ.

MSc/Diploma in Psychodynamics of Human Development, with Birkbeck College, University of London, Dept of Psychology, Birkbeck College, Malet Street, London WC1E 7HX.

Lincoln Centre for Psychotherapy, 19 Abbeville Mews, 88 Clapham Park Road, London SW4 7BX, offers *Postgraduate Diploma/MA in Observational Studies and Application of Psychoanalytic Concepts to Work with Children, Young People and their Families.*

Merseyside Psychotherapy Institute, Aldey Hey Hospital, Liverpool 12, offers courses in *Communication with Children, Child Observation*, etc., and with the Tavistock Clinic the *MA in Psychoanalytic Observation Studies.*

Scottish Institute of Human Relations, 56 Albany Street, Edinburgh EH1 3QR, offers a course in *Working with Children.*

Centre for Postgraduate Psychology, Uffculme Clinic, Queensbridge Road, Moseley, Birmingham B13 8QD. *Individual work with children and young people and their families in various settings: a psychodynamic approach*, is a one-year part-time course with an optional second year.

The Bridge Foundation for Psychotherapy and the Arts, 12 Sydenham Road, Cotham, Bristol BS6 5SH.

TRAINING IN CHILD PSYCHOTHERAPY

Training in child psychotherapy is long and expensive, and not widely available. The Association of Child Psychotherapists requires potential students to have an Honours degree or its equivalent, preferably including some study of human relations; they must have a suitable personality for the work, and experience of work with children. Training takes a minimum of four years. Each student is required to undergo a personal analysis, to gain insight into their own infantile unconscious conflicts, so they are better prepared to understand children's conflicts. Students develop their skills initially through detailed observation of infants and young children. They learn about child development and psycho-analytic theory, and methods of child psychotherapy. Clinical training consists of the intensive treatment of individual patients of different ages carried out under supervision. Children may be seen for one or more years, for fifty-minute sessions, between one and five times a week.

Theoretical approaches differ between centres. The Tavistock Clinic is influenced by the theories of Melanie Klein, the Anna Freud Centre by the theories of Sigmund and Anna Freud, and the Society of Analytical Psychology by Jung. The *Journal of Child Psychotherapy* (Routledge) gives accounts of work.

The training courses recognized as a qualification to practise by the Association of Child Psychotherapists, 120 West Heath Road, London NW3 7TU, are offered by:

The Anna Freud Centre for the Psychoanalytic Study and Treatment of Children, 21 Maresfield Gardens, London NW3 5SH.

Birmingham Trust for Psychoanalytic Psychotherapy, 96 Park Hill, Mosely, Birmingham B13 8DS.

The British Association of Psychotherapists, 37 Mapesbury Road, London NW2 4HJ.

Scottish Institute of Human Relations, 56 Albany Street, Edinburgh EH1 3QR.

The Society of Analytical Psychology, 1 Daleham Gardens, London NW3 5BY.

The Tavistock Clinic and Portman NHS Trust, Belsize Lane, London NW3 5BA.

OTHER MULTI-DISCIPLINARY COURSES

The reflective listening approach of the Children's Hours Trust has been described in earlier chapters. The Trust may offer training workshops. Contact **The Children's Hours Trust,** c/o White House, Clapham Park Estate, London SW4 8HD, or (for work with disabled children) Helen Cockerill at Guys Hospital Newcomen Centre.

The British Association for Counselling, 1 Regent Place, Rugby, Warwicks CV21 2PJ, has a division for counselling in education and produces a directory of training courses in counselling, some of which are counselling for children. For example, the **Central School of Counselling and Therapy**, 118–120 Charing Cross Road, London WC2H OJR, offers an *Introduction to Counselling Children and Adolescents*.

Some multi-disciplinary academic courses are available. **The Open University**, Department of Health and Social Welfare, The Open University, Walton Hall, Milton Keynes MK7 6AA, offers *Working with Children and Young People*. This is a half credit course (K254) with 220 hours study time, intended for a wide range of practitioners and managers; it includes skills in working with children. The course is also available as a self-contained study pack.

HOSPITAL PLAY SPECIALISTS

The courses give training to those who wish to specialize in play in work with children in hospital. The one-year courses leading to *The Certificate in Hospital Play Specialism* involve one day a week in college and further block study weeks and practical placements. Experience of work with children is necessary, and usually an appropriate qualification. Minimum age is twenty. There is also a *BTEC Hospital Play Specialist* qualification. The following offer courses approved (or * pending approval) by the Hospital Play Staff Examination Board or Education Trust:

Basford Hall College, Stockhill Lane, Nottingham NG6 ONB. (*BTEC)
Bolton College, Hilden St Centre, Bolton, Lancs BL2 1JB.
Charles Keene College, Painter St, Leicester LE1 3WA. (*BTEC)
College of Care and Early Education, Broadlands Drive, Lawrence Weston, Bristol BS11 0QA.
East Antrim Institute of Further and Higher Education, Newtownabbey Campus, 44 Shore Road, Newtownabbey, Co. Antrim BT37 9RS, and Dublin.
North East Surrey College of Technology (NESCOT), Reigate Road, Ewell, Epsom, Surrey KT17 3DS.

North Warwickshire College, Hinckley Road, Nuneaton CV11 6BH.
Preston College, St Vincents Road, Fulwood, Preston PR2 9UR.
(*BTEC)
South Nottingham College, Greythorn Drive, W. Bridgford, Nottingham
NG2 7GA. (*BTEC)
Southwark College, CET Faculty, Surrey Docks Centre, Drummond Road,
London SE16 4EE.
Stanmore College, Elm Park, Stanmore, Middx HA7 4BQ .
Stevenson College, Bankhead Avenue, Sighthill, Edinburgh EH11 4DE.
Sutton College, Lichfield Road, Sutton Coldfield, W. Midlands B74 2NW.
(*BTEC)

Further information can be obtained from **Hospital Play Staff Examination
Board** and **National Association of Hospital Play Staff (NAHPS)**, both
at 40 High Street, Landsbeach, Cambridge CB4 4DT.

THERAPEUTIC PLAY IN NURSERY NURSING AND PLAYGROUP WORK

The *Diploma in Nursery Nursing* gives some introduction to emotional
development and play in its two-year full-time course. NVQs and the
Certificate in Child Care and Education are more basic courses. The part-time
Advanced Diploma in Child Care and Education can include study of
therapeutic play, although this is not a requirement. Further information
may be obtained from **CACHE,** 8 Chequer Street, St Albans, Herts
AL1 3X2.

The *Diploma of Playgroup Practice* is a part-time course over one or
two years. Information about this and other courses for parents and playgroup workers is available from **The Pre-school Learning Alliance**, 69
Kings Cross Road, London WC1X 9LL.

THERAPEUTIC PLAY IN PLAYWORK

Playwork is defined as work with children aged 5 to 15 to facilitate their
development through play. There are **National Centres for Playwork
Education** in Birmingham, Cheltenham, London and Newcastle. Contact
The National Play Information Centre (part of the National Playing Fields
Association), 199 Knightsbridge, London SW7 1DE, or **CACHE** which
validates NVQs in playwork.

Diploma in Higher Education (Playwork) courses are available at:
Leeds Metropolitan University, Calverley Street, Leeds LS1 3HE.
The Sheffield College, The Norton Centre, Dyche Lane, Sheffield S8
8BR.
Thurrock College, Woodview, Grays, Essex RM16 4YR.

University of Northumbria, Dept of Education Studies, Coach Lane Campus, Newcastle upon Tyne NE7 7XA.

MSc/Diploma in Playwork is available at Moray House Institute of Education, Heriot-Watt University, Holyrood Road, Edinburgh EH8 8AQ.

The Children's Play Council, providing a forum for play-related organizations, is based at the National Children's Bureau, 8 Wakley Street, Islington, London EC1V 7QE.

PLAY THERAPY IN OCCUPATIONAL THERAPY

Play therapy for emotionally disturbed children in child psychiatric settings is often provided by occupational therapists, who learn about child development and psychopathology as part of their basic three-year training. Often their play therapy training is by apprenticeship within their unit, although increasingly they attend multi-disciplinary courses – for example, modules in play diagnosis and play therapy may be available at the Institute of Family Psychiatry, 23 Henley Road, Ipswich IP1 3TF (Vicky Hall).

The University of East London, Stratford Campus, Romford Road, London E15 4LZ, offers a two-year part-time *MSc in Paediatric Occupational Therapy*, covering paediatrics, child psychiatry and learning difficulty.

Further information may be obtained from **The College of Occupational Therapists**, 6–8 Marshalsea Road, London SE18 1HL, who also have the contact address for the **National Association of Paediatric Occupational Therapists (NAPOT)**.

THERAPEUTIC COMMUNICATION WITH CHILDREN IN SOCIAL WORK

Some *Diploma in Social Work* courses include training in child observation using the psychoanalytical model. Most social workers develop their skills through post-qualifying training. The Central Council for Education and Training in Social Work (CCETSW), 4th floor, Derbyshire House, St Chad's Street, London WC1H 8AD, lists courses on work with children and families, including child observation and direct work with children. One is the *Diploma in Advanced Social Work (Children and Families)* at Goldsmiths' College, University of London, New Cross, London SE14 6NW. Goldsmiths' course was the basis for the development of *Communication With Children*, a teaching pack widely used on in-service courses.

The University of East London, Longbridge Road, Dagenham, Essex RM8 2AS, offers a *Postgraduate Diploma in Child Care: policy, practice and research*, for social workers and nurses and a *Postgraduate Certificate/ Diploma/MA in Child Protection: Abused Children and their Carers: Assessment, Treatment, Management*, in conjunction with the Tavistock Clinic. **The Tavistock Clinic** also offers *Children in Transition: Frameworks for Assessment and Communication with Children* (10 sessions for fostering and adoption workers).

The *MA in Social Work* at the University of Reading, Bulmershe Court, Earley, Reading RG6 1HY, offers modules on baby and child observation and therapeutic work with children.

The **NSPCC**, National Training Centre, 3 Gilmour Close, Beaumont Leys, Leicester LE4 1EZ, the **British Association for Adoption and Fostering (BAAF)** and **National Foster Care Association (NFCA)** provide courses on skills in work with children. **NCH Action for Children** run courses including communication through play at Stephenson Hall, 85c Highbury Park, London N5 1UD.

Independent social workers may provide consultancy and training sessions and courses. One of the most valuable agencies, working mainly in the area of child sexual abuse, is **SACCS (Sexual Abuse: Child Consultancy Service)**, Mytton Mill, Montford Bridge, Shrewsbury, SY4 1HA. Founded by Madge Bray and Mary Walsh, skills in using play form the core of their approach.

INTEGRATIVE ARTS THERAPY

The Institute for Arts in Therapy and Education, principal Margot Sutherland, The Windsor Centre, Windsor Street, London N1 8QL and Terpsichore, 70 Cranwich Road, London N16 5JD, offers a wide range of courses, including *Certificate in the Therapeutic and Educational Appl ication of the Arts* (level 1 course), *Diploma of the Institute for Arts in Therapy and Education* (level 2 course), *Diploma in Integrative Arts Psychotherapy* (level 3 qualifying course), and also *MEd/BPhil in The Arts in Therapy and Education*. There are also taster days and short courses on art, sandplay, music, drama, puppetry, dance movement, the Education of the Emotions, etc.

ART THERAPY

Courses are approved by the **British Association of Art Therapists**. A prior qualifying training in art is a pre-requisite for embarking on the one-year training courses for a *Diploma in Art Therapy*, although some other courses are open. Courses are based on psycho-dynamic theory, particularly influenced by Klein and Winnicott. The child's own self-healing through creativity in art and play is central to an art therapist's approach. In this respect art therapy training comes close to the ideal training for a play therapist. Art therapists are also expected to keep alive their own creative process. Colleges offering courses in art therapy include:

University of Hertfordshire School of Art and Design, Manor Road, Hatfield, Herts AL10 9TL. Alida Gersie is Director of Studies of the Graduate Arts' Therapies Programme.
Goldsmiths' College, University of London, Lewisham Way, London SE14.
Birmingham School of Art Education, Margaret Street, Birmingham B3 3BX.
Roehampton Institute, Faculty of Arts and Humanities, Digby Stuart College, Roehampton Lane, London SW15 5PH.

Further information can be obtained from **British Association of Art Therapists**, 11A Richmond Road, Brighton BN2 3RL, and **British Institute for the Study of Arts in Therapy**, Christchurch, 27 Blackfriars Road, London SE1.

DRAMATHERAPY, DANCE AND MOVEMENT THERAPY

Courses are available at:

University of Hertfordshire School of Art and Design, Manor Road, Hatfield, Herts AL10 9TL.
Roehampton Institute, Institute of Dramatherapy, Digby Stuart College, Roehampton Lane, London SW15 5PH.
Laban Centre for Movement and Dance, Laurie Green, New Cross, London SE14 6NH.
Sesame Institute, Christchurch, 27 Blackfriars Road, London SE1 8NY (Mary Smail). Training includes *Postgraduate Diploma in Drama and Movement Therapy*.

Further information from:

British Association for Dramatherapists, 5 Sunnydale Vale, Durlston Road, Swanage, Dorset BH19 2HY.
Association for Dance Movement Therapy, c/o Arts Therapies Dept, Springfield Hospital, Glenburnie Road, Tooting Bec, London SW17 7DJ or 99 South Hill Park, London NW3 2SP.

MUSIC THERAPY

Nordoff Robbins Music Therapy Centre, 3 Leighton Place, London NW5 2QL.
British Society for Music Therapy, 25 Rosslyn Avenue, E. Barnet, Herts EN4 8DM.

Appendix 2

Sources of play materials and books

E. J. Arnold, Parkside Lane, Dewsbury Road, Leeds LS11 5TD.

Mike Ayres, Unit 14, Vanguard Trading Estate, Britannia Road, Chesterfield, Derbyshire S40 2TZ. (Sensory environments)

'Being Yourself', 73 Liverpood Road, Deal, Kent CT14 7NN – catalogue of games and materials.

Community Playthings, Robertsbridge, East Sussex TN32 5BR.

Early Learning Centre, South Marston, Swindon SN3 4TJ.

James Galt, Brookfield Road, Cheadle, Cheshire SK8 2PN.

Hestair Hope, St Philips Drive, Royton, Oldham, Lancashire OL2 6AG.

Litework, Unit 2, Woodgate Park, White Lund Industrial Estate, Morecambe, Lancashire LA3 3PS. (Sensory environments)

Nottingham Educational Supplies, 17 Ludlow Hill Road, Melton Road, West Bridgford, Nottingham NG2 6HD.

Rompa, Goyt Side Road, Chesterfield S40 2PH. (Sensory environments)

Tfh (toys for the handicapped), 76 Barracks Road, Sandy Lane Industrial Estate, Stourport on Severn, Worcs DY13 9OB.

Show and Tell Dolls, Sunrise, Museum Hill, Haslemere, Surrey GU27 2SR. (Anatomically complete dolls)

Stockingfillas, Euroway Business Park, Swindon SN38 2NN.

Bridge Child Care Consultancy, 1st floor, 34 Upper Street, London N1 0PN. (Needs Game, My Life in Words & Pictures, for computers)

Forum Bookshop/Bookstall Services, 86 Abbey Street, Derby.

Letterbox Library, 8 Bradbury Street, London N16 8JN. (Multicultural and non-sexist books)

One Parent Families, 255 Kentish Town Road, London NW5 2LX. (Annotated bibliography, *A Guide to Books for Children and Young Adults Living in One Parent Families*)

PLANET Play Leisure Advice Network is a national information resource on play and recreation for people with disabilities. Play leaflets include *Special Play for Special Children*, and *Positive Images of Disability in Children's Playthings*.

Play Matters (National Toy Libraries Association), 68 Church Way, London NW1 1LT. (Publishes annual *Good Toy Guide*)

REACH National Resource Centre for Children with Reading Difficulties, formerly National Library for the Handicapped Child, Wellington House, Wellington Road, Wokingham, Berks RG40 2AG.

Save the Children, Cambridge House, Cambridge Grove, London W6 0LE.

Working Group Against Racism in Children's Resources, 460 Wandsworth Road, London SW8 3L8.

Appendix 3

Useful organizations

Action for Sick Children (NAWCH), Argyle House, 29–31 Euston Road, London NW1 2SD.

Adventure Play for Disabled Children (HAPA), Pryors Bank, Bishops Park, Fulham, London SW6 3LA. (With national information service on play and disability)

Association for Child Psychology and Psychiatry, St Saviour's House, 39–41 Union Street, London SE1 1SD.

BAPSCAN (British Association for the Prevention and Study of Child Abuse and Neglect), 10 Priory Street, York YO1 1EZ.

Barnardo's, Tanners Lane, Barkingside, Ilford, London IG6 1QG.

Boys and Girls Welfare Society, Central Offices, Schools Hill, Cheadle, Cheshire SK8 1JE.

Bridge Child Care Consultancy, 1st floor, 34 Upper Street, London N1 0PN.

British Association for Adoption and Fostering (BAAF), Skyline, 200 Union Street, London SE1 0LX.

Catholic Children's Society, 49 Russell Hill Road, Purley, Surrey CR8 2XB. (One of 5 regional centres)

Children in Scotland (SCAFA), Princes House, 5 Shandwick Place, Edinburgh EH2 4RG.

Children's Legal Centre, The University of Essex, Wivenhoe Park, Colchester, Essex CO4 3SQ.

Children's Society, Edward Rudolf House, Margery Street, London WC1X 0JL.

Council for Disabled Children, at the National Children's Bureau.

Exploring Parenthood, 41 North Road, London N7 9PD.

Family Conciliation Scotland (SAFCOS), 127 Rose Street, South Lane, Edinburgh EH2 5BB.

Family Service Units, 207 Old Marylebone Road, London NW1 5QP.

Home Start UK, 2 Salisbury Road, Leicester LE1 7QR.

Kids, 80 Waynflete Square, London W10 6UD.

KIDSCAPE (Campaign for Children's Safety and the Prevention of Abuse), 157 Buckingham Palace Road, London SW1.

Institute of Family Therapy, 24–32 Stephenson Way, London NW1 2HX.

National Association of Young People in Care (NAYPIC), 8a Stuckey Place, Camden, London NW1 8NJ.

National Centre for Play, Moray House College of Education, Holyrood Road, Edinburgh EH8 8AQ.

National Childminding Association, 8 Masons Hill, Bromley, Kent BR2 9EY.

National Children's Bureau, 8 Wakley Street, London EC1V 7QU.

NCH Action for Children, 85 Highbury Park Road, London N5 1UD.

National Children's Play and Recreation Unit, 359–361 Euston Road, London NW1 3AL.

National Early Years Network (VOLCUF), 77 Holloway Road, London N7 8JZ.

National Foster Care Association, Leonard House, 5–7 Marshalsea Road, London SW1 1EP.

National Playbus Association, 93 Whitby Road, Bristol BS4 3QF.

National Stepfamily Association, Chapel House, 18 Hatton Place, London EC1N 8RU.

National Society for the Prevention of Cruelty to Children (NSPCC), 42 Curtain Road, London EC2A 3NH.

Play For Life, 31b Ipswich Road, Norwich NR2 2LN.

Pre-school Learning Alliance, 69 Kings Cross Road, London WC1X 9LL. Scottish PPA, 14 Elliot Place, Glasgow G3 8EP. Wales-PPA-Cymru, 2A Chester Street, Wrexham, Clwyd LL13 8BD. Northern Ireland PPA, 11 Wellington Park, Belfast BT9 6DJ. Irish PPA, 19 Wicklow Street, Dublin 2.

Save the Children Fund, 17 Grove Lane, London SE5 8RD and Cambridge House, Cambridge Grove, London W6 0LE.

Thomas Coram Foundation for Children, 40 Brunswick Square, London WC1N 1AZ.

Voice for the Child in Care, 4 Pride Court, 80–82 White Lion Street, London N1 9PF.

Voluntary Service Aberdeen, 38 Castle Street, Aberdeen AB11 5YU.

West Indian Concern, Caribbean House, Bridport Place, Shoreditch Park, London N1 5DS.

Who Cares? Trust, 152–160 City Road, London EC1V 2NP.

Young Minds (National Association for Child and Family Mental Health) 102–108 Clerkenwell Road, London EC1M 5SA. (Has telephone advice service)

Appendix 4

Recommended reading in play therapy

Axline, V. (1989 orig. 1947) *Play Therapy*, Edinburgh: Churchill Livingstone.

Carroll, J. (1995) 'The Protection of Children Exposed to Marital Violence', *Child Abuse Review* 3, 1: 6–14.

Carroll, J. (1995) 'Reaching out to Aggressive Children', *British Journal of Social Work* 25: 37–53.

Carroll, J. (1997) *Introduction to Therapy through Play: Practical Help for Troubled Children*, Oxford: Blackwell Scientific.

Cattanach, A. (1992) *Play Therapy with Abused Children*, London: Jessica Kingsley.

Cattanach, A. (1994) *Play Therapy: Where the Sky meets the Underworld*, London: Jessica Kingsley.

Cockerill, H. (1992) *Communication through Play*, The Cheyne Centre, 61 Cheyne Walk, London SW3 5LT.

Crowe, B. (1983) *Play is a Feeling*, London: Allen and Unwin.

Gil, E. (1991) *The Healing Power of Play: Working with Abused Children*, London/New York: Guilford Press.

Gil, E. (1994) *Play in Family Therapy*, London/New York: Guilford Press.

Jennings, S. (1993) *Play Therapy with Children: A Practitioner's Guide*, Oxford: Blackwell Scientific.

Michell, R. and Friedman, H. (1994) *Sandplay Past, Present and Future*, London: Routledge.

Newson, E. (1992) 'The Barefoot Play Therapist; Adapting Skills for a Time of Need', in D. Lane and A. Miller (eds), *Child and Adolescent Therapy: A Handbook*, Buckingham: Open University Press.

Pinney, R. (1990) *Children's Hours: Special Times for Listening to Children*, The Children's Hours Trust, c/o 28 Whitehouse, Clapham Park Estate, London SW4 8HD.

Ryan, V. and Wilson, K. (1995) 'Child Therapy and Evidence in Court Proceedings: Tensions and Some Solutions', *British Journal of Social Work* 25, 2: 157–72.

Ryan, V. and Wilson, K. (1996) *Case Studies in Non-Directive Play Therapy*, London: Baillière Tindall.

Webb, N. (1991) *Play Therapy with Children in Crisis*, New York: Guilford Press.

West, J. (1983) 'Play Therapy with Rosy', *British Journal of Social Work* 13: 645–61.

West, J. (1992) *Child-Centred Play Therapy*, London: Arnold.

Wilson, K., Kendrick, P. and Ryan, V. (1992) *Play Therapy: A Non-Directive Approach for Children and Adolescents,* London: Baillière Tindall.

Appendix 5

Books for children

GENERAL

Ahlberg, J. and A. (1977) *Burglar Bill*, Heinemann.
Blume, J. (1985) *The Pain and the Great One*, Heinemann. (Siblings)
Foreman, M. (1987) *Panda's Puzzle*, Penguin. (Identity)
Harmin, M. (1976) *This Is Me!* and *Got to Be Me! A Book to Grow With*, Argus Communications. (Sets of workbooks and cards)
Hughes, S. (1977) *Dogger*, Bodley Head/Fontana. (Regression)
Larsen, H. (1979) *What Are You Scared Of?*, A & C Black.
McAfee, A. (1987) *Kirsty Knows Best*, J. MacRae. (Bullying)
McKee, D. (1982) *Not Now, Bernard*, Sparrow.
Maximé, J. E. (1987) *Black Like Me*, workbook one, *Black Identity*, Emami Publications,125 Avenue Road, Beckenham, Kent BR3 4RX.
Meyer, M. (1976) *There's a Nightmare in My Cupboard*, Dent.
Oram, H. (1982) *Angry Arthur*, Anderson/Puffin.
Ormerod, J. (1984) *101 Things to Do with a Baby*, Viking Kestrel. (Regression)
Ross, T. (1987) *Oscar Got the Blame*, Anderson. (Imaginary friend)
Sendak, M. (1967) *Where the Wild Things Are*, Bodley Head. (Picture book)
Striker, S. and Kimmell E. (1978) *The Anti-colouring Book*, Hippo Books. (Also, *The Second Anti-colouring Book*, *The Anti-colouring Book of Masterpieces*, etc.)
Tomlinson, J. (1973) *The Owl Who Was Afraid of the Dark*, Puffin.
Waddell, M. (1988) *Can't You Sleep Little Bear?*, Walker.
Willis, J. and Varley, S. (1986) *The Monster Bed*, Anderson.

BEREAVEMENT

Alexander, S. (1986) *Leila*, Hamish Hamilton.
Althea (1988) *When Uncle Bob Died*, Dinosaur.
Crimmin, A. and Perkins, G. (1991) *Remembering Mum*, A & C Black.
Egger, B. (1987) *Mary and Her Grandmother*, Viking Kestrel.
Hollis, S. and Sireling, L. (1989) *When Mum Died* and *When Dad Died*, St George's Hospital and Silent Books, Swavesy, Cambridge CB4 5RA.
Hoy, L. (1981) *Your Friend, Rebecca*, Bodley Head.
Keller, H. (1987) *Goodbye Max*, Julia Macrae.
Krementz, J. (1983) *How It Feels when a Parent Dies*, Victor Gollancz. (Eighteen personal accounts from black and white children)
Little, J. (1985) *Mama's Going to Buy You a Mocking Bird*, Viking Kestrel.
Madler T. (1982) *Why Did Grandma Die?*, Blackwell Raintree.

Marlee, B. and A. (1983) *Grandpa and Me*, Lion.
Perkins, G. and Morris L. (1991) *Remembering Mum*, Black.
St Christopher's Hospice (1989/90) *Someone Special Has Died*. (A special booklet for grieving children, Hospice Social Work Department, 51–9 Lawrie Park Road, London SE26)
Sanders, P. (1989) *Let's Talk About Death and Dying*, Watts.
Simmonds, P. (1987) *Fred*, Cape/Penguin. (Death of a cat, comic strip)
Smith, D. B. (1987) *A Taste of Blackberries*, Penguin. (Older children)
Stilz, C. (1988) *Kirsty's Kite*, Lion. (Picture book)
Varley, S. (1985) *Badger's Parting Gifts*, Armada. (Picture book)
Ward, B. (1987) *Good Grief: Talking about Loss and Death*, and (1989) *Good Grief: Exploring Feelings, Loss and Death with Under-elevens, a Holistic Approach*, Good Grief, 19 Bantree Road, Uxbridge, Middx UP8 1PT. (Resource books with activities)
Wilhelm, H. (1985) *I'll Always Love You*, Hodder and Stoughton. (Death of his dog)
Wilkinson, T. (1991) *The Death of a Child – a Book for Families*, Julia MacRae.

DIVORCE AND STEP-FAMILIES

Althea (1980) *I Have Two Homes*, Dinosaur.
Baum, L. (1987) *Are We Nearly There?*, Magnet.
Blume, J. (1972) *It's Not the End of the World*, Piccolo.
Boyd, L. (1987) *The Not-so-wicked Stepmother*, Viking Kestrel.
Brown, L. K. and Brown, M. (1987) *Dinosaur's Divorce*, Collins.
Erup, B. (1979) *Suzanne's Parents Get Divorced*, A & C Black.
Family Conciliation Scotland (SAFCOS) (in press) *Me and My Changing Family*, 127 Rose Street, South Lane, Edinburgh EH2 5BB.
Fine, A. (1989) *Goggle-eyes*, Hamish Hamilton. (About a parent's possible re-marriage)
Galloway, P. (1985) *Jennifer Has Two Daddies*, Womens Press.
Gydal, M. (1976) *When Gemma's Parents Got Divorced*, Hodder and Stoughton.
Hogan, P. (1982) *Mum, Will Dad Ever Come Back?*, Blackwell.
Krementz, J. (1984) *How It Feels when Parents Divorce*, Gollancz.
McAfee, A. (1984) *The Visitors Who Came to Stay*, Hamish Hamilton.
Mark, J. (1985) *Trouble Half-way*, Viking Kestrel.
Petty, K. and Kooper, L. (1988) *Splitting Up (First Timers)*, Franklin Watts.
Raintree, L. and Coale, H. (1980) *All about Families the Second Time Around*, Peachtree Publishers. (Workbook)
Sinberg, J. (1978) *Divorce Is a Grown-up Problem*, New York: Avon Books, available from Sisterwrite, 190 Upper Street, London N1. (Includes colouring book)
Snell, N. (1983) *Sam's New Dad*, Hamish Hamilton.
Townsend, S. (1984) *The Diary of Adrian Mole*, Avon.
Wilson, J. (1986) *The Other Side*, Oxford.

FOSTERING, ADOPTION, AND CARE

Althea (1984) *My New Family*, Dinosaur.
Althea (1987) *Jane Is Adopted*, Souvenir Press.
Alton, H. (1987) *Moving Pictures*, BAAF. (Trigger pictures)
Ashley, B. (1979) *The Trouble with Donovan Croft*, Oxford University Press. (Fostering)
Aston, E. (1981) *Getting to Know You*, BAAF. (Book and poster set)
Bawden, N. (1986) *Princess Alice*, Methuen Magnet.
Byars, B. (1980) *The Pinballs*, Puffin.

Crompton, M. (1978) *The House where Jack Lives*, Bodley Head.

Feltham, H. and Robson, M. (1986) *Children's Home*, A & C Black.

Feltham, H. and Goodman T. (1987) *About You and Fostering*, National Foster Care Association.   (Workbook for teenagers)

King, P. (1988) *Talking Pictures*, BAAF.   (Pictures to complete)

Koch, J. (1985) *Our Baby – A Birth and Adoption Story*, Perspectives Press.

Krementz, J. (1982) *How It Feels to Be Adopted*, Victor Gollancz.   (Nineteen children's experiences)

Lapsley, S. (1974) *I Am Adopted*, Bodley Head.

Macliver, C. and Thom, M. (1990) *Family Talk*, BAAF.   (Picture sheets for children whose family is adopting or fostering)

National Foster Care Association (1990) *My Book about Me*.   (Also available from BAAF)

Orritt, B. (1990) *Dennis Duckling – Going into Care*, The Children's Society.

Paterson, K. (1979) *The Great Gilly Hopkins*, Penguin.   (Fostering)

Snell, N. (1985) *Steve Is Adopted*, Hamish Hamilton.

Thom, M. and Macliver, C. (1986) *Bruce's Story*, The Children's Society.   (Workbooks – care, adoption)

Van der Meer, R. and A. (1989) *Joey*, National Foster Care Association.   (Fostering)

Wagstaff, S. (1981) *Wayne Is Adopted*, A & C Black.   (Mixed parentage)

SEXUAL ABUSE

Bray, M. (1989) *Suzie and the Wise Hedgehog Go to Court*, London: Hawkesmere.

Children's Legal Centre (1991) *Being a Witness*.   (Information sheet for the child witness)

Hessell, J. and Nelson, M. (1988) *I'm Glad I Told Mum (formerly What's Wrong with Bottoms?)*, Hutchinson/Beaver Books.

Hindman, J. (1983) *A Very Touching Book*, Durkes, Oregon, McClure-Heindmann.

Lennett, R. with Crane, B. (1985) *It's OK to Say No!*, Bridlington, Peter Haddock Ltd/Thorsens.   (Colouring and activity book)

Lewis, C. S. (1959) *The Lion, the Witch and the Wardrobe*, Puffin.   (Good and evil)

Morgan, L. (1982) *Daniel and His Therapist*, Papers Inc.

Morgan, L. (1986) *Katie's Yucky Problem*, Papers Inc.   (Picture book for young children)

Morgan, L. (1987) *Megan's Secret*, Papers Inc.   (For older children)

Otto, M. L. (1987) *Tom Doesn't Visit Us Any more*, Women's Press, Can.   (Picture book on child abuse)

Peake, A. (1989) *My Body, My Book*, London: Children's Society.

Rayner, C. (1979) *The Body Book*, London: Pan Books.

Rouf, K. (1989) *Secrets*, London: Children's Society.   (Different versions with white or black family)

Rouf, K. (1989) *Mousie*, London: Children's Society.   (Picture book for young children)

Wachter, O. (1985) *No More Secrets for Me*, Viking Kestrel.

HOSPITAL

Althea (1986) *Going into Hospital*, Dinosaur.

Althea (1986) *Special Care Babies*, Dinosaur.

Althea (1989) *I Have Cancer*, Dinosaur.

Bowden, J. (1989) *When I Went to Hospital*, Little Mammoth.   (For young children/multicultural)

Civadi, A. and Cartwright, S. (1986) *Going to the Hospital*, Usborne.

Cork, B. T. (1989) *First Experiences*, Going to Hospital, Octopus.

Cowlishaw, S. (1989) *Jenny Has a Tumour*, available from Malcolm Sargent Cancer Fund social worker, Queen's Medical Centre, Nottingham NG7 2UH.

Cunliffe, J. (1990) *Big Jim, Little Jim*, Deutsch.

Davies, S. and Bentley, D. (1989) *My Visit to the Hospital*, Wayland.

Gillespie, J. (1989) *Brave Heart*, Hutchinson.   (By a nine-year-old)

Janosch, (1986) *Little Tiger, Get Well Soon*, Hippo.

Jessel, C. (1983) *Going to Hospital*, Methuen, and *Paul in Hospital*, Octopus.

Mercer, G. (1988) *Inside a Hospital*, Kingfisher.

National Association for the Welfare of Children in Hospital (NAWCH) *When I Went to Hospital*.   (Colouring sheets, and photographic leaflet in different languages)

Reuter, E. (1989) *Christopher's Story*, Hutchinson.   (Cancer)

Rodin, J. and Shelley, P. (1989) *Sammy Goes to Hospital*, NAWCH.   (Comic format)

Wade, B. (1982) *Linda Goes to Hospital*, A & C Black.   (Tonsillectomy)

Watts, M. (1978) *Crocodile Plaster*, Deutsch.

Wells, P. (1985) *Talk about Going to Hospital*, Ladybird.   (Multicultural)

DISABILITY

Althea (1985) *I Can't Hear Like You*, Dinosaur.   (In same series, (1982) *I Can't Talk Like You*, (1983) *I Have Asthma*, (1988) *I Have Eczema*, also *I Have Epilepsy*, *I Use a Wheelchair* and *I Have a Mental Handicap*)

Anderson, R. and McNicholas, S. (1988) *Jessy Runs Away*, and also *Best Friends*, A & C Black.   (Down's syndrome)

Brearley, S. (1991) *Adventure Holiday*, A & C Black.   (Wheelchairs)

Dowling, P. (1985) *My Special Playgroup*, Hamish Hamilton.

Gillham, B. (1981) *My Brother Barry*, André Deutsch.

Hearn, E. (1986) *Race You Franny*, Women's Educational Press.   (Wheelchair) (In same series, *Good Morning Franny*; also *Franny and the Music Girl*, Magi)

Jessel, C. (1975) *Mark's Wheelchair Adventures*, Methuen.

Laird, E. (1988) *Red Sky in the Morning*, Heinemann.   (Older children)

Larsen, H. (1974) *Don't Forget Tom*, A & C Black.

Merrifield, M. (1990) *Come Sit by Me*, Women's Press.   (HIV/AIDS)

Peterson, P. (1986) *Sally Can't See*, A & C Black.

Pettenuzzo, B. (1987) *I Have Spina Bifida*, Franklin Watts.   (In same series (1987) *I Am Deaf*, *I Have Diabetes*, *I Have Down's Syndrome* (1988) *I Have Asthma*, *I Am Blind*, *I Have Cystic Fibrosis*, *I Have Cerebral Palsy*)

Rooke, A. (1986) *I'm Louise*, Learning Development Aids.   (Picture book on Down's syndrome)

Shyer, M. (1981) *Welcome Home, Jellybean*, Granada.   (Severe learning difficulties)

Slatford, J. (1987) *Our Family Has Huntington's*, Association to Combat Huntington's Chorea.

Spence, E. (1976) *The October Child*, Oxford University Press.   (Autism)

Yeatman, L. (1986) *Buttons, The Dog Who Was More Than a Friend*, Hippo.   (Deafness)

Yeatman, L. (1986) *Pickles*, Piccadilly.   (Disability through accident)

Yeatman, L. (1987) *Perkins, The Cat Who Was More Than a Friend*, Piccadilly.   (Visual disability)

Young, H. (1980) *What Difference Does It Make Danny!*, Deutsch.   (Epilepsy)

Bibliography

Ahmed, S., Cheetham, J. and Small, J. (eds) *(1986) Social Work with Black Children and Their Families*, London: Batsford/BAAF.

Aldgate, J. and Simmonds, J. (eds) *(1988) Direct Work with Children*, London: Batsford/BAAF.

Alton, H. and Firmin, C. (1987) *Moving Pictures*, London: BAAF.

Atkin, J. (1985) 'Imaginative Play in Early Childhood Education', Update 2, OMEP.

Atkinson, I. and Mead, A. (1981) 'Play Therapy with a Mother and Child', in S. Martel, *Direct Work with Children*, London: FSU/NCVO.

Axline, V. (1947 and 1989) *Play Therapy*, Boston: Houghton Mifflin, and Edinburgh: Churchill Livingstone.

Axline, V. (1964a) *Dibs: In Search of Self*, Harmondsworth: Penguin.

Axline, V. (1964b) 'Recognition and Reflection of Feelings', in M. Haworth, *Child Psychotherapy*, New York: Basic Books.

Ayres, J. (1985) *Sensory Integration and the Child*, Los Angeles: Western Psychological Services.

Baker, A. (1986) 'Child Abuse – The Power of Play', *Community Care* 23 January: 14–16.

Banks, E. and Mumford, S. (1988) 'Meeting the Needs of Workers', in J. Aldgate and J. Simmonds, *Direct Work with Children*, London: Batsford/BAAF.

Bannister, A. (1989) 'Healing Action – Action Methods with Children Who Have Been Sexually Abused', in H. Blagg *et al.* (eds), *Child Sexual Abuse: Listening Hearing and Validating the Experiences of Children*, London: Longman.

Bannister, A. and Print, B. (1988) *A Model for Assessment Interviews in Suspected Cases of Child Sexual Abuse*, NSPCC Occasional Paper 4, London: NSPCC.

Bateson, G. (1973) 'A Theory of Play and Fantasy', in *Steps Towards an Ecology of Mind*, London: Paladin.

Batty, D. (ed.) *(1986) Working with Children*, London: Batsford/BAAF.

Batty, D. and Bailey, N. (1984) *In Touch with Children*, London: Batsford/BAAF.

Belson, P. (1989) 'Play: An Instant Route to Recovery', National Children's Bureau, *Concern* 70: 6–7.

Bentovim, A. (1977) 'The Role of Play in Psycho-therapeutic Work with Children and their Families', in B. Tizard and D. Harvey (eds) *The Biology of Play*, London: Heinemann.

Bentovim, A., Elton, A., Hildebrand, J., Tranter, M. and Vizard, E. (1988) *Child Sexual Abuse within the Family – Assessment and Treatment*, London: John Wright.

Berry, J. (1972) *Social Work with Children*, London: Routledge and Kegan Paul.

Bettelheim, B. (1978) *The Uses of Enchantment: The Meaning and Importance of Fairy Tales*, Harmondsworth: Penguin.

Binney, V. (1991) 'Relationship Play Therapy – Improving Mother–Child Attachments in 4–6 Year Olds with Serious Relationship Difficulties', lecture to Oxford ACPP Conference on the Application of Attachment Theory and Ethology to Clinical Problems, 18 March.

Bion, W. R. (1962) *Learning from Experience*, London: Heinemann.

Black, D. (1990) 'Averting a Crisis', *Social Work Today* 15 March, 11.

Blagg, H., Hughes, J. A. and Wattam, C. (eds) (1989) *Child Sexual Abuse: Listening Hearing and Validating the Experiences of Children*, London: Longman.

Blunden, P. (1988) 'Diagnostic Interview Using Family Tasks', NAPOT newsletter, Spring.

Boston, M. and Daws, D. (eds) *(1977) The Child Psychotherapist and Problems of Young People*, London: Wildwood House.

Boston, M. and Szur, R. (eds) *(1983) Psychotherapy with Severely Deprived Children*, London: Routledge and Kegan Paul.

Bowen, B. and Nimmo, G. (1986) 'Going Over the Bridge – A Practical Use of Metaphor and Analogy', *Journal of Family Therapy* 8, 4: 327–37.

Bowlby, J. (1969 and 1982, 1973, 1980) *Attachment and Loss*, vol. 1, 'Attachment', vol. 2, 'Separation, Anxiety and Anger', vol. 3, 'Loss, Sadness and Depression', London: Tavistock, Hogarth Press, and Harmondsworth: Penguin.

Bowyer, R. (1970) *The Lowenfeld World Technique*, London: Pergamon.

Boyce, L. and Anderson, S. (1990) 'A Common Bond – Group Therapy with Children Who Have Been Sexually Abused', *Social Work Today* 3 May: 38.

Bradley, C. (unpublished paper) 'Management of Therapeutic Play in a Residential Setting'.

Braithwaite, C. (1986) 'Art Always Reveals Truth ...', *Community Care* 31 July.

Bray, M. (1986) 'Communicating with Young Children', *Childright* 31 October.

Bray, M. (1988) *Monsters and Rainbows*, Everyman Programme, BBC video.

Bray, M. (1989) *Susie and the Wise Hedgehog Go to Court*, London: Hawkesmere.

Bray, M. (1991) *Poppies on the Rubbish Heap – Sexual Abuse: the Chiid's Voice*, Edinburgh: Canongate.

Brodzinsky, D. *et al.* (1984), Children's Understanding of Adoption, quoted in A. Burnell (1990), 'Explaining Adoption to Children Who Have Been Adopted', Post Adoption Centre Discussion Paper 3, January.

Brummer, N. (1986) 'White Social Workers, Black Children: Issues of Identity', in S. Ahmed, J. Cheetham and J. Small (eds), *Social Work with Black Children and Their Families*, London: Batsford/BAAF.

Bruner, J. (ed.) (1966) *Studies in Cognitive Growth*, New York: Wiley.

Bruner, J. (1983) 'The Functions of Play', address to the Pre-school Playgroups Association conference at Llandudno, in *Contact*, December.

Bruner, J. S., Jolly, A. and Sylva, K. (eds) *(1976) Play: Its Role in Development and Evolution*, Harmondsworth: Penguin.

Burch, M. (1990) personal communication.

Burke, C. (unpublished working notes) Catholic Children's Society, and personal communication.

Burnell, A. (1990), 'Explaining Adoption to Children Who Have Been Adopted: How Do We Find the Right Words?' Post Adoption Centre Discussion Paper 3, January.

Burnham, J. B. (1986) *Family Therapy*, London: Tavistock.

Carpenter, J. and Treacher, A. (1989) *Problems and Solutions in Marital Work and Family Therapy – a Practical Handbook*, Oxford: Blackwell.

Carroll, J. (1990, unpublished paper) 'Meeting the Needs of Children'.

Case, C. and Dalley, T. (eds) *(1990) Working with Children in Art Therapy*, London: Routledge.

Cass, J. E. (1971) *The Significance of Children's Play*, London: Batsford.

Catholic Children's Society (1983) *Finding Out about Me*, Purley: CCS.

Child, E. (1985) *General Theories of Play*, London: National Children's Play and Recreation Unit.

Christopherson, J., Furniss, T., O'Mahoney, B. and Peake, A. (eds) (1989) *Working with Sexually Abused Boys*, London: National Children's Bureau.

Cleveland, M. *et al.* (1981) 'Family Groupwork', in S. Martel, *Direct Work with Children*, London: FSU/NCVO.

Cohen, D. (1987) *The Development of Play*, London: Croom Helm.

Copley, B. and Forryan, B. (1987) *Therapeutic Work with Children and Young People*, London: Robert Royce.

Crompton, M. (1980) *Respecting Children: Social Work with Young People*, London: Arnold.

Crompton, M. (1991) *Attending to Children: Direct Work in Social and Health Care*, London: Arnold.

Crowe, B. (1974) *Playgroup Activities*, London: Pre-school Playgroups Association.

Crowe, B. (1980) *Living with a Toddler*, London: George Allen and Unwin.

Crowe, B. (1983) *Play Is a Feeling*, London: George Allen and Unwin.

Curtis, P. (1982) 'Communicating through Play', *Adoption and Fostering* 6, 1: 27–30.

Dalley, T. (1985) *Art as Therapy*, London: Tavistock.

Dare, C. and Lindsey, C. (1979) 'Children in Family Therapy', *Journal of Family Therapy* 1: 253–69.

Dartington, T. Henry, G. and Menzies Lyth, I. (1976) 'The Psychological Welfare of Young Children Making Long Stays in Hospital', report from Tavistock Institute, London.

Dearling, A. and Armstrong, H. (1989) *The Youth Games Book*, IT Resource Centre, 19 Elmbank Street, Glasgow G2 4PB.

Deco, S. (1990) 'A Family Centre: A Structural Family Therapy Approach', in C. Case and T. Dalley (eds), *Working with Children in Art Therapy*, London: Routledge.

Dellar, S. (1989) 'Working with Sexually Abused Children through Games', *Practice* 3, 1: 66–79.

DHSS (1976) *Expert Group Report on the Role of Play for Children in Hospital* (Platt Report), London: HMSO.

DHSS (1984) *Guide for Guardians ad Litem in the Juvenile Court*, London: HMSO.

DHSS (1988) *Report of the Inquiry into Child Abuse in Cleveland 1987* (Butler-Sloss Report), London: HMSO.

Dockar-Drysdale, B. (1968a) *Therapy in Child Care*, London: Longman.

Dockar-Drysdale, B. (1968b) 'Play as Therapy in Child Care', in *Therapy in Child Care*, London: Longman.

Dockar-Drysdale, B. (1968c) 'The Process of Symbolization Observed Among Emotionally Deprived Children in a Therapeutic School', in R.J.N. Tod (ed.), *Disturbed Children*, London: Longman.

Dockar-Drysdale, B. (1990) *The Provision of Primary Experience: Winnicottian Work with Children and Adolescents*, London: Free Association Press.

Donaldson, M. (1978) *Children's Minds*, London: Fontana.

Dorfman, E. (1951) 'Play Therapy', in C. Rogers, *Client-Centred Therapy*, Boston: Houghton Mifflin.

Doyle, C. (1985) 'The Imprisoned Child – Aspects of "Rescuing" the Severely Abused Child', NSPCC Occasional Paper 3, London: NSPCC.

Doyle, C. (1987) 'Helping the Child Victims of Sexual Abuse through Play', *Practice* 1, 1: 27–38.

Doyle, C. (1988) 'Three Little Bags', *Community Care* 24 March: 30–1.

Doyle, C. (1990) *Working with Abused Children*, London: Macmillan.

Dunn, J. and Kendrick, C. (1982) *Siblings; Love, Envy and Understanding*, Oxford: Blackwell.

Eaker, B. (1986) 'Unlocking the Family Secret in Family Play Therapy', *Child and Adolescent Social Work* 3, 4: 235–53.

Eichenbaum, L. and Orbach, S. (1983) *Understanding Women*, Harmondsworth: Penguin.

Eimers, R. and Aitchison, R. (1978) *Effective Parents, Responsible Children – A Guide to Confident Parenting*, McGraw Hill.

Erikson, E. H. (1965) *Childhood and Society*, Harmondsworth: Penguin.

Erikson, E. H. (1976) 'Play and Actuality', in J. Bruner, A. Jolly and K. Sylva, *Play – Its Role in Development and Evolution*, Harmondsworth: Penguin.

Fahlberg, V. (1981a) *Attachment and Separation*, London: Batsford/BAAF.

Fahlberg, V. (1981b) *Helping Children When They Must Move*, London: Batsford/BAAF.

Fahlberg, V. (1982) *Child Development*, London: Batsford/BAAF.

Fahlberg, V. (1988) *Fitting the Pieces Together*, London: Batsford/BAAF.

Family Advisory Centre, Ealing. (1989) 'Stimulating the Sensory-impaired Child', *Talking Sense* 35, 3: 6–7.

Feynman, R. P. (1985) *Surely You're Joking, Mr Feynman*, London and New York: Norton.

Finklehor, D. (1984) *Child Sexual Abuse – New Theory and Research*, New York: Free Press.

Foster, S. and Harwood, L. (1981) 'The Watson Family Group', in S. Martel, *Direct Work with Children*, London: FSU/NCVO.

Fraiberg, S. (1959) *The Magic Years*, New York: Scribners.

Freud, A. (1936) *The Ego and the Mechanisms of Defence*, London: Hogarth Press.

Freud, A. (1965) *Normality and Pathology in Childhood*, Harmondsworth: Penguin.

Fundudis, T. (1989) 'Children's Memory and the Assessment of Possible Sexual Abuse – Annotation', *Journal of Child Psychology and Psychiatry* 30, 3: 337–46.

Gardner, D. (1981) 'Mutual Story-telling Technique', in C. Schaefer (ed.), *The Therapeutic Use of Child's Play*, New York: Jason Aronson.

Garvey, C. (1977) *Play*, London: Fontana.

Garwood, F. (1989) *Children in Conciliation*, Scottish Association of Family Conciliation Services, 127 Rose Street, South Lane, Edinburgh EH2 5BB.

Garwood, F. (1990) 'Involving Children in Conciliation', National Children's Bureau, *Concern* 73: 6–7.

Gesell, A., Ilg, F. A. and Ames, L. B. (1977) *The Child from Five to Ten*, New York: Harper and Row.

Gibran, Kahlil (1972) *The Prophet*, London: Heinemann.

Gill, E. (1991) *The Healing Power of Play – Working with Abused Children*, New York/London: Guilford Press.

Gillberg, C. (1990) 'Infantile Autism: Diagnosis and Treatment', *Acta Psychiatra Scandinavica* 81: 209–15.

Gillespie, A. (1986) 'Art therapy at the Family Makers project', *Adoption and Fostering* 10, 1.

Glaser, D. and Collins, C. (1989) 'The Response of Young, Non-sexually Abused Children to Anatomically Correct Dolls', *Journal of Child Psychology and Psychiatry* 30, 4: 547–60.

Glaser, D. and Frosh, S. (1988) *Child Sexual Abuse*, Basingstoke: Macmillan/BASW.

Gordon, R. (1986) 'Working with Children of Separating Parents', *Marriage Guidance* Summer: 24–7.

Gorell Barnes, G. (1984) *Working with Families*, London: Macmillan.

Gregg, J. (1988) personal communication.

Guerney, L. (1984) 'Play Therapy in Counselling Settings', in T. D. Yawkey and A. D. Pellegrini (eds), *Child's Play: Developmental and Applied*, New Jersey: Lawrence Erlbaum.

Harvey, S. (1984) 'Training the Hospital Play Specialist', *Early Child Development and Care* 17: 277–90.

Harvey, S. (1987) 'Value of Hospitalized Children's Artwork', *The Journal, National Association of Hospital Play Staff* 2: 3–8.

Harvey, S. and Hales-Tooke, A. (1972) *Play in Hospital*, London: Faber.

Haworth, M. (ed.) *(1964) Child Psychotherapy*, New York, Basic Books.

Hemmings, P. (1989) 'The Game which Helps Children Come to Terms with Death', *Barnados Today* 5.

Hemmings, P. (1990) 'Dealing with Death', *Community Care* 809, 12 April: 16–17.

Hendry, E. (1988) 'Play-based Work with Very Young Children', *Journal of Social Work Practice* 3, 2: 1–9.

Hogg, C. (1990) *Quality Management for Children: Play in Hospital*, London: Play in Hospital Liaison Committee.

Holmes, A. and McMahon, L. (1978) *Learning from Observation*, London: Pre-school Playgroups Association.

Howard, J. and Shepherd, G. (1987) *Conciliation, Children and Divorce – A Family Systems Approach*, London: Batsford.

Hoxter, S. (1977) 'Play and Communication', in M. Boston and D. Daws (eds), *The Child Psychotherapist and Problems of Young People*, London: Wildwood House.

Hoxter, S. (1983) 'Some Feelings Aroused in Working with Severely Deprived Children', in M. Boston and R. Szur, *Psychotherapy with Severely Deprived Children*, London: Routledge and Kegan Paul.

Huizinga, J. (1949) *Homo Ludens: A Study of the Play Element in Culture*, London: Routledge and Kegan Paul.

Hulsegge, J. and Verheul, A. (1987) *Snoezelen – Another World*, Goyt Side Road, Chesterfield: Rompa.

Hunter, M. (1986) 'The Monster and the Ballet Dancer', *Journal of Child Psychotherapy* 12, 2.

Isaacs, S. (1933) *Social Development in Young Children*, London: Routledge and Kegan Paul.

Ixer, G. (1988) 'Life Story Books Can Damage Your Health', *Social Work Today* 18 August: 26.

Jaques, P. (1987) *Understanding Children's Problems*, London: George Allen and Unwin.

Jefferies, B. and Gillespie, A. (1981) 'Art Therapy with the Emotionally Frozen', *Adoption and Fostering* 106, 4: 9–15.

Jeffree, D. M., McConkey, R. and Hewson, S. (1985: 2nd edition) *Let Me Play*, London: Souvenir Press.

Jeffrey, L. I. H. (1981, unpublished fellowship thesis) 'Exploration of the Use of Therapeutic Play in the Rehabilitation of Psychologically Disturbed Children', *British Association of Occupational Therapists*, 20 Rede Place, London.

Jeffrey, L. I. H. (1984) 'Developmental Play Therapy: An Assessment and Therapeutic Technique in Child Psychiatry', *Occupational Therapy* March: 70–4.

Jenkins, A. (1988) 'The NEWPIN Project – Recognizing and Treating the Hurt Child within Parents', talk to Association for Child Psychology and Psychiatry, Oxford, 26 April.

Jenkins, A. (1989) 'NEWPIN – A Lifeline', BBC Horizon programme, 19 June.

Jewett, C. (1984) *Helping Children Cope with Separation and Loss*, London: Batsford/BAAF.

Johnston, J. (1990) 'Talking Helps', National Children's Bureau *Concern* Summer, 3.

Jones, D. P. H. (1988) 'Some Reflections on the Cleveland Affair', *Association for Child Psychology and Psychiatry Newsletter* 11, 2: 13–18.

Jones, D. P. H. and McQuiston, M. (1988) *Interviewing the Sexually Abused Child*, London: Gaskell.

Jordan, W. (1972) *The Social Worker in Family Situations*, London: Routledge and Kegan Paul.

Judd, D. (1989) *Give Sorrow Words – Working with a Dying Child*, London, Free Association Books.

Kerr, A., Gregory, E., Howard, S. and Hudson, F. (1990) *On Behalf of the Child – The Work of the Guardian ad Litem*, Birmingham: BASW, Venture Press.

Kezur, B. (1981) 'Play Therapy as a Mode of Treatment for Disturbed Children', in S. Martel, *Direct Work with Children*, London: FSU/NCVO.

King, P. (1988) *Talking Pictures*, London: BAAF.

King, R. (1988) 'Hospital Play Specialist on a Bone Marrow Unit', *The Journal, National Association of Hospital Play Staff* 4: 11–13

Klein, M. (1937) *The Psychoanalysis of Children*, London: Hogarth.

Klein, M. (1986) 'The Psychoanalytic Play Technique', in J. Mitchell, *The Selected Melanie Klein*, Harmondsworth: Penguin.

Kolvin, I. (1981) *Help Starts Here – The Maladjusted Child in the Ordinary School*, London: Tavistock.

Krasner, S. M. and Beinart, H. (1989) 'The Monday Group: A Brief Intervention with the Siblings of Infants Who Died from Sudden Infant Death Syndrome (S.I.D.S.)', *Association of Child Psychology and Psychiatry Newsletter* 11, 4: 11–17.

Kubler-Ross, E. (1970) *On Death and Dying*, London: Tavistock.

Lansdown, R. (1988) 'Helping Children Cope with Needles', *The Journal, National Association of Hospital Play Staff* 3: 13–16.

Lansdown, R. and Goldman, A. (1988) 'The Psychological Care of Children with Malignant Disease', *Journal of Child Psychology and Psychiatry* 29, 5: 555–67.

Lear, R. (1990) *More Play Helps*, London: Heinemann Medical.

Leicestershire Court Welfare Service (undated) *What about Me?*, 38 Friar Lane, Leicester LE1 5RA.

Leverton, B. (unpublished papers) 'Play Therapy' and 'Family Therapy'.

Lieberman, F. (1979) *Social Work with Children*, New York: Human Sciences Press.

Lindquist, I. (1977) *Therapy through Play*, London: Arlington Books.

Longhorn, F. (1988) *A Sensory Curriculum for Very Special People*, London: Souvenir Press.

Lowenfeld, M. (1979) *The World Technique*, London: George Allen and Unwin.

Lund, M. (1984) 'Research on Divorce and Children', *Family Law* 14: 198–201.

McConkey, R. (1986a) 'Changing Beliefs about Play and Handicapped Children', in P. K. Smith, *Children's Play*, London: Gordon and Breach.

McConkey, R. (1986b) 'Play It Again, Chum', *Special Children* October.

McFerran, A. (1989) 'Rescue at Hand for Children of the Marital Storm', *Guardian* 29 March.

Macliver, C. and Thom, M. (1990) *Family Talk*, BAAF.

McMahon, L. and Cranstoun, Y. (1981) *Talking with Children – Resource Materials for Tutors and Group Leaders*, London: Pre-school Playgroups Association.

Martel, S. (ed.) *(1981) Direct Work with Children*, London: Family Service Units, Bedford Square Press of NCVO.

Masheder, M. (1989) *Let's Play Together – Cooperative Games*, Green Print, Merlin Press, 10 Malden Road, London NW5 3HR.

Matterson, E. (1989) *Play with a Purpose for the Under-sevens*, Harmondsworth: Penguin.

Maximé, J. (1986) 'Some Psychological Models of Black Self Concept', in S. Ahmed, J. Cheetham and J. Small (eds), *Social Work with Black Children and Their Families*, London: Batsford/BAAF.

Maximé, J. (1987) *Black Like Me*, workbook one – *Black Identity*, Beckenham: Emani Publications.

Meekums, B. (1988) 'Back in Touch: Parent–Child Relationship Building through Dance', videotape and training manual, Leeds Family Service Unit, 15 Lavender Walk, Leeds LS8 8TX.

Millar, S. (1968) *The Psychology of Play*, Harmondsworth: Penguin.

Minuchin, S. (1974) *Families and Family Therapy*, London: Tavistock.

Minuchin, S. (1981) *Family Therapy Techniques*, Cambridge: Harvard University Press.

Mitchell, A. (1985) *Children in the Middle: Living through Divorce*, London: Tavistock.

Mitchell, J. (ed.) *(1986) The Selected Melanie Klein*, Harmondsworth: Penguin.

Moore, J. (1985) *The ABC of Child Abuse Work*, London: Gower.

Moustakas, C. (1964) 'The Therapeutic Process', in M. Haworth, *Child Psychotherapy*, New York: Basic Books.

Moustakas, C. (1973) *Children in Play Therapy*, New York: Aronson.

Muir, E., Speirs, A. and Tod, G. (1988) 'Family Intervention and the Facilitation of Mourning in a Four-year-old Boy', *The Psychoanalytic Study of the Child* 43: 367–83.

Mulberry Bush School (1989) published information.

Murray, L. (1987) 'Depressed Mothers and Their Babies', lecture to Oxford Association for Child Psychology and Psychiatry, 14 July.

Murray, L. (1991) 'Post Natal Depression: Prevention of its Adverse Effects on Mother–Infant Relationship and Infant Development', lecture to Oxford ACPP Conference on the Application of Attachment Theory and Ethology to Clinical Problems, 18 March.

National Association for the Welfare of Children in Hospital (NAWCH) *Keypoints* (1984) 1. Involving Parents in Hospital Play, (1989) 2. Messy Play in Hospital, 14. Value of Play in Hospital.

National Association of Hospital Play Staff, *Let's Play* leaflets, 1. Babies in Hospital, 2. Toddlers in Hospital, 3. In the Out-patients Department, 4. Children in Isolation, 5. Children from Different Ethnic Groups, 6. Adolescents in Hospital, 7. Preparation for Surgery and Unpleasant Procedures, 8. In the X-Ray Department, London, NAHSP.

Neusner, J. (1981) 'Peter', in S. Martel, *Direct Work with Children*, London: FSU/NCVO.

Newson, E. (1983) 'Play Therapy – An Alternative Language for Children and Their Social Workers', *Foster Care* December.

Newson, E. and Hipgrave, T. (1982) *Getting through to Your Handicapped Child*, Cambridge: Cambridge University Press.

Newson, J. and Newson, E. (1979) *Toys and Playthings in Development and Remediation*, London: George Allen and Unwin.

Nicol, A. R. *et al.* (1988) 'A Focused Casework Approach to the Treatment of Child Abuse: A Controlled Comparison', *Journal of Child Psychology and Psychiatry* 29, 5: 703–11.

Nilman, I. and Lewin, C. (1989) 'Inhibited Mourning in a Latency Age Child', *British Journal of Psychotherapy* 5, 4: 523–32.

Noble, E. (1967) *Play and the Sick Child*, London: Faber.

Nover, A. G. (1985) 'Mother–Infant Interactive Play', *Journal of Child and Adolescent Social Work* 2: 22–35.

Oaklander, V. (1978) *Windows to Our Children*, Utah: Real People Press.

O'Brien, A. and Loudon, P. (1985) 'Redressing the Balance – Involving Children in Family Therapy', *Journal of Family Therapy* 7: 81–98.

Opie, I. and Opie, P. (1969) *Children's Games in Street and Playground*, London: Oxford University Press.

Orlick, T. (1972) *The Cooperative Sports and Games Book*, London: Writers' and Readers'.

Orlick, T. (1982) *The Second Cooperative Sports and Games Book*, Pantheon Books.

Owen, P. and Curtis, P. (1988) *Techniques for Working with Children*, 59 Cedar Avenue, Buxton, Chorley, Lancashire.

Panmure House staff team (undated) *A Handbook of Group Games and Techniques*, Panmure House, Lockend Close, Canongate, Edinburgh.

Parkinson, L. (1987) *Separation, Divorce and Families*, London: BASW MacMillan.

Peake, A. (1989) *Working with Sexually Abused Children – A Resource Pack for Professionals*, London: The Children's Society.

Pearce, J. (1990) 'Case studies', *Journal of the National Association of Hospital Play Staff* 8.

Peller, L. (1964) 'Developmental Phases of Play', in M. Haworth, *Child Psychotherapy*, New York: Basic Books.

Pennells, M. and Kitchener, S. (1990) 'Holding Back the Nightmares', *Social Work Today* 1 March: 14–15.

Piaget, J. (1951) *Play, Dreams and Imitation in Childhood*, London: Routledge and Kegan Paul.

Pinney, R. (1983) *Bobby – Breakthrough of an Autistic Child*, Harvill.

Pinney, R. (1990) *Children's Hours*, Children's Hours Trust, 28 Wallace House, Caledonian Estate, 410 Caledonian Road, London N7 8TL.

Pithers, D. (1990a) 'Expressing Feelings', review in *Community Care* 4 January.

Pithers, D. (1990b) 'Stranger Than Fiction', *Social Work Today* 22, 6: 20–1.

Pitman, E. (1984) *Transactional Analysis for Social Workers and Counsellors*, London: Routledge and Kegan Paul.

Pre-school Playgroups Association (1982) *Families in Playgroups*, London: Pre-school Playgroups Association.

Pre-school Playgroups Association (1986) *Adults Learning in PPA*, London: Pre-school Playgroups Association.

Prescott, E. and Jones, E. (1975) *Assessment of Child Rearing Environments: An Ecological Approach*, Pasadena, California: Pacific Oaks.

Prestage, R. O. (1972) 'Life for Kim', in E. Holgate, *Communicating with Children*, Harlow: Longman.

Prevezer, W. (1990) 'Strategies for Tuning in to Autism', *Therapy Weekly* 18 October.

Randall, K. (1989) 'The Luxury of Knowing Who You Are', *Social Work Today* 2 November.

Redgrave, K. (1987) *Child's Play – Direct Work with the Deprived Child*, Boys' and Girls' Welfare Society, 57a Schools Hill, Cheadle, Cheshire SK8 1JE.

Robertson, J. (1970) *Young Children in Hospital*, London: Tavistock.

Robertson, J. and Robertson, J. (1976) *Young Children in Brief Separation*, London: Robertson Centre.

Robertson, J. and Robertson, J. (1989) *Separation and the Very Young*, London: Free Association Books (26 Freegrove Road, London N7 9RQ)

Rogers, C. (ed.) (1951) *Client-centred Therapy*, Boston: Houghton Mifflin.

Rose, M. (1990) *Healing Hurt Minds – the Peper Harrow Experience*, London: Tavistock Routledge.

Ross, J. (1985) 'The Place of Children in the Conciliation Process', *The Scottish Child* 7: 10–13.

Rustin, M. and M. (1988) *Narratives of Love and Loss*, Verso, 6 Meard Street, London W1V 3HR.

Ryan, T. and Walker, R. (1985) *Making Life Story Books*, London: BAAF.

Satir, V. (1964) *Conjoint Family Therapy*, Science and Behaviour Books.

Save the Children Fund (1989) *Hospital: A Deprived Environment for Children*, London: Save the Children Fund.

Schaefer, C. and O'Connor, K. (eds) *(1982) Handbook of Play Therapy*, New York: Wiley.

Schaefer, C. E. (1986) 'Play Therapy', in P. K. Smith, *Children's Play*, London: Gordon and Breach.

Schaffer, R. (1977) *Mothering*, London: Fontana.

Sexual Abuse: Child Consultancy Service (SACCS) (1990) *All About Us* (Brochure), and *Nightingale Books* (Catalogue of Resource Products for Communicating with Children), PO Box 40, Shrewsbury SY1 1ZZ.

Shamroy, J. A. (1987) 'Interviewing the Sexually Abused Child with Anatomically Correct Dolls', *Social Work* 32, 2: 165.

Shearer, A. (1987) 'Finding the Way Home', *Guardian* 23 December.

Shephard, M. (undated) 'In Tune with Each Other', videotape, Milton Keynes: Pace Productions.

Shephard, M. (1989) *Music Is Child's Play*, London: Longman.

Sherborne, V. (1990) *Developmental Movement for Children: Mainstream, Special Needs and Pre-school*, Cambridge: Cambridge University Press.

Sheridan, M. D. (1975) *From Birth to Five Years – Children's Developmental Progress*, Windsor: NFER Nelson.

Shier, H. (1991) *In Service Training and Professional Development in Playwork*, London: National Children's Play and Recreation Unit.

Shires, A. (1989) 'Making Amends – Simple Play Therapy with Young Sexually Abused Children Using Techniques of Fantasy and Analogy', *Child Protection* 4, 1: 14–17.

Silveira, W. R., Trafford G. and Musgrave, R. (1988) *Children Need Groups*, Aberdeen: University Press.

Sinason, V. (1988) 'Dolls and Bears: From Symbolic Equation to Symbol', *British Journal of Psychotherapy* 4, 4: 349–63.

Sinason, V. (1990) 'The Heart Torn Out of Teddy', *Guardian*, 23 June.

Skynner, R. and Cleese, J. (1983) *Families and How to Survive Them*, London: Methuen.

Sluckin, A. (1989) 'The House–Tree–Person Test', *Changes* 6, 4: 128–31.

Smith, M. (1991) 'Play Specialists: A Vital Part of the Team', *Nursery World* 91, 3246: 22–3, 17 January.

Smith, P. K. (ed.) *(1986) Children's Play: Research Developments and Practical Applications*, London: Gordon and Breach.

Southwark College (1988) *Syllabus for Hospital Play Specialist Course*, Tanner Street, London SE1 3DP.

Stainton Rogers, W., Hevey, D. and Ash, E. (1989) *Child Abuse and Neglect – Facing the Challenge*, London: Batsford/Open University.

Stallibrass, A. (1974) *The Self-respecting Child*, London: Thames and Hudson.

Striker, S. and Kimmel, E. (1978) *The Anti-colouring Book*, London: Hippo Books.

Sylva, K. (1986) 'Coping with Stress in Families with Young Children', lecture to Organization Mondiale pour l'Education Pre-scholaire (OMEP), London, October.

Sylva, K. and Stein, A. (1990) 'Effects of Hospitalization on Children', *Association for Child Psychology and Psychiatry Newsletter* 12, 1: 3–8.

Sylva, K., Roy, C. and Painter, M. (1980) *Childwatching at Playgroup and Nursery School*, London: Grant McIntyre.

Thom, M. (1984) 'Working with Children: The Violet Oaklander Approach', *Adoption and Fostering* 8, 3: 34–5.

Tod, R. J. N. (ed.) *(1968) Disturbed Children*, London: Longman.

Triseliotis, J. (1983) 'Identity and Security in Adoption and Long-term Fostering', *Adoption and Fostering* 7, 1: 22–3.

Truax, C. B. and Carkhuff, R. R. (1967) *Towards Effective Counselling and Psychotherapy*, Chicago: Aldine.

Turner, S. (1988) unpublished notes on art therapy.

Valentine, C. W. (1956) *The Normal Child and Some of His Abnormalities*, Harmondsworth: Penguin.

Vizard, E. (1986) *Self-esteem and Personal Safety – A Guide for Professionals Working with Sexually Abused Children*, The Great Ormond Street Hospital Child Sexual Abuse Treatment programme, Tavistock publications.

Vizard, E. (1987) 'Self Esteem and Personal Safety: Comments on Secondary Prevention

Group Work with Young Sexually Abused Children', *Association for Child Psychology and Psychiatry Newsletter* 9, 2; 16–22.

Vizard, E., Bentovim, A. and Tranter, M. (1987) 'Interviewing Sexually Abused Children', *Adoption and Fostering* 11, 1: 20–5.

Walczak Y. and Burns, S. (1984) *Divorce: The Child's Point of View*, London: Harper and Row.

Walford, G. (1989) 'Group Therapy for Sexually Abused Children', *Association for Child Psychology and Psychiatry Newsletter* 11, 6: 7–13.

Wallerstein, J. and Kelly, J. B. (1980) *Surviving the Breakup*, London: Grant McIntyre.

Walrond-Skinner, S. (1976) *Family Therapy*, London: Routledge and Kegan Paul.

Walters, T. (1991) 'The Magic of the White Room', *Nursery World* 2 May.

Ward, B. (1987) *Good Grief, Exploring Feelings, Loss and Death with Under Elevens, a Holistic Approach*, Good Grief, 19 Bantree Road, Uxbridge, Middlesex UP8 1PT.

Waterhouse, S. (1987) *Time for Me – A Resource Book to Help Guardians ad Litem*, 3 Banbury Lane, Byfleet, Northants NN11 6OX.

Webb, N.B. (1991) *Play Therapy with Children in Crisis*, Guildford Press.

Webb, S. (1991) 'Safe Kids', *Social Work Today* 30 May.

Weinstein, J. (1987) 'Working with Sexually Abused Children – A Response to the Article by Celia Doyle', *Practice* 3: 283–6.

Weller, B. and Oliver, G. (1980) *Helping Sick Children Play*, London: Bailliere Tindall.

Wells, J. (1989) 'Powerplays – Considerations in Communicating with Children', in H. Blagg *et al.* (eds), *Child Sexual Abuse: Listening Hearing and Validating the Experiences of Children*, London: Longman.

West, J. (1983) 'Play Therapy with Rosy', *British Journal of Social Work* 13, 6: 645–61.

West, J. (1984) 'Ending or Beginning?' *Changes* 2: 80–4.

West, J. (1990) 'Children in Limbo', *Adoption and Fostering* 14, 2: 11–15.

White, M. and Epston, D. (1989) *Literate Means to Therapeutic Ends*, Melbourne: Dulwich Centre Publications.

Wilkins, R. and Loudon, P. (1986) *A Therapist's Thesaurus*, Philadelphia: Croom Helm.

Winnicott, C. (1964) *Child Care and Social Work*, Bookstall Publications, Codicote Press.

Winnicott, C. (1968) 'Communicating with Children', in R. J. N. Tod (ed.) *Disturbed Children*, London: Longman.

Winnicott, C. (1977) 'Communicating with Children', *Social Work Today* 8, 26: 7–11.

Winnicott, D. W. (1964) *The Child, the Family, and the Outside World*, Harmondsworth: Penguin.

Winnicott, D. W. (1971) *Playing and Reality*, London: Tavistock.

Winnicott, D. W. (1980) *The Piggle: An Account of the Psychoanalytic Treatment of a Little Girl*, Harmondsworth: Penguin.

Wolff, S. (1973) *Children Under Stress*, Harmondsworth: Penguin.

Wood, A. (1988) 'King Tiger and the Roaring Tummies: A Novel Way of Helping Young Children and Their Families Change', *Journal of Family Therapy* 10, 1: 49–63.

Wood, D., McMahon, L. and Cranstoun, Y. (1980) *Working with Under Fives*, Oxford: Blackwell.

Woolfson, R. (1990) 'Using Play as Therapy', *Nursery World* 90, 3217: 16–17.

Worden, J. W. (1983) *Grief Counselling and Grief Therapy*, London: Tavistock.

Wright, E. (unpublished) 'Communicating with Children who have been Sexually Abused'.

Wright, E. and Portnoy, S. (1990) 'Helping Mothers in Crisis', *Community Care*, 25 January.

Wright, Y. (1991) 'Improving Attachments Through Relationship Building Play', NAPOT newsletter, Spring.

Young Bruehl, E. (1989) *Anna Freud*, London: Macmillan.

Zwart, C. (1988) 'Mulberry Bush: Where Children Grow from Small to Big', *Oxford Education Times* summer edition.

Name index

Subject index